WE PROPOSE:
A MODERN CONGRESS

We Propose:
A Modern Congress

Selected Proposals by the House Republican Task Force on Congressional Reform and Minority Staffing

James C. Cleveland, M.C., Chairman

Foreword by Thomas B. Curtis, M.C.
Introduction by Gerald R. Ford, M.C., Minority Leader

Edited by Mary McInnis

McGraw-Hill Book Company
New York   Toronto   London

1234567 – FH – 9876

58845

FOREWORD

by Thomas B. Curtis, M.C.*

The need for congressional reform is urgent if our society is to retain the Congress as a study and deliberative body charged with making crucial social judgments and maintaining the traditional separation and balance of governmental power essential to the preservation and further development of human freedom.

Ideally, Congress is a mechanism for gathering together the knowledge and wisdom existing within the society to make judgments to solve the problems facing the society. Assembling the necessary data and background information occurs through three primary processes. First, the distilled wisdom (*i.e.*, that which has been reduced to books and other units of storage) contained in the Library of Congress is further refined for Members of Congress by the Legislative Reference of the Library. Second, the current wisdom of the society is collected through the standing committees of Congress with the help of professional staff employed by the committees. It is in these forums that the knowledge of experts in the executive branch and in the private sector is brought to bear on public problems and national goals. The testimony is received in public hearings with the witnesss under cross-examiniation and their statements subject to rebuttal. Third, from the letters and conversations of constituents and self-interest groups in the society, Members of Congress gather knowledge of the subject upon which the individual citizens are uniquely expert: how the laws as written and administered affect them.

The deliberative process in Congress also has three essential parts. The committees, each assigned jurisdiction over particular subject-matter areas, study the mass of assembled data and arguments obtained from the sources described above. These data and arguments are then boiled down into written reports, containing majority and minority views, to accompany the legislation for the next stage of deliberation, the floor debate. The floor debate is essen-

* Mr. Curtis represents the 2nd Congressional District of Missouri. He was first elected to Congress in 1950 and has been a member of the House Ways and Means Committee since 1953. He is a member of the Joint Committee on Internal Revenue Taxation, and the ranking Republican House Member of the Joint Economic Committee and the Joint Committee on the Organization of the Congress. He has been a staunch advocate of congressional reform for many years.

tially among the members of the committee responsible for conducting the study and issuing the printed report. The rest of the members sit somewhat as a jury, albeit with the power of interrupting to ask questions and to contribute collateral knowledge and arguments. Finally, a deliberation occurs between "managers" of both houses to strike a common version of the usually divergent versions resulting from the decision-making processes which go on in both houses of Congress. There is a possible further deliberation in the event that the President vetoes the ultimate judgments reached and the Congress decides to override the President's veto.

There is another theory of Congress, a competing theory which is increasingly winning supporters and which has already weakened the Congress as a study and deliberative body. This theory seeks to retain the Congress as a mechanism for recording decisions which have been made previously and elsewhere in the society through different processes. Those presently advancing this radical theory of the Congress think of these decisions as being made in the executive branch of the federal government, but once the Congress is structured as a conduit these decisions could as easily be made in Wall Street, along the Charles River, or wherever the powers within the society may rest. The legislative process under the conduit theory is reduced to a system whereby the decisions, wherever they are made, would be forced through the Congress by whatever methods may be necessary. These methods in practice bypass the techniques of appealing to facts and fair argument. The great fault of the conduit theory for reaching decisions is that is does not permit Congress to avail itself of the greatest amount of knowledge and wisdom within the society. Indeed, the actual decision-making is conducted behind closed doors, frequently in guarded or unknown buildings. The gathering of the data and the deliberations are not made public. Who gives the information, what arguments are advanced, remain secret. Members of Congress as well as the general public are left in the dark and given only the data and arguments which support the judgments made.

I think it is obvious that total implementation of this theory ultimately would destroy the Congress as a study and deliberative body. The Congress under this concept would be basically a super computer machine, a public opinion computer, to record and reflect the pressures which have been built up within the society through propaganda campaigns. Propaganda results when the experts and spokesmen for various points of view do not confront each other in a common forum and are not subjected to cross-examination and rebuttal.

This book is a collection of papers prepared by pragmatists in the field of legislation who are dedicated to the ideal that Congress be a study and deliberative body. It is our belief that not only is freedom preserved by maintaining an effective Congress, but in the long run the judgments rendered by the people's representatives through the deliberative process prove to be wiser and of more benefit to mankind.

CONTENTS

INTRODUCTION

by Gerald R. Ford, M.C.*

The willingness of all Members of the 89th Congress to undertake a study of their institution is on record: the resolution creating a Joint Committee on the Organization of the Congress was passed by a unanimous vote in both houses.

The extent to which Congress was willing to clean out its closets was, however, sharply limited by this language of the resolution: "Provided, That nothing in this concurrent resolution shall be construed to authorize the committee to make any recommendations with respect to the rules, parliamentary procedures, practices, and/or precedents of either House . . ."

A two-party system, to operate in the public interest regardless of which party holds temporary power, imposes on members of the minority party two concurrent responsibilities: to check any tendency toward excess or abuse of majority rule, and to compensate for deficiencies or deliberate inaction on the part of the majority. The Joint Committee was to be composed of twelve members, an equal number from each house, equally divided between the parties. In fact, it is a distinguished, hard-working group. But it should be pointed out that the co-chairmen of the Committee are *both* members of the majority party.

The Republican Task Force on Congressional Reform and Minority Staffing was created in part to assure that every significant aspect of the operation of the House of Representatives would be studied and to serve as a reservoir of recommendations should the Joint Committee fail to report out a

---

* First elected to Congress in 1948, Mr. Ford served as a Member of the House Appropriations Committee and in a number of party leadership positions before his election as House Minority Leader in 1965. He represents the 5th Congressional District of Michigan.

comprehensive set of proposals for modernizing the machinery and strengthening the role of Congress in the twentieth century.

Additionally, the new Task Force was to continue the constructive efforts of the old Schwengel Committee (88th Congress) to correct the imbalance in staffing of House committees and to focus public attention on remaining handicaps under which the minority party labors to fulfill its responsibilities.

Last, the appointment of a task force, as opposed to a committee or study group, grew out of a recognition that since Members of Congress are alone responsible for making needed improvements in the operation of their institution, they ought themselves to sweat out the research and study necessary to render wise judgments.

Happily, the co-chairmen of the Joint Committee have been both gracious in inviting and patient in listening to testimony of all witnesses irrespective of the language of the Committee's charter. In a rare display of harmony and cooperation, the staffs of the Committee, the Democratic Study Group, and our Republican Task Force have swapped and shared bits of information dug up by each to supplement the research efforts of the other. Although this book goes to press in advance of the Committee's Final Report, it is expected that a number of strong and fair recommendations will be put before Congress as a result of the dedicated labors of all three groups.

Our book does not present a comprehensive set of blueprints for modernizing Congress. In those areas in which we feel adequate research obviates specific conclusions, Members have gone forward with their recommendations in legislative form (*e.g.*, Joel Broyhill's bill to abolish the "basic rate" method of determining clerk hire; Bob Ellsworth's bills to permit telecast and broadcast coverage of proceedings on the floor of the House and of public hearings of House committees). In other areas, Members have reached solid conclusions but are waiting for the Final Report of the Joint Committee before introducing corrective measures of their own. In yet other areas, we admit that we have barely scratched the surface in relation to the amount of research that ought to be done, and we have no firm conclusions to offer at this time. (In these areas, we have tried to present the problem, at least, and to discuss a few of its ramifications.)

The world, the nation, and the relations between the U.S. Executive and Congress have undergone great changes in the turbulent twentieth century. "Important principles," Lincoln said, "may and must be inflexible." It is another matter, however, to decide how best to guarantee that the principles will be upheld while government moves swiftly, as it often must, to protect the rights of all citizens, look to the needs of the nation's underprivileged minorities, and combat the "thorns of progress" at home while fighting the Communist menace abroad. "Reform" is a tricky word; change *per se* is not necessarily the same as progress. Each and every proposal for reform of Congress must be weighed against other suggested reforms, and all must be weighed in the balance of power between the branches of government.

Mute witness to the complexity of congressional reform may be seen in the expansion of our original task force of eight members to one comprising twenty-one members. "The more you unwind," as our staff complained one day, "the bigger the ball gets." Finally, we had to say this is the day we go to press. Our work is unfinished, but if we wait until 1984 to publish, it may be too late for the book to do any good. We will present our findings to date, limited as they are, with the hope that others will join this common cause to finish the work we have begun. If we have succeeded in stirring public discussion on the role of today's Congress, we have made a meaningful contribution to the continuing experiment in American democracy. We hope that some of our recommendations will be acted upon without further delay, for, as Dr. George Galloway has said:

> Representative government is the keystone of the democratic arch. The eyes of the world are upon it and the way it works. If Congress is to save itself from the antidemocratic forces which are challenging it at home and abroad, then it must act promptly to improve its efficiency and democratize its methods.
>
> (*The Legislative Process in Congress*)

* * * * *

While the authors of this book have done the bulk of the research in each specific area and the conclusions presented are entirely their own, we would be less than candid to imply that the writing is even "90 proof." We have discovered, with painful (but recoverable) damage to the ego, that it is one thing to argue in committee or deliver remarks on the floor of the House—and quite another to write a book.

Therefore, we gratefully acknowledge the assistance of the many individuals who assisted in the research, translated our drafts, and edited the manuscript.

To Doctors Ernest S. Griffith, George B. Galloway, and Walter Kravitz, particularly, we express our deep thanks for their immeasurable patience and meticulous care in reviewing the manuscript. Dr. Griffith, Dean of the School of International Service, American University, was the director of Congress' Legislative Reference Service for 18 years. He is the author of *Congress: Its Contemporary Role*. Dr. Galloway, Senior Specialist in American Government and History for the Library of Congress, has written the official *History of the U.S. House of Representatives*, the classic book on *The Legislative Process in Congress*, and has contributed as well to the actual rules of the House as staff director of the LaFollette-Monroney Committee from which came the Legislative Reorganization Act of 1946. Dr. Kravitz, Analyst in History and Government for the Library of Congress, has scarcely begun his own writing career, but his research efforts for Members and committees of Congress offer promise of brilliant writing in the field.

Additionally, we would like to thank the following distinguished authorities for their consistently tactful and constructive criticism: Dr. Douglas

Bailey, Harvard University; Dr. Charles O. Jones, University of Arizona; Dr. Samuel C. Patterson, University of Iowa; Dr. Robert L. Peabody, Johns Hopkins University; Dr. John S. Saloma, III, Massachusetts Institute of Technology, and Dr. William B. Prendergast, Staff Director of the House Republican Conference.

The small, hard-working staff of the Joint Committee has been helpful in many ways and at all times, and we thank Mr. DeVier Pierson, Hon. George Meader, Dr. Nicholas Masters, Mr. Melvin Sneed, Mrs. Dorothy Tenenbaum, Mrs. Jane Peigler, and Miss Marilyn Jarvis for services rendered. We acknowledge our gratitude also to Dr. Edward Wenk, Jr., and Mr. Robert L. Chartrand of the Legislative Reference Service, and to Mr. Harry McGill, Chief of the House Disbursing Office, for expert help at various points.

The following Congressional staff aides have provided invaluable assistance throughout the project: Mr. David Blanton, III, Mr. Marion Burson, Mr. William Casselman, Mr. William Copenhaver, Mr. James Cromwell, Mr. Clifton Enfield, Mr. James Fairchild, Mr. Glenn Freeman, Miss Carrie Johnson, Mr. Homer Krout, Mr. Bruce Ladd, Miss Linda Lee, Mr. Virkler Legate, Mrs. Barbara Ludden, Mr. Sol Mosher, Mr. Don Olson, Mr. Leonard Pliska, Mr. Timothy Smith, Mr. William Spencer, Miss Ruth Widmayer, and Mr. Alan Woods. Additionally, we would like to record our thanks to Miss Madeleine Marceau and the staff of Rep. James Cleveland, and to Mrs. Marilyn Early and the staff of Rep. Thomas Curtis, for superb logistical support.

Finally, we extend our thanks to the able young men and women who assisted our efforts while serving internships in various Republican Members' offices: Miss Susan Anderson (Mt. Holyoke '66), Ronald Burnett (Peabody Conservatory '68), Charles Daney (M.I.T. '66), Clem Dinsmore (Princeton '65), Michael Hofmayer (Yale '65), William Hyde (U. of Utah '66), William Loos (U. of Utah '66), Miss Jean McInnis (Southwest Missouri State '66), John Meisel (Yale '66), Clarence Pride (U. of Vermont '66), Mark Simpson (Columbia '65), John Sterling (Stanford '67), and Vern VanderWeide (U. of Michigan Law '65). Without the cooperation of these alert scholars (who became known as the "Little League Task Force on Congressional Reform") the survey of congressional offices by the American Political Science Association would never have been completed. Also, we thank Edward Blair, Jr., (Stanford '66), Gary Cunningham (U. of Michigan '66), Miss Susan Daniels (Otterbein '67), Miss Nancy Grover (George Washington '68), Schuyler Henderson (Princeton '67), Miss Susan Hosmer (Vassar '69), James Leach (Johns Hopkins '66), Charles McMillan (Princeton '67), C. W. (Quincey) Rogers (Yale Law '67), and Steve Sloca (Dartmouth '66).

And to Mr. Richard B. Fisher, Mr. Morrie Helitzer, and Miss Luna Wolf of the McGraw-Hill Book Company, our apologies for the many delays and gratitude for their patience and understanding.

PART 1
The Committee Structure

JAMES C. CLEVELAND, M.C.
2nd District, New Hampshire

THE NEED FOR INCREASED MINORITY STAFFING

by James C. Cleveland, M.C.*

Introductory Note

The adequacy of congressional staffing in a broader sense involves the continuing efficacy of Congress *vis-à-vis* the President. The survival of representative government is directly at stake.

In many areas of the world during recent years, we have witnessed a decline in the power of established parliments and a shift of that power to the executive. The subordination of the power of newly established parliments to the executive in the emerging nations of Africa and Asia underscores that trend. One of the most notorious instances of a decline in the power of an established parliment occurred recently in France, where the French people, with apparent willingness, accepted the transfer of important powers from the legislature to the executive.

It should be pointed out to those who can watch a drift away from representative government with equanimity, that it was such a trend which paved the way for the ascendency of Hitler. Lack of representative government is also a characteristic of the Communist-dominated countries of today.

The need for establishing new rules in Congress to insure the minority party an adequate supply of professional staff on committees is of overriding

* Mr. Cleveland represents the 2nd Congressional District of New Hampshire. Before his election to Congress in 1962, he served 12 years in the New Hampshire State Senate where he was Majority Floor Leader for four years, Chairman of the Judiciary Committee and, at various times, a member of eight additional committees. In Congress he is a member of the House Public Works Committee and was recently named to the Joint Committee on the Organization of Congress succeeding former Rep. Griffin, now a U.S. Senator. Mr. Cleveland's wife, Hilary, teaches Government and History at Colby Junior College for Women in New London, N. H., the Cleveland's home.

importance. It must be met promptly if Congress is to fulfill its constitutionally assigned functions as a co-equal branch of government.

This is a problem that has engaged and troubled many minds, inside Congress and out, in partisan and nonpartisan context, for many years. The work of this chapter is founded on much preceding labor by many hands as well as on my own experience and observations.

While it would be impossible for me to acknowledge everyone who has contributed to the development of this issue, I do wish particularly to acknowledge the work of the Honorable Fred Schwengel of Iowa, who was Chairman of the old House Republican Conference Subcommittee on Increased Minority Staffing, the predecessor to the present Task Force. I also wish to acknowledge the invaluable work of Miss Mary McInnis, staff assistant to the present Task Force.

* * * * *

The serious threat to an effective Congress, and therefore to representative government itself, which is posed by the lack of adequate staff for the minority has not been fully understood, even by some members of the minority. Interest and concern is growing, however, and the time is not far off when, I believe, the majority of both parties in Congress will realize what adequate minority staffing would really mean for them in terms of increasing *their* effectiveness—and that of representative government.

One of the best statements of the issue was published on March 15, 1963, by the Schwengel Subcommittee and signed by the following political scientists: Dr. Robert J. Huckshorn, Bethesda, Maryland; Dr. Howard Penniman, Chairman, Department of Government, Georgetown University; Dr. Franklin Burdette, Bethesda, Maryland; Dr. Brownlee S. Corrin, Goucher College, Baltimore, Maryland; Dr. George Carey, Georgetown University; and Dr. Russell Ross, University of Iowa. I quote it here in full:

POLITICAL SCIENTISTS' STATEMENT
ON MINORITY STAFFING

The committee staff function at the congressional level is not being fulfilled. And a failure to do so is not only unfair, but it is a threat to the tradition of representative government. Responsibility for this condition falls upon the Democratic Party leadership in Congress.

To deny the Minority in Congress access to adequate representation on Committee staffs eliminates the opportunity for a minority to act responsibly after a careful examination of the problems under consideration. Congressmen, in this difficult and complex period of our history, require access to data and evaluation in those subject areas to which they are given responsibility as Committee members. It is obvious that this work cannot be placed regularly with their own office staffs, which have functions very different from those of a Committee. It is obvious, in light of policy formulation patterns at all levels of government, that the adversarial technique of law and politics in this country requires a personal relationship in which a congressman can develop confidence with the professional staff members. This is why, of course, the President has a high degree of control over his White House Staff, as well as at many policy-making levels in the Executive Departments.

Some have argued that an increase in minority staffing of congressional committees would jeopardize the recent "professionalization" of these staffs. We do not believe that this is true. There is no reason why such "professionalization" cannot take place in a bipartisan framework. What is needed are professional staff members separately responsible to the majority and the minority. The demand that a substantially larger portion of the professional staff be responsible to the minority members is wholly reasonable and within the best democratic traditions.

Congressional committee staff members are not intended to serve the same function as staff members in the Legislative Reference Service. Nor should they. The Committee staff must possess high levels of competence. It is equally important, however, that there exists mutual confidence between the congressmen and the staff members. This confidence is not possible when a minority party, be it Democrat or Republican (and there is always the possibility of reversal of role), does not have access to adequate and qualified professional staff members of its own selection.

The existing position is more than unfortunate; it is a subtle denial of freedom of effective speech, of which Congress as a body purports to be justly proud. It hinders reasoned debate that alone can lead to just solution of legislative problems. It prevents the minority from carrying out its major democratic function of knowledgeable criticism.

The country cannot afford gamesmanship or petty, cheap politics at the congressional level. Yet, we are witnessing an outstanding example of partisan pettiness in the denial to the minority in Congress the right to exercise its legislative function by refusing to grant it necessary staff support.

The issue has also engaged the earnest attention of thoughtful members of the present majority party. In his testimony before the Joint Committee on the Organization of Congress, Rep. John S. Monagan (D., Conn.), stated:

The capacity of the minority to examine and criticize should not be abridged, but should be preserved as a basic strength of our system.[1]

In the course of these same hearings, Rep. David S. King (D., Utah), expanded this line of thought:

. . . a formula must be found for balancing the personnel of the committee staffs more equitably between the majority and minority parties. . . . In my opinion, the balance of personnel between the two parties on the committee staffs should more nearly approximate the division of party strength in the House itself. . . . [2]

One more quotation will help set forth the urgency of the issue. Dr. James A. Robinson, professor of political science at the University of Ohio, writes:

. . . It is not fairness, however, that constitutes the most compelling argument for providing minorities with a staff almost equal in number with that of the majority. The best argument is that the improved performance of the minority members helps to strengthen the legislative way of life. If the majority party becomes increasingly aligned with the executive branch . . . then we must look to the minority to check the majority and in so doing to provide the necessary counter-balance to executive power. Hence, generous allocations of minority staffing are essential to the normative theory of Congress. . . . [3]

The present situation is deplorable. Although precise figures on majority-minority divisions among committee staffs in the House have proven impossible to obtain, research into committee payrolls, conducted both by the old Schwengel Subcommittee and my own Task Force, establish a general ratio of about 10 to 1 in favor of the majority.

Some committees—e.g., Armed Services, House Administration, and the Un-American Activities Committee—list no personnel as responsible to the minority.

One rough measure of the discrepancy in staffing is that counsel assigned to the minority often do not receive as much pay as majority counsel. Naturally, this creates difficult recruitment problems for the minority. There has never been any suggestion that minority members of Congress should be paid less than Congressmen belonging to the majority party, and the principle is precisely the same in the case of staff. It makes no more sense to pay minority staff personnel less for equal work than majority staffers than it would to pay less to minority Congressmen themselves.

In fairness, however, it must be conceded that minority leaders on committees do not always press as hard as they should to obtain salary equity for minority counsel. This condition, however, merely reinforces the need to establish the equal pay principle by legislation.

Even in the cases of committees which do list staff members as assigned specifically to assist the minority, those employees are ultimately responsible to the committee chairman, who is always a member of the majority party. By that I mean that they cannot be hired without the chairman's approval; their salaries are subject to the approval of the majority, and often their physical location is determined by the majority. *Thus, nowhere in the House does the minority party have guaranteed to it an unobstructed conduit to information vital to the success of its adversary role under our two-party system.*

We Republicans, currently in the minority, are often accused of mere obstructionism and are charged with failure to come up with constructive alternatives. Under the extremely hampering conditions in which we must operate, it is remarkable that we have done as well as we have. When the majority party not only controls all committee personnel but, as is the case at present, has exclusive access to the vast resources of advice, information, and power in all the federal agencies, the minority party is at a terrible disadvantage. This is very bad for representative government, because it chokes off responsible criticism and seriously cramps the capacity of the public to find out what is going on so it can form independent judgments. The ability to reach sound policy decisions for the nation, both in foreign and domestic affairs, is critically hobbled in these circumstances.

In spite of its handicaps, the Republican Party is doing a creditable job in its present minority status in the House. This is reflected in the increase in the number of Minority Views and Supplemental Views by Republicans appearing in committee reports on various bills. These minority views perform a vital function under the adversary system and represent a valuable distillation of opposition views. Often they form the basis of future legislation or corrections to existing programs.

In my own Committee on Public Works, I use this vehicle quite frequently even when I am in accord with the general purposes of the particular legislation. They are the best means of establishing for the permanent record an assessment of flaws in generally acceptable legislation and, of course, they serve to expound detailed arguments in opposition to legislation deemed unacceptable.

They can be used quite dramatically to capture attention for minority positions that otherwise tend to be overlooked by the news media, which tend to concentrate on the activities of the majority party. I put into verse my supplemental views opposing the legislation authorizing an official mansion for the Vice-President.[4] This poetic device had never been used before in an official congressional report on a bill and that fact was what got the most attention. At the same time, however, my reasons for opposing the bill also received wide publicity—that we couldn't afford it at this time and that it was singularly inappropriate to build a luxurious mansion for the Vice-President while the country was at war and our servicemen are badly housed in many parts of the country. After the bill was approved, the President ordered an indefinite halt to the project, using much the same reasoning.

Minority views have frequently influenced the course of legislation. Notable examples include the Manpower Development and Training Act, which was almost completely rewritten on the basis of Republican proposals before it was passed; the Civil Rights Act of 1964; and Medicare, among many others. Minority views on the anti-poverty program and the Participation Sales Act have had great impact in the country and will almost certainly lead to future reforms, if not in this Congress, then hopefully in the next.

The Legislative Reorganization Act

The Legislative Reorganization Act of 1946 streamlined committee jurisdictions and reduced the number of standing committees of the House from 48 to 19. As a result of the Act, provisions for more uniform procedure were written into the standing Rules of the House, including the provision that each committee, other than the Committee on Appropriations

... is authorized to appoint by majority vote of the committee not more than four professional staff members on a permanent basis without regard to political affiliations and solely on the basis of fitness to perform the duties of the office.

Rule XI further provides that:

> Professional staff members shall not engage in any work other than committee business and no other duties may be assigned to them.

In actual practice, both the spirit and letter of the law have been violated. (One of the most flagrant examples of such a violation occurred in my own Committee on Public Works when it was under control of the previous chairman, former Representative Charles Buckley of New York. We discovered that the committee payroll contained the names of nine persons who were never known to have done any work for the committee or had never even been seen in Washington. They were assigned to work for the chairman in his own Congressional District in the Bronx. I condemned the situation publicly and this exposé perhaps was a contribution to the chairman's defeat in a party primary.[5] With this defeat, the problem ended. Under its new administration the Public Works Committee is operating fairly once again and is one of the committees which gives reasonable, though not adequate, consideration to the minority membership in the matter of staff. Eight employees are assigned to the miniority out of a staff of around 40. (However, the chairman insists upon paying minority staff members substantially less than majority personnel performing similar duties.)

I question the wisdom of ever incorporating into the standing rules governing any legislative body such specific language as that contained in Rule XI, which, to repeat, provides that each committee may appoint "not more than four professional staff members." Twenty years ago the authors of the Reorganization Act could not even foresee the need for a standing committee on Science and Astronautics (which was added in 1958). Today this committee, which must oversee one of the largest Government agencies, the National Aeronautics and Space Administration, with an annual budget totaling over $5 billion, operates with one of the smallest staffs in the House. Other committees have augmented their staffs through extra authorizations by the House Administration Committee for "investigative" or additional professional personnel. The Science and Astronautics Committee, however, continues to function with only four professional staff employees. In the words of one of the Committee's members:

> Anyone who has served on this committee and participated in the markup of the NASA authorization bill knows that, while the desire is there and the intentions good, there are instances when many members must inevitably conclude on a given item that they just don't know with assurance whether or not it is reasonable.[6]

But this is not the whole story. The Committee on Appropriations was carefully exempted from any ceiling on the hiring of employees; yet some of its members suffer from a shortage of expert assistance! The entire federal budget, program by program and agency by agency, goes through this committee—which assigns only one professional staff person to each of its subcommittees with the exception of the Subcommittee on Defense and Independent Offices.

> How does a member know that the post office needs so many trucks, or so many mailbags? How does a member know that a Coast Guard station is obsolete and should be discontinued? We have in the past had to use our common sense and rely on the people who have made a request. But if someone were to come to them and say: "Do you know, or does the committee know, this or that for a fact?" the only honest answer we can give is, "Well, this is how the executive branch justified their request." [7]

Without competent and adequate committee staffing, Congress is at a distinct disadvantage *vis-à-vis* the executive branch. Without such staff assistance, the overwhelming task of checking on the operation of government becomes impossible. And without checking the myriad details, Congress can only pay lip service to its constitutional duty of control over government expenditures.

By law, each of the standing committees is required to report the names, positions and salaries of all of its employees every six months. These lists are duly printed in the *Congressional Record*. Simple enough? Try ferreting out the physical location of all of these people!

"The student of committees," wrote former British M.P. Kenneth Wheare, "has to make a choice. Either he can try to hack his way through the jungle on foot, or he can try to get a bird's eye view of the terrain from the air. If he chooses the first alternative, the most he can hope for is to clear a portion of his territory; if he chooses the second, the most he can hope for is to produce a rough sketch-map of the whole area."[8] How true this is. Our Task Force has tried both approaches.

The push for reform of the minority staffing question is, and has been, hampered by two major underlying fundamental conditions, which must be reported.

First, there is an absence of any consensus among the members of either party as to the proper role of Congress in the 1960's. Should Congress concede its loss of initiative in policy-making and bill-drafting to the executive and become more of an agency for oversight of the administration? Or should Congress attempt to regain some of its initiative in the legislative process and be content with a general overseeing function? The question does not have to be answered to bolster the case for increased committee staffing, because either direction calls for expert assistance and independent sources of information to serve Congress. (Clearly, a national debate over the role of Congress in the twentieth century is in order. The Administration, the academic community, the press, and interested citizens throughout the country should join. This book is an attempt by House Republicans to get the dialogue moving in a meaningful and constructive manner.)

The second condition we found in the committee staffing situation is the prevalent abuse of committee staff people by individual members of both parties. To reiterate the injunction of Standing Rule XI:

> Professional staff members shall not engage in any work other than committee business and no other duties may be assigned to them.

Candor compels me to admit this rule is sometimes violated. Professional staff employees are sometimes commandeered to write speeches or do other chores for individual Members that are not directly connected with the business of the committee, to handle constituent mail on matters of no relevance to the committee, and even to engage in activities directly concerned with the re-election of a Member. We turned up a distressing number of instances in which committee employees were physically quartered, not in the committee staff room, but in the personal offices of committee members. (Part of this sutuation is undoubtedly due to space limitations, however. A staffer may be assigned to a Member's personal office in some instances because there is simply not room for him in the limited committee quarters. Another reason may be that, because of his committee responsibilities, the individual Member may wish to have his staff adviser readily accessible. This would be particularly true where the Congressman's office was located inconveniently far from the committee offices.)

There is also the fact that Members of the minority party have failed to prosecute actively the case for increased staffing. In an extensive survey of Republican Members' attitudes with respect to the work and staffing of their committees, we found roughly two-thirds dissatisfied with the performance of their committee in the exercise of oversight of the Administration. Yet, we are able to document a grand total of only eleven instances in which minority Members were denied requests for additional committee staff help! (One reason, undoubtedly, is that minority Members know from painful experience that it is pointless to make such requests because they have invariably been turned down.) This does not, of course, negate the case for better staffing for the minority; it *does* point up the educational job we have to do on our own side of the aisle as well as generally.

It is hoped that this chapter will form part of this educational process.

The Adversary System

This writer, in common with most responsible political observers, believes firmly in the two-party system. The system has evolved naturally from the early days of our Republic as the best means for organizing disagreement in a diverse society.

The importance of the two-party system goes, indeed, far deeper than simply the "firm belief" of this author or of any other observer. The two-party system is the vital ingredient that has made possible the success of our government. Throughout our history, the interplay between two broadly based, widely inclusive national political parties has enabled the country to overcome, in large measure, those regional differences and conflicts between social and economic interests that, in many other democracies, result in the formation of numerous, specialized parties, none able to speak for the whole nation, or worse, to dictatorship.

The capacity of our two-party system to resist the divisive formation of effective third parties has been the salvation of America. Freed from the worst excesses of enervating factionalism, our country has been able to develop in freedom her enormous natural resources and to achieve fulfillment, in great measure, of the individual rights guaranteed by our Constitution. That document alone could not have provided this result without the proper instruments to carry it into effect. The impotence of mere documents is nowhere better to be seen, for example, than in the Soviet Union, where maximum tyranny reigns under the aegis of one of the world's most liberal written constitutions. In our case, the most effective political instrument for the fulfillment of our Constitution's promise is the two-party system.

The evolution of the system followed logically from our Anglo-Saxon tradition of jurisprudence, which is the root of all American legal institutions.

It is based on the adversary system. The right to counsel and the right to be judged on the facts pertaining to the issue are rights that are stamped indelibly on the minds and hearts of the American people. Through the adversary system, we get more information on which to base our judgments. Under ideal conditions, each side has complete freedom to develop relevant information and present its arguments. The end result is the production of the greatest possible amount of information, and, therefore, the greatest possible understanding for those who must render decisions.

Much the same adversary technique is seen in business competition as well. Competition in business leads to better products at lower cost and to improved public understanding of the products themselves as well as the nature of business. Competition is the economic strength of the nation, and in the marketplace of ideas the principle is of equal importance.

This tradition is as applicable to a legislative body as it is to a court of law. Under free government, each party is permitted to present its views fully. Most important, the system protects the rights of minorities while allowing the will of the majority to prevail.

The success of the adversary system depends on the quality of the debate. To assure the highest possible quality, each side must have equal opportunity to marshal evidence in support of its positions. In a legislative body, it is just as essential that the minority party have sufficient staff assistance as it is for either party in a court of law to have proper counsel.

The present situation in Congress, as the staffing ratio proves, is deplorable with respect to counsel for the minority. When both Senate and House and the Presidency are controlled by the same party, the situation is at the point of maximum danger to representative government. When the minority in Congress is reduced to capitalizing on such mistakes as are made by the Administration (if it can find out about them), effective opposition (if there is any) must come from the ranks of the majority party itself. This is the present trend and it is a very unreliable state of affairs. The business of the Republic demands that the effective expression of minority views not be allowed to rest on the capricious, internal strains within the party that is charged with the responsibility of governing.

In this connection, I wish to mention a Republican-sponsored proposal to give to the minority party control of an investigative committee of the House whenever the majority party controls both houses of Congress and the executive branch. Sponsors of the bill are headed by Minority Leader Gerald Ford of Michigan, and include Congressman Robert H. Michel of Illinois, whose chapter in this book is devoted solely to a detailed explanation of the proposal.

Here I merely want to point out that the adoption of the Republican proposal would ease considerably some of the problems of a minority party seeking to fulfill its functions under the present state of affairs. It would help insure against whitewashes of wrongdoing and gross errors on the part of government officials.

While outsiders and members of the majority party may be forgiven a feeling of suspicion at Republican motives in making the proposal, in refutation of these I point out that there is good Republican precedent for the idea.

In 1923, when both the executive branch and both houses of Congress were controlled by the Republican Party, rumors of improprieties surrounding the leasing of the Teapot Dome oil reserve whirled through the Capital. As they grew to a point requiring formal investigation, Republicans prevailed upon Democratic Senator Thomas J. Walsh of Montana to take charge of the investigation. This is a dramatic example of a case in which Republicans gave to the Democrats control of an investigation into a major scandal involving high-ranking members of a Republican Administration. The results were salutary and of great benefit to the whole country. There should be formal provisions enacted so that this would always be the case.

(It should also be noted that the British House of Commons has a Committee of Public Accounts whose chairman is by tradition a leading member of the Opposition, usually a person who has been Financial Secretary of the Treasury. The committee is charged with responsibility for insuring that all public money is spent in the manner intended by Parliment. It promotes economy and efficiency and helps to maintain high standards of morality in all public financial matters).

In this day and age, more is expected of a minority party than mere criticism, a political platform, and legislative debate. A responsible party must be one in which people have confidence and one to which they will entrust their destiny. It must be prepared to present, in reasonable detail, at least some practical alternatives to the hundreds of complicated and technical issues confronting the country. Offering meaningful alternatives is no simple task. The development of such alternatives requires the services of specialists and technicians, men and women who have devoted their lives to concentrated study of a particular problem.

By the very nature of a Congressman's job, it is very difficult for most Members to become as expert as the problems require. They must be concerned with too wide a range of subjects to permit specialization. Many Members of Congress face still another problem. Most Congressmen feel that they simply do not have the time to study *all* legislative matters and administrative policies. Just to keep up with individual problems of constituents is a huge task. Consider the following examples: A shortage of heating coal, fraud by mail, eligibility for a pension, the impact of a new law, a missing person, a family tragedy, a suspected crime, a missing pension check, harsh treatment at the hands of a government agency, the need for a job, a visa, citizenship for a relative or friend, the impact of a drought, a rate increase, a public transportation problem, a tariff ruling, information concerning the workings of an obscure government agency, a man's draft status, taxes, naming a mountain, a hardship discharge, a promotion, a pay increase —the list is endless.

Besides answering a large volume of mail, greeting constituents visiting the Capitol, attending to the needs of their districts and their party obligations, Congressmen are called upon to exercise leadership and concern in almost every matter involving the federal government. Although some of these areas are beyond the immediate control of Congress, a Congressman frequently must act to rally public opinion or file strong protests on behalf of his constituency. He has an important role in reminding the often smugly insulated federal agencies that they are meant to be the servants and not the masters of the people.

Congressmen have personal staffs to help with some of their tasks, but some responsibilities cannot be delegated. Some commentators have suggested that it would be helpful to the legislative process to remove certain of these tasks from the Congressman's workload by establishing an Ombudsman-type office. This writer is strongly opposed to any such proposal. Dealing with constituent and district problems is the raw material of the legislative process. The Congressman, through the power conferred by his constituents' votes, and acting, in a sense, as a trustee, can cut through red tape and keep our government responsive. Even more important is the fact that as he performs this function the Congressman becomes aware of problems which need legislative action.

Above all, however, a Congressman is a legislator. This most important function begins with his committee work. Although Congressmen are responsible for final judgments in the legislative product of their committee work, their acts are influenced in many ways by the work of the committee staffs. No significant legislation is produced without the aid of experts. The staff supplies the expertise necessary to reduce the extensive time which few Members of Congress can afford to devote to legislative duties. Under the direction and supervision of committee members, the staff suggests investigations, prepares their preliminary groundwork, and often influences their scope and direction. The staff selects witnesses and prepares lines of questioning. The staff collects mountains of data, checks facts, organizes and digests them into manageable proportions. The staff may generate or prepare special studies. Staff people often draft reports upon which the most pivotal committee decisions are based. In short, the staff does that essential spade and leg work few Congressmen have the time to perform.

The demands on a Congressman's time highlight the importance of good staff work. Implicit in this situation is the recognition that many Congressmen cannot devote as much time as they would like to supervising the work of their committee staffs. If this is so, it suggests yet another reason for adequate minority staffing: mindful of human nature, it is conceivable that improperly supervised staffs could exercise undue influence over the work of their committees. A good check on this, obviously, would be an alert minority staff.

Infrequently, the minority is blessed with offers of outside assistance. One memorable example occurred when a task force under the chairmanship of Representative Frank Bow (R., Ohio) and composed of Republican members of the House Appropriations Committee undertook a thorough analysis of the proposed budget for fiscal 1964. Maurice Stans, Director of the Bureau of the Budget under President Eisenhower, and some half dozen former members of that agency, provided valuable assistance to the project. The economy drive which this effort spearheaded resulted in savings of $6.3 billion to the taxpayers of this country. It also permitted economy-minded Congressmen to vote for the tax cut.

It is interesting to note that when Congressman Bow first announced that he thought his task force could recommend substantial cuts in the budget, without damage to necessary programs, he was challenged immediately to itemize the proposed cuts. Congressman Bow refused because he feared that by thus forewarning agencies their public relations sections could man the ramparts and stave off a threatened economy drive by whipping up public opinion as only battle-tested bureaucrats can. I mention this here because it shows how important secrecy is in connection with legislative strategy. Obviously, a minority which relies entirely on a staff responsible to the majority, with lines of communication to the executive departments and agencies, is either naive or lazy or worse.

It should be noted here that where the minority is deprived of its own staff and where members are not as fortunate as Congressman Bow in receiving aid, there is always a temptation to turn to private interests for help. Without discussing the advantages and disadvantages of consulting special interests in regard to legislation which affects them, I shall simply contend that any situation which forces minority Congressmen to turn to special interests for staff work is not in the best interest of sound representative government.

All Members do, of course, have access to the assistance of the Senate and House Legislative Counsel for bill-drafting, and to the Legislative Reference Service of the Library of Congress for research. The primary functions of the Senate and House Legislative Counsel involve the highly technical and specialized task of drafting legislation. The staffs of both offices are composed of qualified and dedicated personnel. The Legislative Reference Service operates exclusively as a nonpartisan research and reference service for Members of Congress. Its staff has grown steadily and in all probability will continue to grow with the increasing need of Congress for specialized research assistance with which to deal with the technologically induced changes in our society and economy. Assuming that Congress maintains a reasonable balance between the legitimate demands for staff assistance from these auxiliary sources and the actual capacity of the staffs to provide such help, it is the committee staff system itself on which Congress must principally rely. While organizations like the Legislative Reference Service greatly assist individual Members in their particular areas, they cannot substitute for committee staffs.

But the needs of congressional committees go beyond the question of sheer size of a staff and reach to the problem of making possible an effective distinction between majority and minority positions in order to facilitate meaningful floor debate and responsible problem-solving. As long as Congress is organized on the basis of a differentiation between majority and minority roles, even at the committee level, it is not realistic to expect adequate legislation to evolve from a "nonpartisan" staff arrangement.

The nonpartisanship of the 1946 Reorganization Act has not, as I have suggested, been a success. Some committee staffs in the House of Representatives are truly nonpartisan, not only in terms of party affiliation but in terms of serving members of both parties equally. On other committees, the principle of appointment and control of tenure by a majority of the committee has led to control of the staff by the Chairman and almost exclusive use of its time by the majority party. Even on the few committees which try to give equal service to members of both parties, it is evident that whoever appoints the staff also controls it. Today, the overwhelming majority of committee staff members are hired, supervised, promoted, and assigned duties by the chairmen of the committees. When the workload of these committees is heavy, the staff naturally feels obliged to give preference to the needs of the majority members on whom they rely for their jobs. Consequently, one can understand why members of the minority party cannot always confide in or depend upon staff members responsible to the opposing party.

Conclusion

The case for increasing the staff available to the minority is overwhelming, in my opinion. It has been brought to the attention of the Joint Committee on the Organization of Congress, which is preparing its report and recommendations as this book goes to press. Very likely the Committee's report will have been issued before this paper is published. However, because many Members addressed themselves to this problem in the course of the Committee's extensive hearings and because our Task Force has worked closely with the Committee's staff, it is expected that the report will contain strong recommendations for immediate action to correct the partisan imbalance in committee staffing.

In discussing what should be done, I do not believe it is necessary to get into a numbers game and try to set up any specific ratios that will meet the problem. The work of every committee is different; accordingly, its personnel requirements are different. Moreover, staffing needs must change in response to new developments.

I strongly believe, however, that the minority on every committee should have the right to hire and fire its own staff personnel, set their salary scales, and locate them without prior approval of the majority.

Last year, minority members of the Public Works Committee asked permission to hire an economist to assist them in consideration of the extremely involved implications of the Appalachian Development Act and the Public Works and Economic Development Act then pending before the Committee. These programs involved many social and economic factors not normally within the purview of the Public Works Committee. We needed to have competent outside advice and counsel. The majority turned us down, and we had no recourse but to swallow this decision and get along as best we could. This is wrong. We should have been able to make our own decision on this point and hire the expert we wanted. While I have no illusion that the final passage of some bills would have been changed, greater public knowledge would have resulted from clearer delineations of portions of them, and it is likely that improvements in the legislation could have been made during the drafting of the bills in committee.

(Another example drawn from the Committee on Public Works is the fact that as of this writing more than eight months have elapsed since a new subcommitte was authorized for the purpose of supervising, overseeing, and investigating the new Appalachian Redevelopment Program and the Public Works and Economic Development Act. Committee members of both parties unanimously adopted the Resolution creating the new subcommittee. This failure to activate the subcommittee, while not directly applicable to the minority staffing question, is further illustration of the need for the minority to have an investigative arm of its own. In this particular situation, even the majority seems powerless to enforce its own formally approved decision.

The minority has no chance at all.) (The subcommittee finally was activated July 13, 1966.—Ed.)

Frankly, I wish to state that this concern on my part does not stem entirely from the fact that I am a member of the current minority party. Although it is true we feel the brunt of this staff deprivation at the moment, I expect to feel no differently when my party is in the majority. Effective criticism from the loyal opposition is essential to good government, regardless of which party is in control. As far as I am concerned, the Republican Party has a commitment when it becomes a majority to see that the minority is provided adequate staffing.

REFERENCES

1. Hearings, Joint Committee on the Organization of Congress, 89th Cong., 1st Sess., Part 1, p. 74.
2. *Ibid.*, Part 4, p. 527.
3. Robinson, James A., *Congress, The First Branch of Government*, American Enterprise Institute, 1965, Library of Congress Catalog No. 66–14193, p. 273.
4. "But over the hill and horizon
   A light is beginning to burn;
   Dissent is getting respectful again,
   Thinking is taking a turn. . . .

   So courage my lonely colleagues,
   Be of good heart and of cheer;
   Minority views are sometimes read
   And the public's beginning to hear."

   From Supplemental Views of Rep. James C. Cleveland on S. 2394. 89th Congress, 2nd Session.

5. I had prepared an article for the *George Washington University Law Review*, which was not published due to the insistence of the faculty adviser that I omit a footnote naming the nine persons and monies received.
6. Rumsfeld, Rep. Donald, (R., Ill.), JCOC Hearings, Part 4, p. 538 (1965).
7. Conte., Rep. Silvio (R., Mass.), JCOC Hearings, Part 2, p. 278.
8. Wheare, K. C., *Government by Committee: An Essay on the British Constitution*, Oxford University Press, 1955.

HON. JOHN V. LINDSAY
Mayor of New York City

THE SENIORITY SYSTEM

*by Hon. John V. Lindsay**

There are three things you can do about the seniority system in Congress: you can attack it directly, you can gnaw at its edges, or you can leave it alone.

The most frustrating part of it is that the practice of elevating to the chairmanship and ranking minority positions the Members longest in point of service on each committee can be stopped at any time by both political parties, without a formal amendment of the rules!

Rule 10 of the Standing Rules of the House states:

> At the commencement of each Congress, the House shall elect as chairman of each standing committee one of the Members thereof; in the temporary absence of the chairman the Member next in rank in the order named in the election of the committee, and so on, as often as the case shall happen, shall act as chairman . . .[1]

Although selection of committee chairmen by seniority is clearly implied in the language "the Member next in rank . . . as often as the case shall happen," there is no actual *rule* of seniority. The Standing Rules provide for election of committee chairmen by the House. The full House, according to the rules, "shall elect as chairman of each standing committee one of the Members thereof . . ." Not necessarily the Member longest in service, but *one of the Members thereof.*

In actual practice, however, the House simply ratifies the decisions which have already been made on the basis of seniority. This is the way it works: Members are appointed to the standing committees by their party's committee on committees. These lists are then approved by the party's conference or caucus and submitted to the House. In the dullest of *pro forma*

---

* Mr. Lindsay was first elected to Congress in 1958 from the 17th Congressional District of New York. He served on the House Judiciary Committee, resigning his seat in Congress in 1965 when he was elected Mayor of New York City.

proceedings, the House "elects" as chairman of each standing committee the Member who was in fact *selected* by his party colleagues to serve as chairman. The sole determining factor in that selection, made in secret caucus, was length of service, or seniority.

How Old Is the Practice?

Dr. George Galloway, eminent historian of the House, marks the birth of seniority at 120 years ago in the Senate and 56 years ago in the House.[2] One of the most memorable speeches on the subject was delivered nearly a century ago, during protracted floor debate over committee assignments in the Senate in the 42nd Congress. The year was 1871, and the speaker was Senator John Sherman of Ohio:

> It has been the custom since I have been a member of the Senate, now more than ten years, for each party to arrange the members of that party on the different committees constitution [sic.] the Senate of the United States. Before I become a member of the Senate it was the common courtesy of the Democratic Senators, then a majority of this body, to allow the minority to fill the places assigned to them on the committees. The division of members of a political party among the various committees was regarded as in the nature of a personal matter, appertaining solely to that party, and not to be controlled or affected by the wishes or desires of the opposing party. . . . That has always been the custom, and therefore time out of mind, at the beginning of every new Congress, a meeting of our political friends has been held and these assignments have been made.[3]

The irony in recalling Sherman's speech is that in only six years the Senator was to become a sorry victim of the very system he had so stoutly defended. Sherman entered the Senate in 1861 and in time became chairman of the Finance Committee. In 1877 he resigned his seat—and his chairmanship of the Finance Committee—to become Secretary of the Treasury in the cabinet of President Hayes. When he returned to the Senate in 1881, he was reassigned to the Finance Committee all right, but at the bottom rung of the ladder.

The seniority system is less entrenched in the House than in the Senate. Prior to 1910, the Speaker of the House generally appointed both members and chairmen of the standing and select committees. That business ended in the revolt against Joe Cannon, when the Speaker was unceremoniously stripped of much of his previous authority, including the authority to appoint members and chairmen of the committees. Unfortunately, the practice of selecting chairmen and ranking minority members on the basis of seniority developed quickly and firmly in the political caucuses of both parties.

How Widespread Is the Practice?

In response to a question put to it by Congressman Morris Udall, the Library of Congress found that "there is not a single State legislature or a free world parliament that operates under this system except the U.S. Congress."

Rep. Udall: "I asked the Library of Congress a couple of years ago to answer me one question, and the question was: How many of the parliaments of the free world, the American States, and the free world parliaments, use this indispensable system? The answer is none; none, except the U.S. Congress. Fifty State legislatures, the British, French, the Swedes, the Australians, no one else uses what we are told is an indispensable system to which we are told there is no alternative."[4]

If imitation is the sincerest form of flattery, the U.S. Congress is not exactly overwhelmed with compliments in the way she selects her leaders. Admittedly, "We're only Number Two" as living democracies go—but do we "try harder?"

In summary, we see that seniority (1) is *not* a written rule of the House but is instead a practice which developed in the political parties; (2) in the House, at least, is of relatively recent origin, and (3) as practiced in the U.S. Congress is a system unique among the world's parliaments and even among the legislatures of our own fifty States.

Why Is the System Bad?

There are some people, of course, who maintain that it is not bad. The standard cliché among Members of Congress is: "The longer you're around here, the better you like seniority." No doubt.

Eighty years ago Woodrow Wilson characterized our federal apparatus as "government by the chairmen of the standing committees of Congress."[5] This was something of an exaggeration then and certainly misses the mark today. But there remains a strong element of truth in the phrase, as illustrated in the following compilation by *Congressional Quarterly* of a committee chairman's powers:

Meetings may be called on short notice, at times when certain members are known to be absent. Or, as a stalling tactic, a chairman can neglect to call meetings.

In most committees, the chairman also controls the agenda. He can bring up a bill without notice, under circumstances in which his recommendation carries great weight because other members do not know what the bill does. . . . He can also refuse to place bills on the agenda.

The chairman also appoints subcommittees and subcommittee chairmen.

He either manages bills on the floor himself or appoints a floor manager. . . . He usually heads the conferees appointed to work out differences on legislation with the other chamber, or influences their appointment.

The chairman has the major voice in hiring committee staff, and he controls the disbursal of authorized travel funds, saying which members may go on field trips. . . .[6]

In America's continuing experiment in democracy, the seniority system operates to elevate men to positions of leadership in Congress without regard to any qualification except length of service. As presently practiced, the system is unsound, inflexible, undemocratic, and certainly discouraging to junior Members of Congress. Even the "law of the jungle" operates on a higher level than the "law" of seniority: the first at least works to assure survival of the fittest; the latter operates only to assure survival of the oldest.

Arguments in Favor of Retaining the System

Let us now examine the arguments put forward to retain the seniority system. First, the argument of Experience: "New Members must learn their way around before they can qualify for chairmanships. There is no substitute for the time that this learning process requires."[7]

No one who has served in Congress will deny that experience is a valuable factor in considering the appointment of a committee chairman. It takes a year or more to unravel the legislative process; most freshman Members would shy away from the reins of a major committee even if they had the opportunity presented to them to grab hold. The fallacy in the Experience argument is that tenure is no guarantee of ability. As the late Estes Kefauver summed it up:

> This much can be said in favor of rule by seniority: the law of averages works in its favor. In many cases, because of knowledge and skill acquired during years of grappling with problems that regularly come before his committee, the man who is handed the chairmanship through seniority in most cases would be chosen for the post by any system of more democratic election that might be devised. But there is abundant evidence to prove that fitness and leadership are not based upon years in office alone.[8]

In the same vein, the argument of Committee Expertise:

> Long service on a committee develops a certain expertise on particular problems which is an essential qualification of the office of chairman. Ranking Members have acquired an acquaintance with most subjects likely to come before the committee and with the personalities and private interests with whom it has to deal. There is also the gain which comes from Members becoming acquainted with one another and learning how to work together. The committee becomes more of a unit as its membership becomes more stable.[9]

Unquestionably, any committee's efficiency would be impaired whose chairman lacked knowledge of its special problems and routine functions. But the point can be made that long service does not *necessarily* produce expertise. Natural ability, devoted interest, and applied study do. I suspect Kefauver was right in predicting that most committee chairmen would be re-elected on the basis of proved expertise whether the system of seniority prevailed or not. But to assume that the man longest in service on a committee is *therefore* the most expert in handling the business of that committee is to present an argument based on something other than hard logic. Expertise, harmony, and continuity from one Congress to the next are all desirable factors in determining leadership positions. However, as Professor Holcombe notes, party leaders

> . . . are not necessarily the ablest members of the party. They may even be grotesquely unsuited for the chairmanship of the important committees on which they happen to serve. They may be out of sympathy with, or even bitterly opposed to, the measures favored by the majority of their fellow partisans. They may be suffering grievously from the infirmities of old age.[10]

Next, the argument that seniority prevents log-rolling and dissension within the political parties:

> Abolition of the rule (sic) would be followed by log-rolling, factional fights, and political trading on a grand scale. "The danger," writes Professor Chamberlain, "that most committee places would go to those who were chosen with specific bills or policies in mind would be real and would be suspected even where it did not exist. The bitter personal feelings engendered by an open contest for committee places would complicate party management, and there would be delay in beginning work in each new Congress until personal and sectional quarrels could be smoothed out." The rule provides a kind of automatic protocol, like one's place at table at a state dinner or the order of appearance of counsel before the Supreme Court, which settles harmoniously the problem of priority without dispute or controversy and without jeopardizing morale.[11]

Galloway effectively rebuts this argument by pointing out that, indeed,

> One of the greatest drawbacks of the seniority system is that it destroys party responsibility or prevents political parties from performing their campaign promises. For if the chairmen of committees owe their places not to their political parties but to the accident of tenure, then they can follow their own inclinations on legislative matters and disregard the platform pledges and legislative program of the party leaders.[12]

Griffith illustrates the point in even more glaring terms (although on balance Dr. Griffith is disposed to favor selection by seniority):

> If one is an advocate of responsible and disciplined party government, the seniority rule is certainly an obstacle. . . . To put the matter in concrete terms, if the Democrats are in control, about 60% of the committee chairmen are from the South, which is in general its conservative sector. If the Republicans control, about 60% of the chairmen are from the Middle West, which is usually more conservative. . . . If leadership is, as it should be, a reflection of the general will of the majority of a legislative body, then such overweighting is a serious matter.[13]

As for seniority providing a "kind of automatic protocol," it is precisely the rigidity and complacency which any automatic method of selection imposes or conduces that we are trying to get away from. The problem of "jeopardizing morale," it should be noted, will remain as long as Congress refuses to deal with the conduct of its Members at least by establishing a code of ethics and grappling with the actual, not talked about, restructuring of its organization and procedures in keeping with the changing times.

The Insulation argument runs as follows:

> Committee chairmen are reelected to Congress because their constituents desire to retain the power and prestige of their office. Long and continued service in Congress and the local benefits derived therefrom would be discouraged by abolition of the seniority system.[14]

Proponents of this theory argue that because Members from so-called "safe" districts are in almost no danger of being removed from office, they are free to exercise judgment that will result in legislation in the national interest.

The argument would have some validity if we could accept the premise that Members representing non-marginal districts were insulated, also, from the pressures of important lobby groups and sectional bias. Unfortunately, Members are often removed from fear of reprisal at the polls only because they share the parochial prejudices of their constituents, which may or may not coincide with the national platform of the Member's party or reflect a national concensus. As Professor Dahl writes,

> Such validity as this argument has must apply entirely to the question of rationality, not that of responsibility. For often enough, it may be the old and senior member who is most at odds with the bulk of his party and the platform on which that party was elected to govern the country. By erecting seniority into a principle, committees may be converted, in effect, into associations of members responsible only to their own constituents, not, in any meaningful sense, to the national electorate as a whole.[15]

A study by *Congressional Quarterly* of Urban-Suburban-Rural House Districts in 1963 showed the following distribution of House chairmanships and ranking minority positions in the second session of the 88th Congress:

	Urban	Suburban	Rural
Chairmen (Democrats)	4	1	17
Ranking Minority (Republicans)	3	4	15

These statistics hardly reflect an equitable representation of the two Americans out of every three who live in and around the nation's cities!

From a compilation of roll call votes in the 87th Congress on which the President's position was ascertainable, *Congressional Quarterly* found that only three of the chairmen of the twenty standing committees of the House supported the leader of their party as often as 75% of the time.[16]

A thorough statistical analysis of the 85th Congress by George Goodwin elicited this less forceful yet still disconcerting conclusion:

> (My) statistical analysis does not make as clear a case against seniority as many of the critics of the system seem to claim. Chairmen are older on the average than their colleagues, and yet with luck a number of younger men are singled out for chairmanships. The districts which produce chairmen are not as stagnant as is often suggested, and the degree of party unity and presidential support among chairmen is not as low as many believe. The picture, however, is far from the ideal held by the proponents of majority rule.[17]

Occasionally, arguments by supporters of the seniority system attempt to justify it by pointing out that "It is no more than fair or just that Members who have been in Congress a long time should be rewarded with committee chairmanships."[18] As far as I am concerned, this argument has been demolished in one memorable sentence by Senator Gore:

> A rule by which a member for no reason except seniority automatically becomes chairman of a committee and so remains until death or defeat is indefensible in principle.[19]

As for the last-ditch cry that "The seniority rule is neither absolute nor invariable; on many occasions the House has ignored this rule and designated members of low committee rank as chairmen," Dr. Galloway was able to record in his authoritiative book only one such deviation—and that occurred in 1921—since the practice of seniority took root in the House in 1910.

Finally, it is argued that "Members with long service have greater prestige and influence than new members." To dispute this, Senate historian George Haynes has written:

> There is this much of logic in the seniority rule: it usually brings to the headship of the committee a man who has had many years of experience in handling the special problems in its domain. . . . (But) servile compliance with the seniority rule involves gamblers' chances. It is a limited appeal to the lot. It implies merely duration of service on the committee—not in the least does it guarantee superior ability or fitness for leadership.[21]

Gnawing at the Edges

Testifying before a Senate committee during hearings 18 years ago to evaluate the Legislative Reorganization Act of 1946, Senator Robert LaFollette, chairman of the joint committee from which the Act had come, plaintively told his colleagues:

> We were unable to get any substantial agreement on methods to improve the seniority system in the selection of committee chairmen. . . . The committee had a great many suggestions made to it . . . but frankly, I have never seen a solution which I thought was better than the disease.[22]

Unfortunately, the result of the 1946 Act was to treat the symptoms rather than the disease. This is illustrated in the following excerpts from testimony of George H. E. Smith, former staff director of the Senate Republican Policy Committee, in the course of these same hearings:

> Under the Reorganization Act . . . the power of the chairman is shared by the committee as a whole. He cannot appoint the staff without committee approval . . . He cannot work by proxies . . . He cannot report a measure unless a majority of the committee were actually present . . . He must conduct all hearings in public . . .
>
> In the light of these limitations on the power of committee chairmen and opportunities afforded to others regardless of seniority, the matter of seniority loses much of its former importance. At the same time, the usefulness of the seniority

rule in solving conflicting claims is retained and no satisfactory substitute has been found.[23]

Smith's argument that "the matter of seniority loses much of its former importance . . . in the light of these limitations on the power of committee chairmen" holds only to the degree the limitations imposed *actually curtail* the authority of committee chairmen. In fact, the symptoms persist because the "disease" is still with us. For example, Rule 11 of the Standing Rules of the House provides that committee staff shall be appointed

by majority vote of the committee . . . without regard to political affiliations and solely on the basis of fitness to perform the duties of the office . . .

In spite of this language, committee chairmen may and do appoint staff without approval of the full committee. Again, the Rules clearly state that

No measure or recommendation shall be reported from any committee unless a majority of the committee were actually present.

In spite of this language, committee chairmen may and do work by proxies. "The fault," Cassius reminded Brutus, "is not in our stars, but in ourselves, that we are underlings."

Another form of gnawing at the edges is seen in the proposals to limit the number of terms a committee chairman may serve, or to force him to retire at a certain age. Again, as in the attempt to limit the chairman's powers, the attempt to limit his length of service attacks only the periphery of the problem. Granted, a limitation of terms or age does have merit, but *not* as a "solution" to the seniority problem.

Alternatives to the Seniority System

Postulating three basic prerequisites—"ability, which embraces knowledge, training, and experience; loyalty to the national interest rather than to local or sectional interest; and a sense of political responsibility to execute party covenants with the people"[24]—Galloway poses seven conceivable methods of selecting committee chairmen:

1. Automatic elevation by seniority.
2. Election from the floor.
3. Selection by a committee on committees.
4. Appointment by the Speaker of the House and the presiding officers of the Senate (or by the majority leaders in each chamber).
5. Automatic rotation in office at periodic intervals.
6. Secret election by committee members.
7. Secret election by party caucus.

We may eliminate the first three possibilities, as the system now in effect is a combination of this trio: committee chairmen are "elected" from the floor, *after* the respective committees on committees have submitted their lists, which were dictated in party caucus by application of the "law" of seniority.

Appointment by the Speaker (No. 4) has flunked the test of history, as seen in the 1910 revolt against Speaker Cannon.

The rotation plan has a great deal of merit, notwithstanding its automatic feature. According to the Atomic Energy Act, the chairmanship of the Joint Committee on Atomic Energy must alternate between House and Senate in succeeding Congresses. Three Senators and three Representatives have filled the post with distinction in the ten years of the committee's existence. Testifying before the Joint Committee on the Organization of Congress last year, present JCAE Chairman Chet Holifield noted:

> Each of my colleagues in the chairmanship has brought talents and ideas and resourcefulness to the job. Each has gained valuable experience in the chairmanship role. Each has been responsive to and considerate of other committee members' ideas and suggestions. The understanding that the chairman's tenure was alternating rather than continuous prevented the growth of complacency and inspired each chairman to excel in performance.[25]

This would be an acceptable alternative to selection by strict seniority.

Two other methods seem to me to present attractive alternatives to the seniority system: election of committee chairmen by secret ballot within the respective party caucuses, and election by secret ballot within each committee. The former has the advantage of strengthening the role of the parties in the legislative process, but it carries some dangers of potential factionalism and swapping of state delegations. However, this alternative has been advanced by the highly respected American Assembly of Columbia University, by many political scientists, and by some Members of Congress. Certainly, it is vastly preferable to the strict application of seniority.

I am personally inclined to favor selection of committee chairmen by secret ballot of the members of each committee. Each of the standing committees of the House is a semi-autonomous body with its own unique problems and special norms. Committee members, by observing each other at close range in the daily operations of the committee, would seem to me to be in the best position to judge the qualifications necessary for their chairman, and they certainly are aware of intelligence or personality traits which are often important to a smooth-working relationship. Committees are the workshops of Congress; their members should determine who should be seated at the head of the worktable.

However, this warning applies to any and all methods of selecting committee chairmen: as long as Members of Congress agree among themselves to elevate their colleagues according to length of service, no amendment of House rules will abolish the rite. Neither will the problem be solved by such peripheral attacks as the attempt to establish uniform procedures for all committees or to force chairmen to retire at a certain age. As we have seen from the operation of the 1946 Act, the first cannot be enforced; the second, unfortunately, is directed at senility rather than seniority.

Speakers, majority leaders and minority leaders, have long been elected by the usual democratic process of casting a ballot, with each party electing its own. It is a tribute to the ability and integrity of the Members that highly qualified men have uniformly emerged in these positions of general leadership. It would seem that a similar system in the committee structure would serve to strengthen the operations of the legislative branch. A responsible legislative body must make every effort to avoid even the occasional disaster that is caused by the blind application of the seniority "rule." The contention has been made that perhaps ambitious and unscrupulous members would trade their votes for the next twenty years in exchange for votes to become chairman. That has never been the operation of the Congress as a whole in the election of minority and majority leaders or the Speaker, and there is absolutely no basis for believing that it would happen in the individual committees.

In closing, the words of Douglass Cater seem to me to present a most eloquent argument for abolishing the seniority system:

> Mostly the reporter comes to accept a certain amount of mystery about the way the House works. He observes the numerous impediments that have been placed in the way of majority rule and the cumbersome procedures for getting around these impediments. But he can never be sure when the seeming frustration of majority rule is simply the working of a silent majority within the membership. One thing is clear. More than in the Senate, raw power in the House is vested in a group of chieftains, a dozen or so, who are pretty much unknown to the public at large. Men of vast seniority, they mostly represent small rural districts where their seignioral rights are seldom challenged. They tend to view their power as a personal accomplishment . . .[26]

It is a little difficult to say with pride that ours is a government of laws and not of men when power and prestige in Congress are not won, as they should be, through diligent, intelligent achievement, but are rather "awarded" to the winners of the continuing race against time.

REFERENCES

1. *Rules of the U.S. House of Representatives*, 89th Congress, 1st session. This provision was adopted April 5, 1911, and continued in the Legislative Reorganization Act of 1946, 60 Stat. 812.
2. Galloway, George B., *Congress at the Crossroads*, New York, Thomas Y. Crowell Co., 1946. "Seniority in point of service has been the prevailing principle governing both committee assignments and the selection of Chairmen since 1846 in the Senate and 1910 in the House." p. 187.
3. Quoted by Galloway in "History of Seniority System in the Senate," Legislative Reference Service, 1959, unpublished.
4. U.S. Congress, Joint Committee on the Organization of Congress, Hearings, 89th Congress, 1st session, Part 1. For full testimony of Rep. Udall (D., Ariz.), see pp. 132–165.
5. Wilson, Woodrow. *Congressional Government*. Originally published in 1885.

6. *Congressional Quarterly*, Special Report on "Congressional Reform: An Examination of the Structure, Operation, Rules and Customs of Congress, and Proposals for Revision," revised April 1, 1964.
7. From a compilation by Frederick L. Scott, Legislative Reference Service, "Seniority as the Basis for the Selection of Committee Chairmen." 1954, unpublished.
8. Kefauver, Estes, and Dr. Jack Levin, *A Twentieth-Century Congress*, New York, Duell, Sloan, & Pearce, Inc., 1947.
9. *Congressional Digest*, August–September, 1945. From a compilation of arguments in favor of retention of the seniority system by the Committee on Congress of the American Political Science Association.
10. Holcombe, Arthur M., *Our More Perfect Union*, Cambridge, Harvard University Press, 1950.
11. *Congressional Digest*, *op. cit.*
12. Galloway, *op. cit.*
13. Griffith, Ernest S., *Congress: Its Contemporary Role*, New York, New York University Press, third ed., 1961.
14. *Congressional Digest*, *op. cit.*
15. Dahl, Robert A., *Congress and Foreign Policy*, New York, Harcourt, Brace & World, 1950.
16. *Congressional Quarterly* Special Report, *op. cit.*
17. Goodwin, George, Jr. "The Seniority System in Congress," *The American Political Science Review*, June 1959. For the 85th Congress, Goodwin found that "the 109 most urban districts produced 21 per cent of the House chairmen, the 108 next most urban produced 5 per cent, the 110 next most urban 16 per cent, and the 108 least urban 58 per cent."
18. Scott compilation, L.R.S., *op. cit.*
19. Rep. Albert Gore, in testimony before the Joint Committee on the Organization of Congress, 1945.
20. Galloway, George B., *History of the U.S. House of Representatives*, New York, Thomas Y. Crowell Co., 3rd printing, 1962.
21. Haynes, George Henry, *The Senate of the United States: Its History and Practice*, Boston, Houghton Mifflin Co., 1938.
22. U.S. Congress, Senate, Committee on Expenditures in the Executive Departments, Hearings, 80th Congress, 2nd session (1948).
23. *Ibid.*
24. Galloway, *op. cit.* In summary, Galloway states: "Of the seven possible methods listed above, the only ones that seem most likely to result in the selection of chairmen of ability, public interest, and party accountability are selection by party caucus, by the committee on committees, or by the presiding officer or majority leader. Men of undoubted ability and devotion to the public interest might be chosen by the other methods, but they fail to satisfy the important test of party responsibility. Major importance is attached to this test because, unless political parties can be held responsible for fidelity to their campaign pledges, then party platforms are a snare and a delusion and public confidence in the party system will wither away."
25. U.S. Congress, Senate. Hearings before the Joint Committee on the Organization of Congress, Part 2, May 17, 1965.
26. Cater, Douglass, "Spotlight on the House," *The Reporter*, September 28, 1961.

58845

ROBERT P. GRIFFIN,
U.S. Senator from Michigan

RULES AND PROCEDURE OF THE STANDING COMMITTEES

by Robert P. Griffin, U.S. Senator*

The twenty standing committees of the House and their subcommittees perform the difficult and time-consuming work relating to the economic, social, technological, scientific, military, and foreign affairs problems which face the country today. If the committees are properly structured, if they are adequately staffed and are ably and fairly directed, if the rules of the committees are so written as to assure full participation by all members, and if all Members recognize their duty to serve as an effective check upon the Executive Branch and to represent the individual citizen in organized society, then the House will properly serve its historical function as the co-equal branch of government closest to the people.

The trouble is that committees of the House (and of the Senate) are not performing effective service today. They have failed to arm themselves with the necessary staffs to meet the Executive Branch on its own terms; data retrieval, computer technology, and communications advances are ignored or ill-used. Appointment of Members to committees and selection of committee chairmen are not made on the most rational basis; scheduling and floor procedure frequently impede effective action. Additionally, the use and misuse of committee rules decisively contribute to the general debilitation of representative government.

In some respects, committee rules glorify the chairman in a manner which diminishes the contribution that could be made by more junior Members of

* Sen. Griffin, first elected to Congress in 1956 from the 9th Congressional District of Michigan, served as second ranking minority Member of the House Education and Labor Committee, the Government Operations Committee, and the Joint Committee on the Organization of Congress. In May, 1966, he resigned his House seat to accept appointment as Senator from Michigan.

his own party. In other cases, committee rules are misused by a chairman or a majority of a committee in a way which defeats the purpose of Congress. Equally important, committee rules are so fashioned as to hamper the effectiveness of the minority party.

The latter point is far more significant than one may initially conceive. We are taught that we have a tripartite form of government, complete with a series of checks and balances. To some extent, this is true. But when the President and the majority in Congress are of the same political party, there develops an affinity of political purpose and mutual assistance, and in periods of history when a domineering President exists, as is the case today, there is an even greater tendency for the majority party in Congress to become subservient to the will of the President.

The subservience of the majority party in Congress to the executive branch can be seen in innumerable ways. Chairmen of committees will not routinely schedule hearings unless the Administration has sent up a bill. This is so even though Members of the chairman's own party have introduced related legislation and have requested hearings. If the Administration is opposed to certain proposed legislation, it is most unusual for a committee to proceed independently. A committee will rarely investigate objectively and fully any conduct by the Administration which might prove embarrassing to the majority party. The Administration will deliberately withhold information Congress needs and is entitled to, or it will fail to enforce legislation or spend money Congress has enacted or appropriated without much more than a murmur from the majority party.

The majority party in Congress tends to look upon itself more as a political ally and supporter of a President of the same political party than as a separate and independent branch of government, standard behavior whether Republicans or Democrats are in control.

A few Congressional uprisings have occurred recently over courses of action taken or proposed by the Administration—protests by the Armed Service Committees, resolutions and speeches by Members opposed to activities in Vietnam, disputes concerning disarmament negotiations or NATO operations, etc.—but the prominence given to such activities by the communications media demonstrates how rare and unusual these eruptions have become.

In short, the party controlling Congress generally does not offer an effective check on the Executive Branch, and the rules of committees are so fashioned as to hinder the efforts of the minority party to offer such opposition.

The rules of the House provide in detail for the conduct of business by committee. In addition, House Rule XI, clause 26(a), authorizes committees to adopt additional rules not inconsistent with the House Rules. This authority is so broad, and the House Rules are in most instances so general in nature, that a majority of a committee may easily ride roughshod over the rights of the minority. Equally significant is the fact that almost every committee divides itself into subcommittees, which, in turn, perform the major work of a committee. Yet nowhere in the Rules of the House are subcommittees even mentioned, let alone regulated. Perhaps of greatest importance, the Rules of the House and the rules and practices of committees grant the chairmen of committees wide-ranging authority so that little effective opposition can be developed within a committee if a chairman believes that it will embarrass the Administration of which he is a senior party member.

To understand how chairmen acquire such authority and how the operations of the minority are thwarted, we must examine the Rules of the House and of the committees. Eight of the twenty standing committees of the House (*i.e.*, those that have the authority to report legislation as well as conduct investigations) have not adopted separate committee rules.[1] But the absence of rules does not alter to any appreciable extent the manner in which committees operate.

Rule XI provides that all proposed legislation and related matters shall be referred to the particular standing committee having jurisdiction over the subject matter of the proposals. From this authority, as well as authority generally considered to run with the prerogatives of chairmanship, eight standing committees have given to the chairman alone the right to refer bills to or recall them from subcommittees. One standing committee provides that such bills shall be referred to particular subcommittees unless a majority of the committee otherwise directs. Another committee grants such authority to either the chairman or a majority of the committee. Three committees, in adopting separate rules, make no provision on this matter, while eight committees have no separate committee rules.

Thus, a majority of the committees has formally given the chairman total control over the consideration of matters that may come before the committee. The same authority has been found to exist in those committees not having separate committee rules or which have issued no rule on this matter. In spite of language to the contrary, the two committees providing for alternative means of referral have, in practice, permitted the chairman to exercise such authority.*

In the same vein, eight committees by rule have granted the chairman sole authority to schedule hearings, while the remaining twelve have either informally extended to him such power or have done so through committee resolution.

The breadth and importance of such authority can only be appreciated fully when one examines how it is used to regulate the activities of the entire House. In the Education and Labor Committee, on which I formerly served as second-ranking member, the minority received notice one day last year

*The committees that have adopted additional rules are: Agriculture, Armed Services, Banking and Currency, District of Colombia, Education and Labor, Foreign Affairs, Government Operations, Interior and Insular Affairs, Post Office and Cival Service, Public Works, Science and Astronautics, and Un-American Activities. In addition, certain committees adopt limited rules through resolutions at the beginning of each Congress.

that a full Committee meeting was to be scheduled within a few hours. A $100-a-plate fund-raising dinner at which the President was to speak had been scheduled by the majority party for that evening. The meeting was called to consider the higher education bill. Even though hundreds of millions or even billions of dollars were involved, the chairman of the Committee permitted only 15 minutes of debate on the bill before it was put to a vote and reported out of Committee. Following this most irregular course of action, the President was able that evening to announce a great accomplishment at the dinner.

Another example of the chairman's power was seen recently in the Banking and Currency Committee. A notice of a Committee hearing on the proposed Participation Sales Bill was given to the minority one day in advance. Copies of the bill were not made available until 15 minutes before the hearings commenced. No subcommittee hearings had been held. Only two Administration witnesses were scheduled to testify. No member was permitted more than five minutes for interrogation. Many members were not allowed to complete their questioning. After about two hours and a half, the hearing was closed and the bill was reported. This was a major piece of legislation. It authorized the Administration to sell about $4.2 billion in federally-owned loans to private parties at an interest rate approximately 2 per cent higher than the government was paying, with the government making up the difference in interest payments.

Still another example of this type of activity occurred in 1964, when the House Post Office and Civil Service Committee scheduled a meeting on an important and costly federal salary bill one day after the bill had been introduced. The Committee held no hearings on the bill; not one witness appeared before the Committee to testify on the measure. The meeting convened at 10:35 A.M., and at 11:30 A.M. discussion was cut off and the bill was reported to the House by the majority.

Almost every bill introduced in Congress contains flaws, both of substance and of form. This is especially true of the important, lengthy, costly, and technically complicated bills. They need to be corrected in committee after hearings and after the testimony of witnesses has been digested.

A chairman who is granted control over the referral of all business and the scheduling of meetings obviously has it in his power to prevent a matter from being considered. In the Government Operations Committee, for example, where I also served as second-ranking member, a number of majority and minority members have been pushing for enactment of the Intergovernmental Cooperation Act, which was passed by the Senate in the last session of Congress. This Act would require Congress to review federal grand-in-aid programs periodically, strengthen the ability of States to administer and coordinate financial operations, encourage greater planning by metropolitan and regional organizations in the use of federal financial assistance, and provide for additional improvements in federal-state relationships. Although the bill has bipartisan support and has been praised by many private and public organizations associated with regional and local government planning, it remained buried in Committee until the President expressed some interest. Even then, however, only limited hearings have been held and it appears the bill may die.

In the same Committee, the minority party members have proposed establishment of a new Hoover-type commission to investigate inefficiency in the organization and operation of government. The Government Operations Committee is regularly faced with reorganization proposals sent up by the President. These are usually dreamed up by the Bureau of the Budget and few people can understand the underlying rationale or the standards used for them. As a consequence, the organization of the Executive Branch becomes more confused and disrupted. There is a definite need for a high-level and bipartisan examination of such organization. But these proposals remain dormant.

Rule XI, clause 25, of the House Rules does require that each standing committee fix regular weekly, biweekly, or monthly meeting days for the transaction of business. Additional meetings may be called by the chairman. If the chairman fails to call a meeting, a majority of the committee is granted authority to do so.

None of the twenty standing committees, however, consistently hold regularly scheduled meetings. Of the twelve committees that have adopted formal rules of their own, nine specify days for such regular meetings, but they frequently ignore such rules. Similarly, many of these committees' rules appear to violate the House rule. For example, the Committees on Agriculture, Banking and Currency, Science and Astronautics, and Armed Services permit the chairman on his own authority to dispense with calling a regularly scheduled meeting, while the Post Office and Civil Service Committee grants such permission to the chairman if concurred in by the ranking majority and minority members. The Public Works Committee specifies that the committee shall meet at such times as the chairman may designate. The House rule is also ignored by those committees which do not adopt formal rules.

It is possible for a majority of the committee to call a special meeting under the House rule if the chairman fails to do so. Recently a majority of the Banking and Currency Committee overcame the chairman's efforts to block Committee consideration of a bill relating to the establishment of procedures for reviewing proposed bank mergers. Similarly, instances have occurred where a chairman, faced with the threat of majority revolt, has relented and called a hearing in order to avoid losing control of his committee. This happened in the 88th Congress, in the Judiciary Committee, when a majority of its members wished to consider a resolution to investigate the manner in which the Department of Justice was conducting certain criminal investigations.

However, this authority is rarely used because members of the majority are either in tune with the chairman's action or are extremely reluctant to challenge his authority. It is only when a chairman has grown so dictatorial or erratic in his behavior or when he obstinately and persistently stifles the will of the majority that this rule is utilized. Rarely, it may be added, will this rule be of any use to the minority party, particularly when minority members are seeking to check the authority of the Administration.

The need exists, then, for rules to protect the rights of the minority party to receive adequate notice of and participation in the deliberation of legislation and to have proposed legislation considered.

In regard to the first point, a rule of the House should be adopted that no matter shall be taken up by a committee or a subcommittee unless three days advance notice is given to all members of the committee. Second, every member should be entitled to at least a half-hour examination of each witness if he so desires. Third, a minimum period of three days should be required between reporting a bill from subcommittee and consideration of it by full committee. Moreover, the rule should provide that the three-day provision could be waived only by unanimous consent. (The Agriculture, Armed Services, and Science and Astronautics Committees presently require such delay, but it is often waived.) Fourth, adequate provision should be made for the right of members to call witnesses.

In many instances, it is difficult to enforce rules even when they seem precise on their face. This has been the case regarding the scheduling of regular meeting days. To remedy this, a provision should be included specifying that a point of order will lie against a committee's proceeding if the rules are violated. Through this means, the matter could be blocked from consideration on the Floor of the House until the rule had been complied with.

Concerning the other aspect of this problem, a rule of the House should be adopted providing that on a set day once a month, each member of the committee shall have the right to call up one bill and ask for a hearing on it. If he is supported by a majority vote, the day and a minimum time would be set for the hearing. Each member would be entitled to call up one bill at each meeting and, if voted down, would have the right to call up the same bill at the next meeting. This provision somewhat resembles the Calendar Wednesday procedure for consideration on the House floor of bills stymied in the Rules Committee or sidetracked by the House leadership. The monthly meeting should not be dispensed with, except by unanimous consent, to avoid majority domination. In the event a meeting is not held, any member should be authorized to call up one bill, as a privileged motion, on the floor of the House within seven legislative days after the date when the meeting should have been held. The number of hours for debate on such a bill should also be provided for in the rule. This right to call up a bill by a member, as a privileged motion and without previous consideration in committee, is not inconsistent with established parliamentary procedure. Under the Reorganization Act, any member has such a right involving reorganization proposals sent down by the President.

Among the dominant powers possessed by chairmen of committees is that of control over the time allotted for hearings and who shall testify at such hearings. Equity demands that a rule be established giving each member the right to examine each witness for at least one-half hour, and permitting members to call witnesses.

Chairmen of a number of committees arbitrarily, and in my opinion unwisely, limit debate on important pieces of legislation. In the interest of upholding representative government and of affording an effective check upon a domineering President, it is essential that debate not be emasculated. The latent ability of all chairmen to exercise this power means that even the fairest chairmen may be under pressure at some time in the future to act arbitrarily when there is the greatest need to examine a proposal at length.

There is nothing in the Rules of the House directly authorizing committee chairmen to restrict the time of debate or of examining witnesses. However, of the twelve standing committees that have adopted formal rules, five provide that the chairmen may limit each member to five minutes in examining a witness; three provide for ten-minute periods; and two simply provide that the chairmen may limit the time according to the time available, importance of subject matter, etc. As for debate, one committee provides for a five-minute period; three provide for ten-minute periods; and two provide for time limitations without specifying exact time periods. In addition, chairmen of certain of the committees which do not have formal rules also impose time limits upon the members.

In actual practice, most committee chairmen seldom enforce these time limitations. Those who do usually are fair in extending equal time to the minority members. But even when time limits are imposed fairly, the minority is frequently unable to develop an adequate record. This is so because the committee will usually be considering an Administration proposal which has been widely propagandized in advance through Presidential messages, press releases, news stories, etc. Similarly, since the chairman controls the scheduling of witnesses, the Administration witnesses will be given a major share of the time to develop their case. To attempt fully to explore a technical piece of legislation, demonstrate its weaknesses, develop alternatives, or challenge its necessity is almost impossible in five minutes or even sixty minutes.

Therefore, each member of a committee should be entitled by right to examine each witness for one half hour. In addition, each member should be entitled in executive session (where passage of a bill is being considered) to address the chair for one half hour. This right would not be unconscionable because the majority of legislation develops little controversy and members would have little inclination to use the time. Similarly, hearings are usually conducted in subcommittees where a small number of members are present. Experience shows that the privilege of reasonable examination or debate is rarely abused in those committees which do not impose strict time limitations. The proposed rule would provide members with a reasonable period of time to explore important and involved legislative proposals and would permit the development of a solid record.

Closely related to this matter is the right to call witnesses. Nothing in the Rules of the House relating to committee operations directly provides for the calling of witnesses, with one exception discussed below. The rules of those committees which have adopted their own rules are also strangely silent on this matter. In practice, the chairman of a committee exercises this right as part of his residual powers to schedule hearings and regulate the course of business. (The House Rules do contain a group of provisions relating to the appearance of witnesses before committees, but these have been included for the protection of witnesses or for the preservation of orderly procedure.)

The exception to the absence of authority in the House Rules to the calling of witnesses is found in Rule XI, clauses 2, 8, and 18. There, the Committees on Appropriations, Government Operations, and Un-American Activities are given authority to sit while the House is in session, or has recessed or adjourned; and the chairmen and the subcommittee chairmen (or any member designated by such) are authorized to subpoena witnesses and documents. Every other standing committee (except Rules, House Administration, and Ways and Means)[1] must obtain authority at the beginning of each Congress through a House resolution to sit regardless of whether the House has recessed or adjourned, and these resolutions authorize the chairmen of their respective committees (or members designated by them) to subpoena witnesses and documents.

It could be argued, then, that the right of a chairman to subpoena witnesses includes in it the right to request witnesses without subpoena. Such logic is open to question. The right is an inherent part of a committee's authority to conduct hearings and investigations (upheld by courts of law pursuant to Constitutional interpretation). It has gravitated to the chairmen of committees as have most other powers. If this were not an inherent right, it might be added, chairmen of subcommittees who do request the presence of witnesses (without first receiving authority of the full committee chairman) would be acting contrary to House rules.

The fact remains that the chairmen of committees do possess almost exclusive authority to invite witnesses to testify, and this authority can have a detrimental effect upon the rights of the minority.

Examples were presented above describing how, in the Banking and Currency Committee the chairman restricted testimony on the Sales Participation Bill to two Administration witnesses, while no witnesses were called by the chairman of the Post Office and Civil Service Committee on the federal salary bill. Others examples readily come to mind. This year (1966) the chairman of the Education and Labor Committee conducted hearings on the operations of the Poverty Program. He limited testimony to Administration witnesses, business and university representatives who operate Job Corps projects, and a few other non-controversial persons. Minority members on the committee had requested that representatives of the poor be invited to present their side of the story, but to no avail.

The chairman of the Banking and Currency Committee precipitated a new row with many majority and minority members of his committee in 1966 by issuing subpoenas for extensive amounts of confidential information from banks throughout the country. These were issued without first consulting with the other committee members. Although this is not directly related to the scheduling of witnesses for hearings, it is illustrative of the authority of a chairman to influence and guide the course that hearings and investigations will take.

As in other instances, most chairmen are fair in honoring the requests of members, including minority members, that particular witnesses appear and testify at hearings. But the power is there to refuse such requests, and as we have seen occasions arise when requests are refused.

Therefore, a rule of the House should be adopted which would authorize chairmen of committees to request the appearance of witnesses. In addition, the rule should also provide that at any hearing each member of the committee should have the right to request the appearance of one witness.

In a related manner, the Rules of the House ought to be amended to authorize every committee to sit when the House has recessed or adjourned, and for every committee chairman to have the right to issue subpoenas, subject to approval from a majority of the committee.

Rule XIII, clause 2, of the House Rules provides that "all reports of committees, . . . together with the views of the minority, shall be delivered to the clerk for printing" and referred to the proper calendar under the direction of the Speaker.

The right of the minority party to explain fully and precisely its reasons for opposing a particular piece of legislation, to propose alternative solutions to problems, and if necessary, to point out where the majority party or the Administration has attempted to railroad a matter through Congress, is essential if we are to preserve representative government and a free society. In many instances, however, the minority is not given sufficient time to prepare such reports.

Under the present rule, no set period of time is allowed for the filing of committee reports—majority or minority. Here again, the chairman, with the concurrence of the majority members of the committee, is given free rein. Of those committees which have adopted formal rules, only four make any reference to the subject, and in each of these cases the reference is either very general or is directed toward expedition.

Thus, the Government Operations Committee's rules merely provide that members not concurring in the majority report may file minority or additional views. The same general language is employed by the Public Works Committee. The Interior and Insular Affairs Committee, on the other hand, directs that minority views shall be prepared (but without delaying the majority report), while the Post Office and Civil Service Committee requires that minority views be submitted no later than three days after the majority report is ready for filing.

Committee chairmen are generally reasonable in permitting the minority adequate time to file its reports, but sometimes they are not. A good example was reported in the minority views of the Public Works Committee in relation to the Highway Beautification Act of 1965. In their views, the minority stated:

> A majority of the committee agreed to report it (the bill) out on Tuesday morning, just minutes before the members of the committee were required to be on the floor of the House to take up the Conference Report on the Water Quality Act of 1965 and to debate the Omnibus Rivers and Harbors and Flood Control Act of 1965. As if this were not enough, it was directed that the report be filed not later than midnight Wednesday, which allowed less than a day and a half for preparation of the report, including minority views, on this complex and controversial measure. During this day and a half, the members and the staff were almost totally absorbed in the debate on the Ominibus Rivers and Harbors and Flood Control Bill which was then going on.[2]

Similar instances could be cited for a number of other standing committees where only one, one and a half, or two days are permitted the minority for filing their views. When one considers how important and technically complicated many of these bills are, how understaffed the minority is, and how pressing other committee or floor business may be, one begins to realize how difficult it is to draft meaningful minority views.

To correct this abuse, the Rules of the House should be amended to provide that any Member shall have a minimum of five legislative days after the approval of a matter to file minority or additional views.

A matter closely related to committee reports has to do with the issuance of committee prints or staff studies by chairmen of committees. Nowhere in the Rules of the House or of the committees is explicit authority granted for such prints or studies. Certain committees, such as Merchant Marine and Fisheries, have granted such authority to the chairmen in committee resolutions.

As in other matters, this privilege is not generally abused. But some prints or studies have reflected unfairly upon the minority. Because of typography, the average reader may well be fooled into believing that these prints are endorsed by the entire committee. In fact, however, they have been prepared by staff at a chairman's direction and are frequently printed and released without the knowledge of other members of the committee.

A startling example of the misuse of committee prints occurred in connection with reporting the Housing and Urban Development Act of 1965. Minority members on the Banking and Currency Committee filed minority views concerning the proposed Rent Supplement Program. After their views had been filed, a committee print was issued, for which the chairman of the House Subcommittee took responsibility, which sought to rebut the views of the minority. This print, believed to have been written by the Housing and Home Finance Agency for the chairman, contained many distortions of the minority's views. Not only did minority members not have an opportunity to review the print in advance and thereby object to the distortions, but they only learned about it through a press release on a Sunday, although the print was dated the previous Friday!

Similar examples, although far less discriminatory or underhanded, have occurred in other committees. Committee prints are frequently released, at a chairman's direction, which are unduly laudatory of the Administration, or which analyze particular pieces of proposed legislation, or which condemn some segment of the economy. Since these prints appear to be submitted by the committees as a whole, the outsider may gain the impression that all members endorse certain Administration action or condemn certain aspects of the economy when in fact they may not.

To correct this discrimination, a rule of the House should be adopted requiring that no committee print or staff study be printed unless approved by majority vote of the committee. Any member should have five days to submit minority or additional views.

Turning to committee budgets, supervision over expenses, and requests for appropriations, under present conditions, the chairmen of committees have almost complete control over these matters by right of their position. Only the Post Office and Civil Service Committee actually includes such authority in its committee rules. In other committees, the right is assumed. In most committees, the advice of subcommittee chairmen is asked; such advice is required under the rules of the Post Office and Civil Service Committee. Ranking minority members are also advised of the budgets and requests for authorizations in a number of committees. But such solicitation is done more as a matter of courtesy and as an effort to maintain harmony.

There are other committee activities which can work to the disadvantage of the minority and to the disruption of effective representative government. These relate to proxy voting, attendance at meetings, and records of committee action.

Rule XI, clause 26(a), of the House Rules procides that "no measure or recommendation shall be reported from any committee unless a majority of the committee were actually present." While the import of this rule is clear, namely, that there must be a majority of the committee present when a matter is reported out, it does not preclude certain objectionable practices. In the first place, although all committees in theory require the presence of a majority to establish a quorum for the transaction of business, some committee meetings are conducted without such a quorum. Generally, a quorum will be established, but by the time the members get around to voting, it has vanished. This does not invalidate the measures recommended by the committee, however, because no one sees fit to challenge the absence of the quorum.

Perhaps a more objectionable practice is the use of proxies. Nowhere in the rules of the House is proxy voting authorized. In fact, a valid argument can be made that the use of proxies in committee contravenes the House rules. Yet eleven of the twelve committees that have adopted formal rules authorize proxy voting, while most others permit it informally or through committee resolution. Only a very few committees bar it, among them Rules and Veterans Affairs. It is true that no committee permits proxy voting to establish a quorum, but equally questionable practices result from its use.

Proxy voting is objectionable because it enables members to cast votes without participating in the debate which precedes the voting. It also enables a member to follow the lead of the chairman or other member who receives his proxy without having to acquaint himself with the issue being voted upon. Some committees actually go through entire sessions without the appearance, or with the rare appearance, of one or more of their members. Yet, when the votes are counted, there are the proxy votes of those members. It is not unusual at a committee meeting for a majority of the members present to be outvoted by proxies!

This is certainly contrary to democratic government and the maintenance of an effective representative system. In addition, the minority is particularly hindered by such a practice because the greatest number of proxy votes is cast by majority party members. Frequently, the minority is taken by surprise. The chairman of the Banking and Currency Committee convened a meeting on the Sales Participation Act so quickly that the minority had little opportunity to obtain proxies from its members, but the chairman had obtained a number from majority members. (Majority members make greater use of proxies because they are more inclined to go along with the chairman and Administration, or because they have spread themselves too thin. Although minority members also resort to proxy voting, they tend to be in attendance to a greater extent, perhaps because they generally must fight an uphill battle to overcome the power of the majority and the Administration.)

To induce more members to participate in committee business, the House rules should be amended to prohibit proxy voting. The rules should also require that the chairman of a committee be placed under obligation to adjourn or recess a meeting at any point when a quorum is lost.

Along the same lines, Rule XI, clause (h), of the House rules specifies that

each committee may fix the number of its members to constitute a quorum for taking testimony and receiving evidence which shall be not less than two.

Of the committees that have adopted formal rules, seven follow the House rule. The District of Columbia Committee provides that "less than a quorum shall be competent to hold hearings," whatever that means; while the committees on Post Office and Civil Service and Science and Astronautics provide that a member of the majority and a member of the minority must be present. In theory, the other committees which have not adopted rules on this point also follow the same requirement. Unfortunately, most committees do violence to this rule at one time or another.

The rule was primarily adopted as a protection for witnesses. It is also of some benefit to effective representative government because it tends to assure at least a degree of attendance by members who afterwards may be required to recommend and vote upon legislation. But even this limited protection is sometimes thwarted. In many instances, only one member is present when hearings are conducted. In fact, it has been discovered that in at least one committee only staff members have been present at times while hearings were going on. (While the rule of the District of Columbia Committee does not seem to be in strict conformity with the Rules of the House, the violation is no greater than that of any other committee. The rules of the Post Office and Science and Astronautics committees are also frequently ignored.)

In order to afford greater protection to the rights of witnesses and to assure that more members of the committees receive first-hand knowledge of the business transpiring, the Rules of the House should be amended to require that a majority of the members of a committee or subcommittee be present while a hearing is being conducted. Moreover, as in the case of reporting out measures, the House Rules should place an obligation upon the chairman of a committee or subcommittee to adjourn or recess any hearing where a majority is not present.

Rule XI, clause 26(b), provides that

> each committee shall keep a complete record of all committee action . . . such record shall include a record of the votes on any question on which a record vote is demanded.

The next clause provides that all Members of the House shall have access to such records and that each committee shall print committee hearings.

Unfortunately, the rules do not require that the actions of individual members be made available to the public. Of those committees that have enacted formal rules, four have specified that the committee's records shall include the Members' votes and also show the members present at each meeting. Nine committees specify the manner in which formal roll call votes may be demanded on particular matters under debate. But only the Committee on Agriculture requires that members' votes be made public, and even it does not require that the presence or absence of members be revealed.

Attendance of Members at committee meetings should be made public, and the reports of hearings should indicate the number of Members in attendance at any particular time during the hearings. In this way, the public would have a greater opportunity to determine the degree of consideration given to particular matters. This arrangement also would induce greater attendance at meetings and hearings.

In addition, the House Rules should be amended to require that each committee report disclose how each member voted. (If proxy voting is permitted, the members who voted by proxy should also be disclosed.)

Subcommittees are creatures of committees rather than creatures of the House. There is no specific authority in the Rules of the House for their establishment. Subcommittees are mentioned tangentially in five different places. Rule XI, clauses 2, 8, and 18 authorize the Appropriations, Government Operations, and Un-American Activities Committees, or any of their subcommittees, to sit while the House is in session, or has recessed or adjourned. Clause 26(g) provides that

> all hearings conducted by standing committees or their subcommittees shall be open to the public, except executive sessions for marking up bills or for voting or where the committee by a majority vote orders an executive session.

Clause 29 requires that each committee report to the Clerk of the House twice a year the name, profession, and total salary of each person employed by such committee or subcommittee thereof.

Subcommittees nevertheless perform most of the yeoman work of Congress. A few committees, such as Rules and Ways and Means, do not have subcommittees, while others, such as Veterans Affairs and Public Works, do a great deal of their work in full committee. The majority of the standing committees, however, delegate most of their business to subcommittees.

This is done for a number of reasons. A committee may be responsible for such detailed and complicated business as to demand a division of work and specialization. A great deal of time may be involved in conducting investigations and hearings. The chairman of a committee may feel that he can better control legislation or obtain desired results by assigning members to particular subcommittees according to their philosophy and loyalty, and then funneling proposals to favorable subcommittees. Members of the majority party may desire more recognition and responsibility, or may claim greater reward for faithful service via subcommittee chairmanships.

Because of the varied reasons for creating subcommittees and also because they are creatures of independent committees, there is little uniformity in their jurisdiction, membership, or operations. Yet, there are a few patterns of similarity.

A committee chairman generally has complete authority to create, abolish, combine, or alter subcommittees. However, the rules of three committees—Interior, Post Office, and Banking—specify that certain named subcommittees be operated. Similarly, long-established subcommittees headed by influential members may be difficult to change. Aside from these, a chairman's authority is nearly supreme in this area.

Chairmen also have a great deal of freedom in assigning members to subcommittees and designating subcommittee chairmen. Seniority and preference are usually followed, but only the Post Office Committee's rules require this procedure. The Education and Banking Committee's rules specify that Members shall retain seniority on subcommittees to which they are appointed. In the appointment of subcommittee chairmen, the rules of the Education, Interior, and Post Office Committees designate seniority, but even here there is some leeway in appointment to special and select subcommittees.

The chairmen of committees generally exercise complete control over the referral of bills and other matters to subcommittees, and over their budgets and staffs. Depending on his intelligence, ability, influence, and personality, therefore, a committee chairman can in most instances work his will through the manipulation of subcommittees.

The objections raised above with regard to committee operations also apply to the operations of many subcommittees. To the extent that they do, the recommendations for changes in the House rules suggested above should be made to apply to subcommittees. Six committees provide that the Rules of the House shall be the rules of the subcommittee. Other committees also follow this requirement, but it would be desirable to spell this requirement out more fully.

The rules of ten committees provide that the chairman and ranking minority member of the committee shall serve as ex officio members of the subcommittees. A number of other committees follow the same procedure through resolution or informal practice. The Interior and Insular Affairs Committee and the Judiciary Committee extend this right only to the chairman, however. Six committees provide in their rules that the chairman and ranking minority member shall have the right to vote in their ex officio capacities; certain other committees extend this right informally. The Banking and Currency Committee, however, denies the ranking minority member an ex officio vote on any subcommittee chaired by the full committee chairman! To provide uniformity and to preserve the rights of the minority, the rules of the House should be amended either to bar ex officio membership or to assure that both the chairman and ranking minority Member have the same rights.

Eight committees provide in their rules that Members of their respective committees may sit but not vote with subcommittees of which they are not members. Other committees generally permit this right informally. Since subcommittees are mere creations of full committees and since this practice is beneficial to effective representation by Members of Congress, the Rules of the House should formally grant this right.

Three committees provide by rule that the ratio between majority and minority members on each of their subcommittees shall approximate the party ratio of the House. Another committee has a similar rule for standing subcommittees. Still others follow these rules in practice. But there are exceptions. In the Judiciary Committee, the chairman's own subcommittee has at times a greater ratio of majority to minority members than that of the House. This imbalance can and has been used unfairly at times to recommend legislation which could not pass the full committee or the House but which might serve political purposes. To correct any abuse of power, the Rules of the House should require that subcommittees have the same ratios as exist between the majority and minority parties in the House.

Another matter that has proved vexatious is the scheduling of subcommittee meetings. Nine committees have adopted rules which, to a greater or lesser extent, attempt to avoid conflicts in scheduling, while other committees attempt to do this informally. (All seek to avoid conflict between subcommittees and full committee meetings.) But the number of subcommittees together with a degree of autonomy by some subcommittee chairmen do sometimes lead to such conflicts. Since a member may serve on more than one subcommittee, many instances occur when a member is forced to miss one or the other of the subcommittee meetings.

Such conflicts are particularly harmful to the minority. For example, a subcommittee of the Agriculture Committee recently scheduled a hearing in Iowa. The chairman of the full committee scheduled a meeting of the full committee for the same day. Minority party members elected to attend the latter. When it was cancelled a day before the meeting was scheduled, it was too late to attend the hearing in Iowa. Meanwhile, at the Iowa meeting it was implied that the minority members were boycotting the meeting!

In order to avoid such conflicts, the Rules of the House should provide that the chairman of each committee should be responsible for coordinating full committee and subcommittee meetings to avoid conflicts. If conflicts do occur, both meetings should be subject to a point of order.

Since many members serve on more than one committee, conflicts of scheduling also develop among committees. Study ought to be given to a requirement that committees must clear the scheduling of hearings through a central office, such as the office of the Clerk of the House, so that conflicts can be eliminated.

Finally, the House should require that the rules of each committee be filed in a central location, such as the Office of the Clerk of the House, so that the public, as well as members and staffs of the House, will know exactly what are the operating procedures of each committee. Twelve committees do publish their rules, but they are little publicized. Other committees adopt resolutions at the beginning of each Congress to govern their procedures, but these are almost completely hidden from public view and, for that matter, from Members and staffs of the House not assigned to one of these committees. Then there are, of course, the committees which operate under informal rules.

Opening the rules to public inspection will improve the workings of the House and prove of some benefit to the minority party. An inspection of the rules has demonstrated that some appear to be in violation of House rules. In other instances, operations outside of established committee rules or in the absence of such rules also seem to violate House rules at times. Central filing will generate efforts by leaders and Members of the House to eliminate these violations. Some committees' rules are fairer to rank-and-file members, particularly minority party members, than others, and bringing these out in the open, too, might encourage efforts to democratize all committees' rules.

When Congress determines to act, it may not act as swiftly as the Executive Branch or as efficiently as a finely run private organization. Congress is not an administrative organization, and does not always construct neat packages or devise neat solutions. What Congress does do is resolve issues through compromise and accommodation, taking into consideration the rights, needs, and interests of individual citizens, along with a concern for the population as a whole. In view of the everincreasing workload and accelerating tendency toward specialization, the committees of Congress must gear themselves to conduct their business in an efficient, open, and fair manner. Toward that end the Congress will be made more effective. Toward that end have I proposed various changes in House Rules.

REFERENCES

1. Exceptions for these three committees were inserted in 1953. See House Rule XI, paragraph 30, annotated.
2. Report No. 1084, 89th Congress, 1st Sess., U.S. House of Rep., p. 46.

F. BRADFORD MORSE, M.C.

5th District, Massachusetts

STRENGTHENING THE COMMITTEE STRUCTURE: THE PROBLEM OF OVERLAPPING JURISDICTION

by F. Bradford Morse, M.C.*

Introduction

Denis W. Brogan, the distinguished British commentator on American life and government, has written that

> the future of parliamentary government is uncertain. . . . [It] can be said that the Congress of the United States is the last really important legislative body.[1]

The Congress certainly is the only major legislative body which relies on the committee system so heavily. Speaker Thomas Reed once called the typical House committee

> the eye, the ear, the hand, and very often the brain of the House.[2]

Due to the number of House Members, the number and complexity of the issues, and the pressures of time and constituency, the standing committees assumed an early importance. Indeed, the extent of their power makes them miniature legislatures with the power to hold hearings, draft and amend bills, and take votes. By the time a bill reaches the floor, the opportunities for amendment may be limited and the weight given the judgment of the committee by other Members of the House is often the key to its passage.

Neil MacNeil has described the importance of House committees:[3]

> The House of Representatives from its first weeks of existence, has found itself dependent on committees as the only way to cope with the infinite detail of its task of legislating for the American people.

* Mr. Morse represents the 5th Congressional District of Massachusetts. He was first elected to Congress in 1960 and serves on the House Foreign Affairs Committee.

All of these factors make it clear that a strong committee structure is essential to a strong House. There is a real question whether the structure established by the Legislative Reorganization Act of 1946 is presently adequate to permit oversight of existing programs, consideration of requests for new authorizations and appropriations, and the development of the resources to anticipate the legislative needs of the future.

In the twenty years since Congress gave careful study to the jurisdiction of its standing committees, two new Cabinet-level departments and dozens of new federal boards and agencies have been created; scores of new federal programs have been enacted; the responsibilities of the United States around the world have grown enormously.

In my judgment, there are three basic questions to be asked about the present committee structure. Are jurisdictional lines now drawn in a manner that contributes to maximum efficiency? Do the committees have adequate access to necessary information? Does the individual Representative have the tools he needs to enable him to be an effective member of his committee?

The answer to each is a deafening no. The House, we must admit, is deficient in performing its legislative and oversight functions. Where we once had too many committees, we now may have too few. Some committee jurisdictions are too narrow, some too broad, some too diverse.

Although it is an axiom that the key to advancement to a position of leadership in the House is good committee work, the Member is limited in this role. Procedures are time-consuming, professional staffs are inadequate; shortsightedness often prevents the Member from using the professional staff of his own office to maximum advantage.

All of these problems stand out with stark clarity when we begin to review our present jurisdictional lines. In the pages that follow, I hope to review the committee system as it presently operates in a few major domestic areas and in foreign affairs, and to suggest some alternatives that in my judgment would strengthen and enrich it.

Urban Affairs

At present, there are eight standing committees of the House of Representatives with jurisdiction over some aspect of urban affairs.

This lack of coordination in the House is paralleled in the executive branch. Despite Administration assurances that the proposed new Department of Housing and Urban Development would provide a focus for coordination of urban problems, the bill itself did little more than elevate the Housing and Home Finance Agency and its constituent agencies to cabinet status. It did not touch the more than sixty other federal programs with urban implications.[4]

Republicans recognized the need for coordination in this field several years ago and introduced legislation to create an Office of Community Development in the Executive Office of the President.[5] It was this legislation that was the basis of the Republican position on the new Cabinet Department in 1965.[6]

The problems already experienced by the new department indicates that the need for coordination is still great. The House has an urgent responsibility to do what the executive branch has failed to do, to streamline its present capacity to deal with urban affairs.

Under the present rules of the House, the Committees on Agriculture, Banking and Currency, the District of Columbia, Education and Labor, Government Operations, Interstate and Foreign Commerce, the Judiciary, and Public Works all have significant areas of jurisdiction over urban problems.[7] Given this wide dispersal of authority, coordination is practically impossible. In some instances our committees may even be working at cross purposes. For example, while the Public Works Committee is considering legislation to build new highways to bring more cars into the central city, the Housing Subcommittee of the Banking and Currency Committee may be working on legislation to improve mass transit facilities in an effort to keep the cars out.

Water pollution is another example. The Banking and Currency Subcommittee has jurisdiction over programs funded by the Community Facilities Administration of the Department of Housing and Urban Development involving new sewage systems, while Public Works has jurisdiction over Water Pollution Control legislation which funds the construction of water treatment facilities. The relationship between these two urban functions is far closer in fact than this jurisdictional arrangement would suggest. The present system makes it next to impossible to consider the interrelationships between housing and education, between transportation and air pollution, between highways and open spaces.

The wise response to this confused situation is to create either a Select or Standing Committee of the House of Representatives on Urban Affairs. In 1961, I introduced a resolution to create a Select Committee on Urban Affairs; I have subsequently reintroduced it in the 88th and 89th Congresses.[8] The Select Committee would be composed of thirteen Members of the House and would be charged with the responsibility to

> conduct full and complete investigations and studies of the problems of urban areas, including housing, urban renewal, slum clearance, prevention and elimination of urban blight, air and water pollution, water supply, sewage facilities, transportation and other problems of urban areas.[9]

It would also be directed to review the implementation and administration of urban programs by the executive branch. Most important, it would have the authority to make specific recommendations to the House

> with respect to the advisability of the establishment of a standing committee of the House having jurisdiction over problems of urban areas.[10]

Partially in response to the creation of the new cabinet department, there has been considerable agitation for a standing committee on urban affairs which would combine the jurisdiction of a number of the present standing committees. I first introduced such a resolution in 1965;[11] a number of my colleagues have introduced similar resolutions since that time.

The value of such a committee was demonstrated early in 1966 when the Administration recommended a Demonstration Cities Act.[12] In a special message to Congress on January 26, the President asked for grants that would include such programs as transportation, housing, urban renewal, welfare, and economic opportunity.[13] House consideration of this proposal could have been much more meaningful if an Urban Affairs Committee, benefiting from the expertise of Members from the eight committees now charged with responsibilities in this field, could have brought their mutual wisdom and understanding to the consideration of this major new legislation.

There was nothing magic in the number nineteen set for House standing committees in the Legislative Reorganization Act of 1946, and the House responded to changing needs in 1958 when it created the new Standing Committee on Science and Astronautics.[14] Urban affairs represents another area where federal involvement has outstripped Congressional efficiency.

Education and Labor

The bulk of the growth in new federal programs has taken place in the field of education. The 88th Congress was known as the "education Congress" because of the significant new programs it adopted for higher education, vocational education, and health professions education. In 1965, the 89th Congress enacted entirely new educational programs for elementary and secondary schools, a scholarship program for college students, and a loan insurance program.

These developments have preoccupied the House Committee on Education and Labor at a time when major legislation to amend the Fair Labor Standards Act and repeal section 14(b) of the Taft-Hartley Act has also demanded time and attention.

In the hearings before the Joint Committee on the Organization of the Congress, Congressman Charles McC. Mathias, Jr., of Maryland proposed that the education and labor functions of the Committee be separated and that to the education programs now handled by the Education and Labor Committee be added the health professions educational efforts now under the jurisdiction of the Health Subcommittee of the House Committee on Interstate and Foreign Commerce.

This appears to be an eminently sensible proposition. It would bring together the vast number of educational programs

under a more logical and a more contemporary grouping. . . .[15]

The new Labor Committee would continue to handle labor problems now before Education and Labor and take on, in addition, labor matters now handled by the Committees on Interstate and Foreign Commerce, Merchant Marine and Fisheries, and Judiciary.[16]

It should be made clear that any efforts to consolidate functional programs into a single committee are positive in nature. They not only increase the efficiency of the Congress in that area, but they also free other committees from peripheral problems. For example, the Committee on Interstate and Foreign Commerce could give greater attention to over-all problems of transportation if it were not burdened with health, education, and related problems.

In other words, a more concentrated workload should not be viewed as downgrading a particular committee, but as increasing the quality and effectiveness of its work.

A similar consolidation should be considered in the health and welfare field. These programs are now scattered among the House Ways and Means Committee, the Education and Labor Committee, the Interstate and Foreign Commerce Committee, and the Agriculture Committee. Despite the obvious advantages of central review of revenue measures in the Ways and Means Committee, it may well be time to consider whether the proposed financing of a new program should be the determining factor in assigning a bill to a particular committee. It may be possible, on the other hand, to improve our capability for analysis in the welfare field through a procedural rather than a jurisdictional change, but at least we should keep an open mind to the problem.

Similarly, the Select Committee on Small Business should be elevated to a standing committee with the power to consider and report all legislation, except tax matters, affecting the nation's 4.7 million small businesses.

Foreign Affairs

Ever since the United States emerged from World War II as a global power, the legislative and executive branches of the United States Government have collectively worried about their capacity to conduct foreign and national security policy. Innumerable reorganization plans, executive orders, and personnel shifts in the executive branch have accompanied our mounting international involvement.

Probably one of the most significant contributions to our administrative capacity in this field was the series of hearings conducted by Senator Henry Jackson of Washington and his Subcommittee on National Policy Machinery.

Almost unnoticed in the reports that emanated from those hearings was an important reference to congressional capability in foreign affairs. On November 15, 1962, the Subcommittee reported:

Although the Subcommittee inquiry was directed toward the executive branch, there is clearly much room for improvement on Capitol Hill.

One major problem is fragmentation. The Congress is hard put to deal with national security policy as a whole.

The difficulty starts with the executive branch. Except in the State of the Union and the budget messages, it presents national security information and program requests to the Congress in bits and pieces.

The present mode of operation of the congressional system compounds the problem. The authorization process treats as separable matters which are not really separable. Foreign affairs, defense matters, space policies, and atomic energy programs are handled in different committees. It is the same with money matters. Income and outgo, and the relation of each to the economy, come under different jurisdictions.

There is no place in the Congress, short of the floors of the Senate and the House, where the requirements of national security and the resources needed on their behalf, are considered in their totality.[17]

Here again the Congress has an opportunity to provide the coordination that has not been achieved by the executive branch.

There has been no lack of suggestions as to how to remedy this problem of "totality." Every session of Congress has produced proposals for Joint Executive-Legislative Councils, Advisory Councils on National Security, and Joint Committees on Cold War Strategy or National Security.[18]

Many of these proposals cite the Joint Atomic Energy Committee as a hopeful example. However, the powerful JCAE cannot really be relied on as a precedent to support greater use of joint committees generally. Its statutory mandate,[19] its authority to consider legislation,[20] and its statutory right to receive information from the executive branch[21] distinguish it from the model. Other joint committees, like select committees, are essentially study groups.

One of the most careful students of the JCAE, Professor Harold Green, has downgraded the influence of the Joint Committee in relation to the strengthening of Congress as a whole.

. . . the JCAE contributes relatively little to the enhancement of the role or power of the Congress except to the extent that any curbing of executive power increases the power of Congress relatively.[22]

At any rate, Green concludes,

it is doubtful that the Congress could, even if it so desired, create another Joint Committee which could function in a manner approaching the JCAE model.[23]

These conclusions suggest that the Congress will have to continue to seek sources of information other than the executive branch.

The problem with all of the various proposals is that they fail to recognize that the problem of national security policy is too broad and too complex to be handled by a single congressional committee.

One of the virtues of the committee system has been its capacity to build expertise; its ability to permit each and every Member to question witnesses and otherwise involve himself in the legislative process. This would be impossible in a committee of more than 100 Members as has been proposed by Professor Lasswell, for example.[24]

It would appear that in the foreign policy field at least, dispersal may not be a bad thing, so long as it is, as Dr. Francis O. Wilcox has argued, accompanied by "satisfactory liaison."[25] In the Senate the liaison problem is often minimized by overlapping membership. It is not unusual for a Senator to serve simultaneously on the Appropriations and Foreign Relations Committees; or on the Aeronautical and Space Sciences Committee and the Armed Services or Government Operations Committees.[26]

In the House, overlap is much less frequent and coordination therefore demands the development of new techniques and practices. One possibility frequently mentioned is greater use of joint hearings by the Foreign Affairs and Armed Services Committees on national security matters, and by the Foreign Affairs and Joint Atomic Energy Committees on disarmament matters. While joint hearings may not always permit individual questioning, they do save the time of both witness and Member and should be used to a greater extent.

Liaison between the professional staffs of the committees should be strengthened. The staff of the Appropriations Committee's Subcommittee on Foreign Operations, the Foreign Affairs Committee, and the Government Operations Subcommittee on Foreign Operations and Government Information should always work closely together.

Subcommittee jurisdiction of foreign affairs-related committees should be reviewed. I think it is imperative, for example, that the House Foreign Affairs Committee establish a subcommittee on U.S.-Canadian affairs, whose professional staff would work closely with committees responsible for our commercial and educational exchange policy. At the present time Canadian affairs are included within the jurisdiction of the Inter-American Affairs Subcommittee, which has been, of necessity, preoccupied with Latin American problems.[27]

An important way for the Congress to obtain sufficient information about the conduct of foreign policy by the Administration is through the adoption of an amendment to the Rules of the House permitting the Secretary of State to come before the House in a carefully operated question period, similar to that in the House of Commons in Great Britain.[28]

As necessary as these proposed changes are in my judgment, they do not meet the problem of dispersal of committee jurisdiction over foreign policy problems.

In addition to the Foreign Affairs Committee, we have the Armed Services Committee with responsibility for raising and maintaining our armed forces; the Ways and Means Committee with jurisdiction over trade bills; the Interstate and Foreign Commerce Committee, which handles international transportation policy; the Merchant Marine and Fisheries Committee, which handles not only shipping matters but the Panama Canal as well; the

Banking and Currency Committee with jurisdiction over U.S. membership
in international banking and financial institutions; the Agriculture Committee, which allocates the two million ton foreign sugar quota each year and has
overseen the Public Law 480 program of distribution of agricultural surpluses;
and the Interior Committee with jurisdiction over the administration of
United States territories abroad.

Each and every one of these committees is making foreign policy decisions, often in circumstances where foreign policy implications receive very
little consideration. A good case in point was the inclusion in the amendments
to the Immigration and Nationality Act of 1965 of a provision that would restrict Western Hemisphere immigration for the first time in our history.[29] It
seems clear that the potential impact of this section on our relations with
Canada and Mexico in particular probably received less attention than did
domestic factors.

While it can be argued that the House Foreign Affairs Committee should
have jurisdiction over legislation proposing a new Food for Freedom and
International Health and Education programs which bear directly on our
foreign policy, there are equally valid reasons for leaving jurisdiction over
these programs to the committees with the substantive expertise. In these cases,
however, the judgment of experts on education, health, and agriculture should
be supplemented by the counsel of Members with knowledge of their international implications. Members of the House Foreign Affairs Committee
should be available as non-voting participants to the Education and Labor
and Agriculture Committees in the consideration of legislation with such an
important relation to U.S. foreign policy. Likewise, when the House Foreign
Affairs Committee considers military aid, Members of the Armed Services
Committee could provide useful counsel on its implications for our defense
posture and our national security arrangements around the world.

Committee Resources

A strong committee structure requires not only rational jurisdiction and
coordination, but strong staff and adequate access to information as well.
Many of our committees presently lack sufficient committee staff for both
majority and minority members. This situation is particularly harsh on
junior Members, who must take second place to the requirements of the
chairman and ranking minority member. Even where committee staffs are
bipartisan, the same person frequently must write both the majority and
minority reports, to the detriment of each.

Staff resources have not kept pace with the committees' requirements for
information. The Legislative Reference Service, which was established to
supplement individual Member and committee staffs, is forced to spend far
too much time collecting material for Members' constituents. If the commit-

tees and Members are to use the Legislative Reference Service to maximum advantage, the Service should be authorized to create a special Constituent Reference Bureau to handle routine requests. At the same time, the Legislative Reference Service should be authorized to increase its professional research staff.

At the present time, the entire legislative branch is forced to rely too heavily on the executive for information regarding pending legislation. The use of data processing techniques, particularly on committees such as Appropriations and Government Operations, and expanded committee and Member staffs, would greatly increase congressional access to necessary data. Committees should be permitted, as are executive agencies, to contract with private firms for research studies.

By the same token, Members should be encouraged and permitted to use their own professional staffs to a greater degree in committee work. Particularly on those committees dealing with foreign affairs and national security, this is now virtually impossible. Because of security regulations, only the Member himself is permitted to see and correct executive session testimony. In some instances he must go to the committee offices to do so.

I have introduced a resolution[30] which would permit each member of the Foreign Affairs, Armed Services, Appropriations, and Joint Atomic Energy Committees to designate a professional staff member to be cleared for access to such information as is made available to the Congressman in his capacity as a member of the committee. This resolution should be enacted promptly.

Of course, the most significant way to bring the Member's staff into the committee structure is to streamline Capitol Hill housekeeping generally. Even a quick review of the allocation of administrative duties between the Architect of the Capitol and the Clerk of the House, between the Sergeant-at-Arms and the Doorkeeper, reveals vast room for improvement.[31] Capitol Hill needs a city manager to increase efficiency in the conduct of housekeeping functions from the supervision of pages to the construction of buildings, and to organize the services available to Members in a manner that would relieve a Member's principal assistants of managerial drudgery.

A New Kind of Committee

If we succeed in adjusting committee jurisdiction and in increasing the effectiveness of committee and Members' staff, we should be able to enlarge the potential of the House to formulate long-range policy. A model for the expansion of House capability can be found in the idea behind the task forces established by the House Republican Conference.

Although the Administration frequently gets bogged down in day-to-day policy problems, the Congress should be able to develop the capacity to stand away from current vexations and assess the future challenges to international and domestic policy.

We should look very carefully at the possibility of creating a new kind of committee: a committee modeled after the present select committees which would be able, without regard to the seniority of its members, to conduct studies and investigations of future policy needs.

Under the proposed system, each Member would serve on a select, or research, committee as well as on a standing committee. The research committees would be staffed with adequate professional people and authorized to contract for research studies. A few areas for research committee consideration include information and intelligence operations, future transportation needs, the function of wage and price guideposts in the U.S. economy, and the role of systems technology in public policy.

The recommendations outlined here cover just one phase of the vast needs of a modern Congress. I reject the counsel of those who argue that the legislative branch cannot be a productive participant in policy-making. We can play a vital role if we have the strength to look beyond our precedents to the possibilities of the future.

REFERENCES

1. Brogan, Introduction to Clark, *Congress: The Sapless Branch*, ix–x.
2. Quoted in MacNeil, *Forge of Democracy*, 149.
3. *Ibid.* at 174.
4. H.Rept. No. 337, 89th Cong., 1st Sess. 46 (1965).
5. H.R. 7839, 88th Cong., 1st Sess. (1963); H.R. 6216, 89th Cong., 1st Sess. (1965); see H. Rept. No. 337, 89th Cong., 1st Sess. 45 (1965).
6. H.Rept. No. 337, supra note; 111 Cong. Rec. 13302 (daily ed. June 16, 1965).
7. See Rule XI, Rules of the House of Representatives, H. Doc. 374, 88th Cong. 2d Sess. (1965).
8. See H. Res. 190, 87th Cong., 1st Sess. (1961); H.Res. 286, 88th Cong., 1st Sess. (1963); H.Res. 532, 89th Cong., 1st Sess. (1965).
9. *Ibid.*
10. *Ibid.*
11. H. Res. 573, 89th Cong., 1st Sess. (1965).
12. H.R. 12341, 89th Cong., 2d Sess. (1966).
13. See XXIV Congressional Quarterly 493 (March 4, 1966).
14. Congressional Quarterly, *Congress and the Nation* 301 (1965).
15. *Hearings Before the Joint Committee on the Organization of the Congress.* 89th Cong., 1st Sess., pt. 10 at 1770 (1965). (hereinafter cited as *Joint Hearings.*)
16. *Ibid.* at 1768.
17. *Joint Hearings*, pt. 8, at 1223.
18. See summary, *Id.*, at 1225–28.
19. Section 201, Atomic Energy Act of 1965, 68 Stat. 956 (1954); 42 USC 2251 (1958).
20. 68 Stat. 956 (1965), as amended, 42 USC 2252 (Supp. IV 1963).
21. *Ibid.*
22. Green, "The Joint Committee on Atomic Energy: A Model for Legislative Reform?", 32 *Geo. Wash. L. Rev.* 946 (1964).
23. *Ibid.* at 945.

24. Professor Lasswell proposed to create in each House a Committee on National Security composed of members "of all Committees whose jurisdiction covers some fragment of the field." *Joint Hearings*, pt. 8, at 1253.
25. *Ibid.* at 1265.
26. See *Congressional Directory*, 89th Cong., 2d Sess., at 289–95 (1966).
27. This is also a problem in the Department of State where Canadian affairs are still handled by the Office of British Commonwealth and Northern European Affairs. See "White Paper on U.S.-Canadian Relations," prepared by a group of Republican Congressmen, 111 Cong. Rec. 24482 (daily ed. Sept. 28, 1965).
28. See testimony of Rep. Ogden R. Reid, *Joint Hearings*, pt. 11, at 1711–25.
29. Section 21 (e), P.L. 89–326 (1965).
30. H. Res. 725, 89th Cong., 2d Sess. (1966).
31. The following exchange between Congressman Flynt and administrative officers of the Capitol is illustrative:

> Mr. FLYNT. To what extent do you supervise the responsibilities and functions of the Superintendent of the House Office Buildings?
>
> Mr. STEWART. The Superintendent of the House Office Buildings comes directly under my office.
>
> Mr. FLYNT. And under the Superintendent of the House Office Buildings would be the elevator operators and the uniformed guards within the buildings?
>
> Mr. HENLOCK. Not the guards, but the elevator operators. By law, the Architect of the Capitol has responsibility for the structural, mechanical, and domestic care of the House Office Buildings, except the police, which are under the Sergeant at Arms. That is true with respect to all three House Office Buildings. The split jurisdiction is in the Capitol.
>
> Mr. FLYNT. Has any consideration been given to assigning to the Superintendent of the House Office Buildings the direction of the security service within those buildings?
>
> Mr. STEWART. Perhaps the Superintendent can enlighten you on that point.
>
> Mr. RIDGELL. Not that I know of, Mr. Flynt. It has always been under the Sergeant at Arms of the House. The furniture, carpets, and drapes are under the Clerk of the House. Mine is the maintenance of the permanent structure and the mechanical and domestic care of the buildings.
>
> Mr. FLYNT. Mr. Stewart, who has jurisdiction of the cafeteria and restaurant service of the House of Representatives?
>
> Mr. STEWART. That comes under my office.

Hearings Before a Subcommittee of the House Committee on Appropriations on Legislative Branch Appropriations for 1966, 89th Cong., 1st Sess. 22–23 (1965).

PART 2
Policy-Making, Lobbying, and Oversight

JOHN B. ANDERSON, M.C.
16th District, Illinois

SCIENCE POLICY AND CONGRESS

by John B. Anderson, M.C.*

I. Evolution of Research and Development into a Three-way Partnership Involving the Academic Community, Private Enterprise, and the Federal Government.

Did you ever stop to realize that the modern conveniences we presently enjoy are the end product of, first, basic or pure *research*, and second, the practical application or *development* into a utilitarian product?

These two factors contribute immensely to our economic growth and well-being. Indeed, they have a direct relationship and causal effect upon our rate of economic growth. Witness the great revolution of today in science and technology, as well as the frequency with which startling new pronouncements of further progress are being made. And look at our fantastic rate of economic growth: our Gross National Product—total output of goods and services—is now expected to jump from the estimated $670 billion in 1965 to $735 billion in 1966, a jump of $57 billion, or eight per cent. The combination of research and development brings new products to the marketplace, improves older products, and makes them more attractive to the buyer in the marketplace. Research and development contribute greatly to our military posture and national defense.

Down through the pages of history, man's fertile brain has been busily opening up new science frontiers. Today's space age would not have been possible without men like Copernicus, Kepler, the Bernoulli family of mathe-

---

* Mr. Anderson is a Member of the House Rules Committee and the Joint Committee on Atomic Energy. He was first elected to Congress in 1960 from the 16th Congressional District of Illinois and previously served on the Select Committee on Government Research, the House Administration Committee, and the Government Operations Committee and GOP Policy Committee of the House.

maticians, Werner von Braun, Dr. Goddard, ad infinitum. The steam engine, the steamboat, and internal combustion engine, the laser, the transistor, Marconi's wireless were all figments of man's imagination at one time. (Incidentally, I have always enjoyed the letter one constituent wrote to her Congressman concerning Marconi's wireless: "What a terrible waste it was before the radio came into being for all that free music to be floating around in space, waiting to be captured by that device which today we call a radio.")

At first, practically all pure research was done at the universities. Then, as plant operations began to enlarge, industry began to hire development specialists. Eventually there evolved a marriage and the first partnership in research and development between the universities and the industrial community was formed.

A man of our own time who exhibited great intellectual capacity and leadership, vision, and foresight, who served as President of the United States and its Commander-in-Chief, brought about one of the earliest marriages of government and private enterprise in research and development. This was none other than the late President Herbert Hoover, who, as Secretary of Commerce during the period 1921–28, had an appreciation of the great value of science and launched a cooperative effort between the Federal Government (namely, the National Bureau of Standards) and private industry, aimed at commercial standardization.

Volume 19 of the 1966 edition of the *Encyclopedia Britannica* (page 196) has this to say about the important role that President Hoover played in one of his early governmental positions:

> The Secretary of Commerce (1921–1928) Herbert Hoover, who had begun his career as a mining engineer, was one of the few major political figures of his time who had a true appreciation of the value of science. He believed his department should carry out scientific research and should also help to eliminate inefficiency from industry operations. Under his guidance the National Bureau of Standards worked with industry to launch a cooperative program of simplified practices and commercial standardization; and by 1924 about 23 industrial trade associations were supporting 29 research associates who worked alongside government scientists at the National Bureau of Standards.

> Hoover appreciated the dependence of industrial research on fundamental research, and he was well aware of the paucity of American fundamental research at that time. Believing that industry should bear some responsibility for fundamental research, and in an effort to redress the balance, he was instrumental in establishing the National Research Fund in 1926. This fund was designed to allow industry to make regular and substantial contributions to a monetary pool to be used as a common source of finance for universities carrying out independent fundamental research. For a variety of reasons the fund was a failure and was discontinued in 1934, but it marked a realization that both government and industry had a responsibility for maintaining a balance between pure and applied science.

During World War II there evolved a more intensified three-way partnership—government, private industry, and the academic community—forging a common pursuit in the national interest.

II. Tracing the Growth of R & D in the United States from World War II.

Prior to the Manhattan Bomb Project, the federal budget contained an infinitesimal amount in comparison to what it allocates today for research and development. Great impetus was given to federal research and development as a result of the federal government, for the first time, directing a massive effort to hasten along the practical application of the fruits of basic, theoretical scientific research conducted by scientists in the private sector in the 1920s and 1930s. I refer to the efforts aimed at trying to unlock the secrets of the atom. In 1945, the first atomic bomb was exploded. Congressman Elliott, in urging the creation of the Select Committee on Government Research, stated in the well of the House on September 11, 1963, in describing the growth in our knowledge gained from research and development, that we need

merely note that the bomb we dropped on Hiroshima is but a pea shooter in today's modern military arsenal.

While in 1940 the federal government spent only $74 million on research and development programs, by 1953 we were spending about $2 billion. Annual research and development expenditures then increased by about $1 billion a year so that today such expenditures approach $16 billion, a sum greater than is allocated to any department or agency of the federal government with the single exception of the Department of Defense.

These funds are not distributed evenly across the fields of knowledge and practice. They are concentrated in the sciences related to weaponry and the conquest of space. Three out of every four federal R & D dollars are paid by the government to private firms or institutions. The government has its own laboratories and experimental stations where about one-fourth of the government's research and development tasks are performed.

An analysis has shown that in 1964 more than $11 billion of the government's $15 billion total for research and development went to nongovernmental laboratories and research centers.

Of those 11 billion federal dollars that went to private hands for research and development, we found that 80 cents of each dollar went to business firms—private, profit-making companies who do the bulk of the government's research and development, especially in defense and space fields.

Some 12,000 firms perform R & D work. Ninety per cent of these have less than 1,000 employees. Three per cent of these firms each have over 1,000 employees. Yet the largest companies—only 3 per cent of the industry—account for 90 per cent of federally financed research and development. The smaller firms, which represent nine out of ten companies in this field, account for only 5 per cent of the federally financed research and development.

We find much the same situation in the case of the 15 to 20 cents out of each research and development dollar that the government passes on, by grant or contract, to colleges, universities, or other non-profit organizations. About 100 institutions of higher learning each do at least a $1 million worth of government research per year. These 100 institutions receive 90 per cent of the federal research money that goes to educational institutions. But for every one of these fortunate 100 institutions, there are another 10 to 15 colleges and universities that are doing very little, if any, government research. Perhaps much useful research could be performed on these other campuses.

Dr. Alan T. Waterman described *The Thirteenth Annual Report of the National Science Foundation* as one covering his final years at NSF's Director. He indicated he was devoting this, his final statement, to a "review and critical analysis of over-all trends in research and development. . . ."

In describing the impact of federal support in the broad basic fields of mathematics, science, and engineering, he went on to say:

> As this support grew, many institutions began to revise and strengthen the central administration of programs and funds secured from outside sources. *At the same time, the rising volume of federal support began to introduce problems:* such as coverage of administrative and operating costs, balanced support among the scientists, engineering, and the humanities, *and a certain loss of independence and flexibility on the part of academic institutions in the planning and carrying out of their own programs.* (My italics.)

Another cautionary note is being sounded. One of the criticisms now directed at higher education in the United States is that labeled by the Carnegie Foundation for the Advancement of Teaching in a report issued in 1964 as *The Flight From Teaching*. The thesis of this report is that with increasing numbers of graduate students, decreased faculty teaching loads (this refers to the teaching of formal courses), increased support of research, and increased use of university scientists in advisory and consultant capacities (especially by the federal government), too many of the better faculty members are being drawn too much away from the undergraduate classroom, and too many undergraduates are therefore being deprived more and more of top-level instruction as a greater share of the instructional load is carried by staff members of lesser accomplishments and lesser training, particularly by graduate teaching assistants. A variant criticism asserts that too much of the teaching done by graduate students is not of high enough calibre, because fellowships and research assistantships are more attractive to the better student than teaching is. As a result, teaching assistantships are filled by less able students. This led the National Science Foundation to comment in a special report for a subcommittee of the Committee on Science and Astronautics in the U.S. House of Representatives as follows:

> Although the evidence in support of these criticisms is not firm and certainly not conclusive, it is clear that these are not capricious criticisms; the critics are serious, and they are concerned.

III. The Need for a More Responsible Role by Congress to Foster a National Science Policy, and the Urgency for a Better Science Policy Apparatus Within the Congress.

Thus we begin to see from the foregoing that more and more signs are emerging to indicate that unless Congress develops a national science policy with greater care, federal channeling of R & D funds to the academic community may result in permanent and lasting harm to the undergraduate classroom. Also, when the taxpayer foots the bill for such studies as "The Social Role of the Aging Ungulate," one cannot help but suggest that it should not be the function of the government to provide funds for "ivory tower" type projects.

Further, in the debate on the floor of the House on March 1, 1966, on H.R. 12889, which authorizes supplemental appropriations during fiscal year 1966 for the procurement of aircraft, missiles, tracked combat vehicles, research and development, and military construction for the Armed Forces, Chairman Rivers stated (*Congressional Record*, p. 4263):

> Normally, in the regular programs, research and development comes to almost half of the total bill. Here the sum of $151,650,000 represents only about 3 per cent of the bill. The reason for this is evident in that the weapons that the men are fighting with and will fight with are the result of research and development carried on in the past. *Actually, the funds in this supplement will be used in every instance to accelerate development projects of particular interest to our operations in southeast Asia.* (My italics.)

I think one can safely conclude here that when the goals are clearly defined, R & D costs can be reduced.

We have discovered that the impact of R & D funds can be either a boon to the economy of a community, or that rapid fluctuations in R & D funds can cause a community's economy to go through unpredictable gyrations with traumatic results in some instances.

In an article in *Reader's Digest* (April, 1966, p. 153), there appears this revealing statement that is condensed from an article in *Time*, September 3, 1965:

> Meanwhile, the technical disciplines—chiefly the sciences—have turned loose such a Niagara of information that even the wealthiest of corporate, collegiate or community libraries simply do not know what to do with it.

To anyone in the federal government, and to us in the Congress in particular, the above statement becomes even more disturbing when we onsider what John Martyn, a British writer, wrote in his article entitled "Unintentional Duplication of Research," which appeared in the *New Scientist*, published in London, February, 1964, p. 338. He had conducted a survey of 647 scientists. On the basis of that survey, he concluded that if these scientists had discovered literature at the beginning of the research which they may have wished they had at that time, approximately 0.9% of the money spent on these researches could have been saved.

After the House of Representatives voted on September 11, 1963, to pass H.R. 504, thereby creating the Select Committee on Government Research on a temporary basis, at our first meeting, Chairman Elliott dramatized with the following statement the challenge Congress faces:

> A suspicion that there may be unjustified duplication of effort arises from the fact that eleven agencies and departments perform research in health and medicine; five agencies perform space research, exclusive of aircraft technology; seven are doing work in oceanography; eight in water research, and fourteen in meteorology. Multiple-agency interest is also apparent in such broad categories as defense, environmental health, natural resources, nuclear energy, and the like. Of course, overlapping is not wasteful per se; in some cases I am sure it can be justified on a number of grounds. In fact, I have heard it predicted that we may find the term "justifiable overlap" taking its place in the government lexicon alongside "wasteful duplication."

Be that as it may, it is not enough that we recognize the undisputed need for scientific research by appropriating many billions of dollars to support it. We in the Congress have the constitutional duty to ourselves and to the tax-paying public to oversee the administration of these great sums, to inform ourselves as to how they are being spent, and to assure ourselves that they are being spent wisely and in the public interest.

Mr. William D. Carey, Executive Assistant Director of the U.S. Budget Bureau, writing in the November 6, 1965, issue of *Saturday Review*, put his finger on a problem which Congress must resolve:

> The question which has repeatedly arisen in Congress is "Who, if anybody, is in charge of coordinating R & D?" What Congress wants more than anything else is evidence that the Executive is running a tight ship and knows what it is doing. Congress in its present incarnation is perfectly capable of making up its mind about the moon program, medical research, and the Mohole. But it is less prepared to certify that twelve or fifteen agencies have their meteorology programs in balance, or that feedback from supported research is being put to good use.

On December 29, 1964, the Select Committee on Government Research of the United States House of Representatives filed its recommendations to Congress for establishing national goals and policies in connection with the annual expenditure of such a sizeable sum as $16 billion a year for federal research and development. Approximately $1.5 billion of that amount goes for basic research.

The Select Committee amassed 1077 pages of hearings, heard from eminent scientists and academicians whose testimony represented the viewpoints of those professing expertise in both private enterprise and the federal government. Periodic progress reports were published. In all, there were ten study reports.

Of particular and significant importance is Study No.- 10. It was the judgment of the Select Committee as expressed therein that four important proposals for congressional implementation be made, namely:

1. A Joint Committee on Research Policy
2. A Select Committee on Government Research
3. A subcommittee on technical problems within the Government Operations Committee
4. Certain procedural changes

The Select Committee placed important emphasis on the recommendation that there be established within the framework of Congress a Joint Committee on Research Policy. Considering that Congress is a bicameral entity, such a joint committee composed of members from both the Senate and House could be expected to operate with the high motivation, efficiency, and success of other joint congressional committees already established by the Congress. Also, it goes without saying how much value a Select Committee on Government Research would have in the House of Representatives.

I subscribe wholeheartedly and enthusiastically to these recommendations. Nowhere under the present legislative process do we have in Congress a central body to foster an over-all science policy. It is true, of course, that the several committees of Congress, acting individually and independently of each other, pay close attention to and exercise legislative oversight in the areas of primary jurisdiction assigned to them by the Legislative Reorganization Act of 1946 and the House and Senate Rules as amended from time to time. However, that kind of legislative oversight is confined within the narrow metes and bounds prescribed by their basic authority set forth immediately above. This gives no rise to the kind of comprehensive, over-all review and direction that are so urgently needed in connection with the expenditure of $16 billion per annum for federal research and development.

On page two of its *First Progress Report*, dated February 17, 1964, the Select Committee on Government Research reported:

> While the House of Representatives may have considered the separate parts of our Government's research and development programs, it made no overall examination of the entire effort—to be sure that it is being properly directed and coordinated, and to insure that the legislative branch of our Government, as the provider of research and development funds, does not act without comprehensive knowledge and a firm sense of direction.

The following lends itself even further in support of what I just quoted from our Select Committee's report. The House Committee on Merchant Marine and Fisheries, on September 17, 1965, in House Report No. 1025, to accompany the Marine Resources and Engineering Development Act of 1965, had this to say:

> Present Federal Organization and Function in Oceanography: The existing federal program is presently conducted under existing statutes in approximately 20 federal departments, independent agencies, and bureaus.

To illustrate further the need for Congress to scrutinize in a more comprehensive manner basic and applied research and development financed by tax dollars, at one time, the Bureau of Commercial Fisheries had approximately 70 different studies going on Pacific salmon.

At the moment, the Appropriations Committees perhaps come closest to providing some semblance of over-all review. But their function is not the same as a committee invested with the authority to define a policy area. They cannot be expected to concentrate as thoroughly as a joint committee on the spectrum that a well-defined national science policy entails. Thus, the need for a Joint Committee on Research Policy.

As the Select Committee on Government Research counseled in one of its study reports, we have a foreign policy, we have an economic policy, and with the advent of the nuclear age and now the nuclear-space age, we do indeed dearly need a well-defined science policy. It is incumbent upon Congress to play a vital role in a national science policy.

Dr. Alan T. Waterman, in writing the introduction to the *Thirteenth Annual Report of the National Science Foundation*, described how quickly the Executive Branch equipped itself with coordinating and supervision functions in its efforts to cope with the spectacular growth in science and technology and the government's enlarged role in research and development.

He mentioned, in addition to the creation in 1950 of the National Science Foundation as significant and explicit recognition of the critical importance in the over-all effort of basic research and education in the sciences, these further important steps within the framework of the executive branch:

1. The President's Science Advisory Committee
2. The Special Assistant to the President for Science and Technology
3. The Federal Council for Science and Technology
4. The Office of Science and Technology in the Executive Office of the President

I am heartened by the fact that the Government Operations Committee of the U.S. House of Representatives has already seen fit to implement recommendation No. 3 made by the Select Committee on Government Research in its Study No. 10. A Special Subcommittee on Research and Technical Programs has been formed within the framework of the Government Operations Committee.

I think we will place even greater reliance on the newly formed Science Policy Research Division established in the Legislative Reference Service of the Library of Congress to fulfill "the growing demand for more and better science advice for Congress," in the words of John Walsh, *Science*, Vol. 145, Sept. 11, 1964, p. 1162.

These are steps in the right direction. But in themselves they still do not provide the basis for the kind of comprehensive, over-all review and direction that are so urgently needed in connection with a national science policy. While research and development programs can continue under existing control arrangements, I think it becomes obvious from the foregoing discussion that if such programs are to be conducted with the greatest possible degree of efficiency, economy, and effectiveness, they must be under the direction of a responsible coordinating body of the Congress itself. This role can be most successfully fulfilled by a Joint Committee on Research Policy.

OGDEN R. REID, M.C.
26th District, New York

CONGRESS AND FOREIGN POLICY

by Ogden R. Reid, M.C.[*]

We live in a nuclear age in which United States foreign policy decisions are singularly important in determining the fate of mankind. The Constitution bestowed a significant role on Congress in the area of foreign policy. Both houses were empowered to raise all the revenues and to appropriate all the monies which are used in the conduct of foreign relations; to raise and support the armed forces and "to make Rules for the Government and Regulation of the land and naval Forces;" to admit immigrants; "to regulate Commerce with foreign Nations," and "to declare War." The Senate, in addition, was made responsible for confirming appointments and consenting to the ratification of treaties.

In spite of the clear powers assigned to Congress in the field of foreign affairs, the fact is that Congress has too often been on the periphery, rather than at the heart, of the foreign policy making process. This is not to deny that the President is clearly responsible under the Constitution for the conduct of foreign policy, nor should his freedom, power, and flexibility in foreign affairs be impaired. But this does not mean major Administration policies should always be initiated, conducted, and furthered without some timely testing in Congress.

To state that Congress can or should have a significant role is not to say that it clearly visualizes the parameters of its authority or its responsibilities. In part this is due to an erosion of Congressional control over warmaking powers almost to the point of invisibility in the area of guerrilla wars, undeclared wars, civil wars and wars of subversion. In part this is due to an accession of Presidential power in the nuclear age—which the executive has welcomed if not sought—in an era when time is foreshortened and when quiet White House decisions, carrying large implications, are often the rule.

---

[*] First elected to Congress in 1962, Mr. Reid is former Editor and President of the *New York Herald Tribune* and served as Ambassador to Israel during the Eisenhower administration. He represents the 26th Congressional District of New York and is a Member of the House Education and Labor and Government Operations Committees.

The Congress in the name of national security is all too frequently faced with decisions already set in train which it is virtually powerless to revoke or substantially alter.

The Changing Role of Congress

In several important respects the role of Congress in foreign policy has been significantly changed in recent times. For one thing, agreements with foreign powers today often take the form of executive agreements rather than formal treaties. Executive agreements, entered into by the executive without requiring the approval of two-thirds of the Senate, have virtually the same effect as treaties.

Executive agreements were used to terminate World War I, to acquire British naval bases in exchange for over-age destroyers, to accept the Atlantic Charter, and for scores of other matters. Most international agreements today are in the form of executive agreements rather than treaties. In 1956, for example, the U.S. concluded 200 international agreements. Of these, only five were actually in the form of treaties. Big and dramatic issues, such as adherence to the UN Charter, NATO, and the Nuclear Test Ban Agreement, are usually honored by the treaty procedure. Consular conventions and extradition agreements are similarly dealt with.

The use of the Congressional resolution has to some extent compensated the Congress in the international sphere for the decreasing reliance on formal treaties submitted to the Senate. Joint resolutions must be passed by a majority of both houses and be signed by the President. They have the same effect as laws. To the extent that they are used in the area of international agreement-making they represent a shift from President plus two-thirds of the Senate to President plus a majority of both houses.

Concurrent resolutions are also passed by both houses but are not referred to the President and have no legal force; they merely express the will and intent of Congress. Simple resolutions go through only one house and, of course, express only the views of that body.

Frequently resolutions are formulated by the State Department and are presented to Congress for approval. If Congressional sentiment goes along with the President, the resolution is forthcoming, as in the case of the Middle East Resolution. This resolution stated that

> the United States regards as vital to the national interest and world peace the preservation of the independence and integrity of the nations of the Middle East.

and it provided that

> if the President determines the necessity thereof, the United States is prepared to use armed force to assist any nation or group of such nations requesting assistance against armed aggression from any country controlled by international Communism; provided, that such employment shall be consonant with the treaty obligations of the United States and with the Constitution of the United States.

Occasionally, real initiative in foreign affairs is taken by Congress and expressed in a resolution. A notable case of this kind was the Monroney Resolution of 1948. The Resolution dealt with the economies of the underdeveloped countries, the more efficient use of surplus local currencies owned by the United States, and possible reduction of United States foreign aid. It called for a study of the feasibility of establishing an International Development Association, which was subsequently created as a result of the interest aroused by this resolution.

Resolutions originating in Congress, even if unsuccessful, when they have widespread support, alert the State Department and other interested groups to important trends in the thinking of Congress.

> There are many times in which Congress can make its views known somewhat irresponsibly without creating the type of severe reaction which would be created if the executive branch through ordinary diplomatic channels or through public pronouncements seemed to be resorting to pressure. The congressional resolution is just what it purports to be, an indication of opinion and attitude, and is not in itself overt in its results or effect. It is, however, often an interesting and significant counterweight or response to the increasing tendency on the part of the President to use the executive agreement as an instrument of international action.[1]

Ever since the advent of extensive foreign aid and international monetary and banking and loan programs by the United States Government requiring large sums of money, Congress has had a role in this field of foreign affairs. Since appropriation bills must originate in the House, this body now has a more significant voice in the determination of our international economic and military policies. However, in another important respect, the combined houses of Congress have seen their powers dwindle away.

> Congressional control of the war-making power has been eroded almost to the point of invisibility.[2]

It is perfectly true that the President as Commander-in-Chief can, and sometimes has, taken responsibility for directing United States military forces to respond to acts of aggression, as in Korea. Nevertheless, until recent decades, the act of declaring war (and holding deliberations regarding responses to hostilities) was still required of Congress, and there were times when Congress took an active part in bringing about hostilities as well as in making the formal declaration of war. The Spanish-American War is the most clear-cut case of the Congress virtually forcing a reluctant President to undertake military action almost against his will.

Since 1945 fighting has taken place in many parts of the world without formal declarations of war. The possibilities of nuclear confrontation have meant that the President must have the right to act almost immediately in the event of aggression against the United States, since there would not be time for consulting Congress in the event of a nuclear attack. Although the military actions in which we have been involved in the nuclear age have not been ones requiring instantaneous response, the formal deliberations which Congress is expected to carry on when military commitments are made have not always taken place.

> . . . It is guerrilla wars, undeclared wars, civil wars, and wars by subversion that now plague the world and are likely to continue as the chief difficulties in the years ahead. It is in this area of policy-making that the people's elected representatives in Congress have largely abdicated their constitutional responsibilities.[3]

Military actions undertaken by the executive, either with or without a declaration of war, should have congressional sanction. The Vietnam war, with more than 400,000 Americans involved in the Southeast Asian theatre, and with some 5,000 North Vietnamese regulars heading south each month, could become as large, indeed potentially larger, than the Korean War. Yet the Congressional role throughout has been on the periphery, not at the center of policy or decision-making, at a time when our commitment has been substantially enlarged, if not changed.

After an ever-deepening involvement in Vietnam and following an attack on our ships in the Gulf of Tonkin, the President in August 1964 asked Congress to go on record as giving him authority to act. A hastily drafted and broad joint resolution giving the President power

> to repel any armed attack against the forces of the United States and to prevent further aggression . . . to take all necessary steps, including the use of armed force, to assist any member of protocol state of the Southeast Asia Collective Defense Treaty requesting assistance in defense of its freedom

was submitted to the relevant committees and passed by Congress with no real deliberation but with overwhelming majorities: 88-2 in the Senate, 416-0 in the House.

> From initiation to Presidential signature, each of these measures (the appropriation bill and the resolution) took only three days. That is not constitutional procedure; it is a caricature of such procedure.[4]

On April 28, 1965, United States marines landed in the Dominican Republic "to protect American lives" and the lives of some 5500 other nationals at the request of their governments. The executive had not fully anticipated a deteriorating situation, had not kept members of the Embassy Country Team at their posts, had not informed the OAS of the U.S. decision prior to the landing of troops, and did not fully appraise the Congress until a sensitive situation had developed. Consultation with congressional leaders took place largely after the decision had been made.

At a somewhat later date the House passed a resolution proclaiming the right of unilateral intervention at the mere threat of "subversive domination." It was as unwise as its predictable effect. It not only confirmed many Latin Americans in their concern over our policy but resulted in the U.S. being unanimously condemned in the legislatures of Colombia and Peru.

What is important to note here is that too often our policy is the result of failure to anticipate; of hurried executive action and lack of constructive Congressional involvement—prior to major decisions—followed by an escalating situation that increasingly defies easy solutions or reasonable progress.

The Congress in the field of foreign affairs is operating under a handicap. The development of foreign policy requires large amounts of highly technical, specialized, sometimes confidential information, much more readily accessible to the executive branch. It has at its disposal all the voluminous reports and analyses of the State Department, which in turn receives daily dispatches and cables from embassies all over the world and the reports of the Central Intelligence Agency. The President also has the authority to make speedy decisions in crisis situations.

Because of these built-in advantages of the executive, much of the initiative in foreign policy must continue to come from the executive branch. Recognizing the need for executive planning and initiative does not, however, reduce the importance of the legislature's role. One of the great functions of Congress, implied in all the grants of power enumerated by the Constitution, is the function of debate and discussion, of making known the will of the people by their elected representatives, and in turn informing and enlightening the citizens back home. Indeed, decisions within the legislature must be arrived at after discussion in committee and on the floor:

> It is probably correct to say that the decision-making process in the legislature, more than in any other significant power institution, is an actual practice conducted by discussion.[5]

Nowhere is the function of discussion more essential than in the domain of foreign affairs. In domestic matters—labor relations, education, farm problems, crime, unemployment—the citizen can often make up his mind based on his own experiences and observations. But when it comes to events and trends in the Congo, Kashmir, Indonesia, Chile, or Communist China, few Americans have real means of evaluation based on direct personal involvement. Most must judge what the United States policy should be in these far-off places based on what they read and hear.

To provide the public with reliable, comprehensive, and comprehensible information about international affairs which are of concern to the United States is one of the most vital responsibilities of Congress but one too often performed in a perfunctory, superficial, or ineffectual manner.

> Aside from simply having more debate on important matters, and less on unimportant ones, it is necessary to improve both the level of discussion and the effectiveness with which it is communicated.[6]

The process of searching floor debate, as a complement to committee hearings, which explores, examines, criticizes, and analyzes will bring to light weaknesses and inadequacies of policies advocated by the executive, and may lead to the proposal of alternatives or to the elimination of the evils or shortcomings uncovered in debate.

No matter how well-intentioned or how wise the policies formulated by the executive, in an area so fraught with life and death significance as our relations with other nations, there must be an opportunity for the American people to hear the various aspects of issues discussed and debated and for alternative proposals to be given a hearing.

There are many reasons why it is not adequate to have major foreign policy determinations emanate from the White House with only cursory debate in the Congress, as is too often the case. The President and the State Department may publicize only the favorable aspects of policies they propose and give the public the information they wish them to have. Even in the event that an Administration policy is the correct one, the democratic process does not flourish if debate and consideration of alternatives play no part in the decision-making. If it is essential in the domestic arena to allow diverse opinions to be expressed, how much more important it is that this be done in the foreign field, where the great bulk of the individual's taxes are spent, where the lives of thousands of men are affected by military service, and where the future of all of us may be decided.

Meaningful, illuminating debate cannot just happen. It must be thoughtfully prepared and there must be proper channels for its expression. Does Congress adequately provide these prerequisites for wide-ranging and penetrating examination of major foreign policy issues? It has some of the means for such debate, but it needs a number of improvements to make this goal possible.

Among the reforms most urgently needed to place Congress in a more significant position in the foreign policy area rather than at the edges are access to independent sources of information, more effective staffing and organization of committees, and the establishment of a direct link between the representatives of the people and the executive.

Better Sources of Information

"Our judgment," said President Kennedy, "is only as good as our information." This is as true of organizations as it is of individuals. Only if Congress is able to correct the appalling imbalance between the information, research, and analysis available to its Members and that at the disposal of the executive branch will it be able to play a truly significant role in evolving effective, far-sighted foreign policy approaches. Otherwise, it will continue in the main to react to policies formulated by the executive.

Because Congress has inadequate sources of information and research of its own, it must rely substantially on the statistics, reports, and analyses of executive agencies. The data supplied by these agencies reflects the views of the department concerning legislation which they, rather than Congress, all too often initiate. As long as Congress has to fall back on the information it receives from the executive branch, it will be something less than a fully autonomous branch of the government, capable of originating fresh and productive ideas and will have to go on accepting, rejecting, and amending executive proposals.

What has been referred to as the "brainpower gap" between the professional staff of the executive and that of much of the legislature is substantial. Congress is sadly lacking in the kind of creative, independent research which the executive avails itself of—both in its own departments and through universities and research institutions.

The present facilities available to Congress do not fully provide Members with the kind of high quality research they require. The Legislative Reference Service was established as a "reservoir of research" for Congress within the Library of Congress. It was to provide information, research and reference materials to Members of Congress, committees and staffs. The enormous growth in the nature and complexity of legislative issues and in the workload of individual Congressmen in recent years has led to a greatly increased demand for assistance from LRS. The Service has also become involved in providing assistance to answer inquiries from constituents.

Most important, LRS does not employ enough highly trained specialists —some of whom should have held serious and responsible positions in foreign affairs—capable of original thinking for the research it should be providing Members and committees of Congress. Some changes can be brought about by administrative decisions within the Library, but Congress cannot ignore its responsibility to provide the necessary funds for increasing the capabilities of the Service.

However, even if the Legislative Reference Service of the Library of Congress is revamped, it will not be in a position to supply all the types of information and analysis which Congress needs. The LRS staff does not have access to classified documents which are vital to studies in the area of international relations. Staff members, as a matter of policy, are not permitted to make recommendations to Members or committees of Congress. What Congress needs is to have creative thinkers to assist it in formulating new foreign policy approaches, not merely to secure information on what has happened in the past. The problem is not only to acquire data and analysis, but also new ideas.

Congress might well consider the feasibility of establishing a foreign policy research and analysis institute of its own, patterned after the Air Force's Rand Corporation. Staffed with eminent experts from a large number of disciplines, trained in the latest scientific techniques, this institute would be able to apply a multi-disciplinary and "systems" approach to complex international problems. It would both respond to requests of Members and would act on its own initiative as well in selecting subjects of inquiry which it considered of vital future importance. The Rand Corporation has frequently taken upon itself studies of problems which the practitioners in the Air Force, deeply immersed in day-to-day matters, did not foresee the need for studying.

Many of the new ideas developed by the Rand researchers have been accepted by the Air Force.

A Congressional foreign policy institute might well undertake studies of such existing problems as the achievement of a lasting peace between Israel and the Arab states in the Middle East, political and economic instability in Brazil and other Latin American areas; it could also offer recommendations regarding emerging problems like the danger of the proliferation of nuclear weapons, and serious and growing unrest in the Republic of South Africa and Rhodesia. On these existing and emergent problems it would bring to bear the expertise of economists, anthropologists, agronomists, geographers, psychologists, sociologists, political scientists, and other appropriate specialists, who would do much of their research in the areas involved. Recommendations would be the result of the findings and conclusions of the combined group of specialists, operating as a cohesive team. They would utilize the up-to-date techniques so fruitfully employed by the Defense Department, Rand, and large-scale private corporations, such as operations research and cost-benefit analysis.

The institute would provide Congress with analyses of proposed foreign policies based on examination of alternative policies, estimates of the probable consequences of each alternative, and indications of the degree of consensus or disagreement among qualified experts on the probable consequences. If Congress had this kind of service available to it, it might well tackle foreign policy issues in a creative way and be able to anticipate trouble spots before they become crises.

This kind of institute would be expensive, but if Congress is willing to allocate some $50 million annually for research in strategic and foreign policy studies for the Defense Department, it ought to be willing to do as much for its own study of broad international issues.

Prior to the establishment of such an institute, or in addition to it, there is no reason why congressional committee staffs cannot contract with private research firms, foundations or universities to explore in depth problems which the staffs do not have the time or facilities to pursue. The Senate Foreign Relations Committee has made some use of this type of research in former years. Executive agencies often utilize the talents of competent scholars and research organizations with rewarding results. Congress should not overlook these resources in the larger community.

The House and Senate Committees on foreign affairs each have several subcommittees dealing with major areas of the world. Some of these are actively concerned with their areas, but others rarely meet or do not have very meaningful sessions when they do meet. Congress' influence on foreign policy would be greatly enhanced if more of these regional subcommittees could be brought to life with Members appointed to them who have a real interest in the area and who would make this assignment one of their chief responsibilities. Such Members should travel to the area regularly, maintain contacts with individuals and groups from this part of the world, and have available to them competent, well-trained and experienced staff people who know the area thoroughly, preferably through first-hand observations and experience in the military service, Peace Corps, diplomatic service, or teaching, and who would be prepared to accompany Members on fact-finding trips and international conferences concerning the area.

Few Members of Congress have the time to become knowledgeable in more than one field of Congressional activity. In the vast and complex field of international affairs, a Member will do well to be thoroughly conversant with the manifold problems of Latin America, the Middle East, or Southeast Asia. Yet he has to pass on matters pertaining to the rest of the world. His ability to deal intelligently with such diverse subjects as trade with Communist countries, foreign aid, and NATO depends to a large degree on the staff assistance available to him. Only if an adequate number of highly qualified people are utilized in the offices of individual Members and in the committee staffs can Congress hope to deal with the enormous variety of legislative matters which it must handle.

Improvement of Committee Organization and Staff

The starting place for all legislation, resolutions, and investigations is a committee. It is here that proposed legislation is weighed and considered and the activities of the executive branch scrutinized through investigations. If committees are inadequately staffed, improperly organized, and poorly attended by their Members, then the chances of the measure being given proper consideration are dim.

Important proposals may never be taken up by the committee in the first place if the Members (particularly the chairman) do not have the acumen to recognize the significance of the measure, or if they have some personal or political reason for keeping it buried.

It has frequently been pointed out with respect to committees that since the chairman has so many crucial functions—such as deciding which bills to take up and in what order, when to call committee meetings, which subcommittees to establish and who to appoint to them—his selection ought not to be left to the vagaries of the seniority system.

The value of competent committee staffs has long been recognized. The efficiency of committees is to a large degree dependent on the calibre of the professional staffs. The committees dealing with foreign policy could use more first-rate staff from the academic community and research institutions with expertise in international affairs. The use of a sufficient number of such persons on the committees would help to permit the members to make independent judgments on many issues without being unduly dependent on the information supplied them by the State and Defense Departments.

The staffing of individual Senators' and Representatives' offices also has a bearing on how well-equipped Members are for carrying on informed discussion either in committees or on the floors of the houses. Staffs which are almost entirely concerned with handling constituents' requests and in keeping up with current legislation may offer no help to the Member who needs competent research assistance for dealing with long-range international problems.

The public hearings and investigations of committees bring into the open the views of various groups in American life through the statements of expert witnesses, including members of the executive agencies, and the questioning of these witnesses by members of the committee. A well-planned and -conducted hearing

> may sometimes be a potent force for influencing opinion in and out of Congress, as witness the enormous importance of the Nye Committee in persuading almost a whole generation to the view that the first World War was entirely a product of the munitions industry.[7]

The investigation of the dismissal of General MacArthur, which began by scrutinizing executive action, ended by focusing attention on our whole Far Eastern policy.

The continuing hearings of the Senate Foreign Relations Committee on our policy in Asia have both outlined what the executive considers our policy now to be and some of the basic questions with regard to it. These hearings have helped to compel national debate, and there should be more hearings of this type.

Congress needs to find ways of integrating and coordinating its activities in more effective ways. This is particularly true in the area of foreign affairs. The various aspects of over-all foreign policy and national strategy are handled in different committees in each body with the result that there is no way to evaluate the problem in its entirety or to develop a comprehensive, unified national policy.

Foreign policy and military policy are both aspects of the same total problem, yet they are considered in separate committees. Many international matters do not go to the Foreign Affairs or Foreign Relations Committees. Foreign trade problems go to the Banking and Currency Committee, tariffs are considered in the Ways and Means Committee, the Food for Peace program is handled by the Agriculture Committee. All measures which require money—and most of them do—must go to the Appropriations Committees of both Houses, as well as to the subject-matter committees.

It is important to remember that no matter how many approvals a bill receives in the subject-matter committees, it will be a failure unless the appropriations committees approve of the money involved. These committees do do not confine themselves merely to expenditures. Instructions are frequently inserted in legislation which in effect modify the policy itself:

> As more and more of our foreign policy is determined by programs of foreign aid, by the size of the armed forces, and by the extent of the appropriations for

the various branches of the State Department itself, so more and more the Appropriations Committees will, in fact, if not in name, constitute themselves a kind of third house of Congress which will play its own role in policy formulation and adoption.[8]

Typical of the handling of many foreign policy issues was the way in which the foreign trade problem was bandied about in one session of Congress:

Ten Committees of the House of Representatives pursued their sometimes inconsistent and usually uncoordinated philosophies in a fraction of one policy area, the area of international trade policy.[9]

Often each committee becomes acquainted with one small facet of a large international issue and like the blind man confronted with an elephant, each of them is aware of one special feature but has no comprehension of the overall phenomenon.

Congress dealing with foreign policy is a Don Quixote riding off in all directions at once. . . . The Senate Armed Services Committee may pull one way, the Foreign Relations Committee another, and the Appropriations Committee still a third.[10]

An example of the fragmentation of subject matter and committee jurisdiction in the Congress is the responsibility for legislative oversight of the intelligence community—primarily the CIA. In both the House and the Senate small subcommittees of the Appropriations and Armed Services Committees undertake this watchdog function. Neither the Foreign Affairs nor Foreign Relations Committees have jurisdiction in this area despite their direct concern in matters affected by foreign intelligence.*

Many Members of both houses have felt increasing concern with regard to more effective oversight of our intelligence activities, especially since there has been a growing apprehension that the CIA may be exceeding its statutory authority—which does not include policy-making. As Professor Ransom, a leading scholar in the area of intelligence matters, put it:

The man, or group, controlling the information available to policy makers does in fact play a major if indirect role in policy making. . . .

It would be unrealistic to suggest that the bright young men of CIA, by training, talent and personality, do not hold strong views on controversial issues of national security policy. If it is granted that knowledge is indeed power, it will be recognized that in reality the CIA, through an increasing efficiency—and consequently rising credit with responsible decision makers—has come to play a major role in creating national security policy.[11]

In theory and by virtue of clear executive orders, the President, the Ambassador, and a small group of advisors at the highest level of government must approve all activities of the CIA in a particular country before they are initiated. But pressure of other responsibilities, the secrecy that has to be main-

* Although the Senate has turned down a proposal to add members of the Foreign Relations Committee to the CIA Subcommittee, the principle is valid as the CIA, acting under Presidential approval, does at times affect foreign policy.—O.R.R.

tained, and the lack of familiarity with the nature of this specialized field may preclude sufficient and clear supervision.

In nearly every session of Congress since the CIA was established there have been proposals for a Joint Committee on Foreign Intelligence. These proposals have been supported by a considerable number of Democrats and Republicans but so far not by a majority. The Mark Clark Special Task Force of the Hoover Commission (1955) also favored greater Congressional surveillance of CIA. This Task Force was concerned about the relative freedom of the CIA from oversight by Congress and recommended a Joint Committee on Foreign Intelligence similar to the Joint Committee on Atomic Energy.

The group expressed the commonly held view that there is a danger that such freedom from restraints could produce laxity and abuses that could prove costly to the American people.

Congress might well expect a Joint Committee on Foreign Intelligence to consider the relations between intelligence gathering on the one hand and so-called special operations on the other. The Committee would likewise review the selection and training of intelligence personnel and undertake studies of over-all intelligence evaluation.

Advocates of a joint committee to keep track of the CIA discount the danger that some of the secret aspects of the organization's work may become public knowledge. Secrecy is also involved in the areas where Congress already has oversight and legislative powers—atomic energy, weapons development, and some aspects of foreign policy. Members of both Houses have shown in the main that they are quite capable of keeping secret information to themselves.

One means of bringing a modicum of order into this confusion and lack of coordination is to have more joint hearings. There are a few encouraging precedents for holding joint hearings on subjects of concern to several committees. During the Cuban crisis and some of the Vietnam crises, the Armed Services Committee met with the Appropriations Committee members. In connection with the Nuclear Test Ban Agreement, joint hearings were held among the Senate members of the Joint Atomic Energy Committee, the Foreign Relations Committee, and the Armed Services Committee. The leadership of both parties was also invited to attend these sessions. In early 1965 the Armed Services Committee met with the subcommittee on Military Expenditures of the Appropriations Committee to take up the matter of defense appropriations.

In the Senate it has been customary for some time for two majority members and one minority member of the Foreign Relations Committee to join the Appropriations Committee as non-voting observers when the Appropriations Committee deals with matters affecting the State Department. This kind of procedure should be broadened in terms of common meetings on a larger number of subjects which concern the two committees and the practice adopted in the House. It is particularly important that there be close coordination between the committees dealing with foreign affairs and those which handle appropriations to prevent the emasculation or transformation of some foreign policy measures.

More joint committee meetings and hearings should be held, not only because they give the Members a more well-rounded and balanced picture of international problems, but because they would save the Secretaries of State and Defense a great deal of valuable time. Sometimes these cabinet officers must leave urgent tasks in their own departments to come to Capitol Hill to testify one day before the Foreign Affairs Committee, a few days later to the Armed Services Committee, and the following week to the Appropriations Committee. The same procedure must be repeated in the other House—and all these appearances deal with virtually the same subject matter.

Those interested in congressional reform hoped that the addition of new staff personnel in committees, provided for by the Legislative Reorganization Act of 1946, would play a part in coordinating committee activities. The expectation was that staff members of one committee would have more communication with those in other related committees. It has not happened, but it should be encouraged.

One means by which Congress could more effectively contribute to the formulation of American foreign policy would be to establish a National Security Committee which would concern itself with foreign and military policies and the interrelationships of various foreign programs. Instead of duplicating the legislative work of the existing committees, the new committee would be largely concerned with the identification and consideration of long-range problems in foreign affairs.

A prototype for such a committee is the Joint Economic Committee; it studies over-all economic problems which are fragmented in other committees. Its main task is to examine the present and future state of the economy and to recommend courses of action. It is not, by and large, a legislative committee, but an idea committee. The Committee's yearly reports on the economy and where it is heading are useful, highly regarded documents.

Such a committee in foreign and military affairs should be kept relatively small, its membership determined on the basis of the concern and interest of Members in its work. Seniority should play a minimal, if any, role with rotating rather than permanent chairmen. Outstanding younger Members of both bodies whose talents are not being fully utilized might well make a valuable contribution to our nation's foreign policy in this committee. If and when a congressional foreign policy institute were established this committee would work closely with it.

Congress As a Public Forum

If Congress is to provide a nationwide forum for the public discussion of issues of international import, both the quantity and quality of debate on the floors of the House and Senate must be on the highest level possible. Debate in these bodies should reflect all the preliminary stages of consideration of a bill—the expert opinions expressed in committee hearings, the findings of research staff, conversations and correspondence with executive officers, personal reflection and study by Members.

Judicious consideration should be given to televising sessions of Congress when high level debate on important and dramatic issues of foreign policy takes place on the floor of the House or Senate. More people in the United States own television sets than telephones, and this medium ought to be utilized to bring to the American people the benefits of Congressional insights —or the lack thereof as the case may be.

In the Senate, where debate is virtually unlimited, all the varied ramifications and implications of a measure can be fully explored if the Members are minded to do so. Senate discussion has on occasion had much to do with changing or modifying certain aspects of policies when thoughtful and convincing arguments were presented. Such discussion characterized the "great debate" over NATO and resulted in the broadening of the membership of the organization by the inclusion of Greece and Turkey and led to the creation of public interest in the defense problems of Western Europe that could not have been aroused in any other way.

Debate in the House is much more limited in scope, generally ranging from one to six hours. This is often far too short to be meaningful, especially on matters involving the whole direction of our foreign policy.

It would be useful if in the House a certain amount of time could be devoted to the discussion of grave international concerns, even when they do not pertain to a specific piece of legislation. Congressmen might wish to discuss events in Rhodesia, Indonesia, or Brazil, not because there is a bill pending on these matters, but because it is important for Members of the House and the general public to realize that historic changes are taking place in these countries which may one day have a vital bearing on our own affairs. To a limited extent, such debate is already possible if a simple resolution is passed, but this procedure is rarely used.

These measures for increasing public awareness of international affairs would make for much more effective debate, but they do not come to grips with one weakness from which our system presently suffers—the lack of a direct link between the representatives of the people and the executive branch. Those conducting debate are not charged with the carrying out of foreign policy, and those responsible for implementing foreign policy are not involved in debate.

This gap in our system is not filled by the Presidential press conference— even when it is not in disarray—nor by committee hearings which serve an important but different function.

The Presidential press conference can serve a vital role in informing the American people on questions of foreign policy through the media of newspapers, television, and radio. It is, however, a dialogue between the Chief Executive and the "fourth estate," not with the legislative branch.

The committee system provides valuable first-hand information, facts, and insights as to our foreign policy, often by members of the Cabinet. It does not do so, however, on a national stage. A Cabinet officer testifying before a congressional committee is not under "a sense of liability of prompt explanation" as Elihu Root once explained. The colloquy in committee does not enjoy the same degree of national interest and sanction it could enjoy on the Floor of the House or Senate.

Should not the American people through their elected representatives have an opportunity through prompt, responsible, and enlightened floor debate to register or withhold a degree of national sanction? This could be effected by the adoption of a simple change in the rules of the House of Representatives and Senate to admit the Secretary of State to the House and Senate Floors to answer private notice questions from Members on this country's foreign policy.

A consensus achieved within the portals of the White House—or national understanding that is skin deep and sometimes furthered by massive access to communications media—is no substitute for understanding that derives from the basic soundness of a program and fundamental understanding— where possible—of opportunities and risks. If the broad goals of foreign policy are not susceptible to national support and at least national understanding, then their viability is in question.

It is thus clear that a necessary, more direct link between the representatives of the people and the executive has been lacking in our Presidential form of government—a link which could provide responsible and elevated debate on great foreign policy questions.

A regular exchange of this character in the well of the House and on the floor of the Senate would at the least illuminate the truth of where our foreign policy is heading. It could test—in a way not now possible—the principles and soundness of foreign policy, and policies in turn could receive public sanction which could help gird the national will.

Private notice questions would be submitted in advance and in writing. The Secretary of State would not be expected to answer questions which are clearly contrary to the national interest, but he would have to so state on the floor.

It is a matter of some interest to note that the United States is virtually the only democracy which does not make provision for executive officers to participate in legislative debate. Other countries maintain, in much greater degree than is suggested here, prodecures whereby executive members may participate in the debates of their legislatures. This includes countries as diverse as Great Britain, India, New Zealand, Australia, Italy, and France.

It is certainly by accident and not by design that Cabinet members have been excluded from floor proceedings of the House and Senate since 1792.

For in the first days of Congress, members of the Cabinet, including John Jay, Alexander Hamilton, Henry Knox, and Thomas Jefferson, did appear on the floor of the House and the Senate for consultation, advice and information. Indeed, President Washington also came before the Congress to answer questions.

Such distinguished Americans as President Woodrow Wilson, Secretaries of State Henry L. Stimson, Charles Evans Hughes, and James Byrnes, and Senators Henry Cabot Lodge, Estes Kefauver, and J. William Fulbright have supported this proposition.

This is a limited proposal. A question period would provide the opportunity to illuminate the broad outlines of foreign policy in a national forum. Debate and responsible clash of opinion would mean that foreign policy could be held up to public view so that reaction thereto could provide constructive responses.

A question period would enable Members of Congress, as popularly elected guardians of the public trust, to consider and to participate in testing American foreign policy. This procedure could enhance the effectiveness and stature of Congress. We should welcome the opportunity to ask difficult questions in an effort to get the best possible thinking on the great problems of our time.

A question period, as distinguished from periodic and off-the-record personal and group congressional briefings, would enable the State Department to benefit from a sense of liability of prompt and public explanation.

Equally important, it would, in the words of Congressman George Pendleton, have further salutary effects:

> Would it not be better that their opinions should be expressed, their facts stated, their policy enforced, their acts defended, in open day, on the floor of the House, in face of the nation, in public speech, in official, recorded statement, where there can be no hidden purpose, no misconception, no misrepresentation?[12]

Our foreign policy must have the consistent understanding and support of the Congress and the people. I am convinced that the best way to get this is for Congressmen to be more closely seized with the great issues of war and peace.

There is a long-term trend which has set in which has substantially reduced the powers of Congress *vis-à-vis* the executive. The answer to this does not lie in consensus politics constructed within the portals of the White House, no matter how skillful the occupant.

The answer lies in the Congress playing a more significant role *vis-à-vis* the executive in the development of legislative initiatives and in a sense of close involvement with the great questions through the thrust and parry of responsible debate.

REFERENCES

1. Griffith, Ernest, "The Place of Congress in Foreign Relations," *The Annals of the American Academy of Political and Social Science*, Vol. 289, Sept., 1953, p. 13.

2. Editorial, *The New York Times*, May 9, 1965.
3. *Ibid.*
4. *Ibid.*
5. Dahl, Robert A., *Congress and Foreign Policy*, New York, 1950, p. 124.
6. *Ibid.*, p. 165.
7. Dahl, *op. cit.*, p. 164.
8. Griffith, *op. cit.*, p. 13.
9. Carroll, Holbert N., *The House of Representatives and Foreign Affairs*, Pittsburgh, 1958, p. 58.
10. Cheever, Daniel S., and Field Haviland, Jr., *American Foreign Policy and the Separation of Powers*, Cambridge, 1952, p. 216.
11. Harry Howe Ransom, *Central Intelligence and National Security*, Cambridge, 1958, p. 201, p. 203.
12. George Pendleton, U.S. Congress, House Select Committee on Admitting Heads of Executive Departments on the Floor of the House of Representatives, entitled Heads of Executive Departments. Accompanied Bill 214, Printed April 6, 1864, 38th Congress, 1st Session, House Report 43, p. 4.

ROBERT McCLORY, M.C.
12th District, Illinois

REFORMING THE BUDGETARY AND FISCAL MACHINERY OF CONGRESS

by Robert McClory, M.C.*

The existing congressional machinery for handling the fiscal business of the Federal Government is antiquated, complex, and wholly inadequate if the Congress is to meet its constitutional and public responsibility. Unless reform occurs in regard to congressional control of revenues and expenditures, the dangers of spiraling inflation and additional raids on the Treasury could seriously impair the economic and political growth and stability of our Nation. Major steps toward reform must be taken now.

It is the purpose of this chapter to examine the entire congressional budget process and to offer recommendations for the improvement of the budgetary and fiscal machinery of Congress. These recommendations have been formulated into a "13-Point Program for Budgetary and Fiscal Reform" demonstrating the need for:

1. Creating a Joint Committee on the Budget.
2. Creating a Budget Information Service.
3. Improving the presentation of the budget—use of a planning-programming-budgeting system.
4. Re-scheduling of the budget.
5. Limiting the use of annual authorizations to short-term programs.
6. "Price-tagging" authorizations.
7. Reducing "fixed" budgetary commitments.
8. Joint Appropriations Committee hearings.
9. Revising appropriations procedure and organization on a functional basis.
10. Increasing Appropriations Committee staffs.

* Mr. McClory is a Member of the House Judiciary Committee and a United States delegate to the Interparliamentary Union. He was first elected to Congress in 1962 from the 12th Congressional District of Illinois and has seen service on the House Government Operations Committee.

11. Restricting the use of executive sessions by the House Appropriations Subcommittees.

12. Improving the "legislative oversight" function of the Government Operations Committee—additional minority staff.

13. Enhancing the place of the General Accounting Office in the Congressional budget process—including a pre-audit role.

The Constitutional Responsibility of Congress in the Nation's Fiscal Affairs—Federal Budgeting and Fiscal Control as a Political Process.

Realizing from English history that the power of the purse must never be given exclusively to the Executive, the Founding Fathers provided for congressional control of revenues and expenditures in Article I of the Constitution. The responsibility of Congress and the primacy of the House of Representatives in the control of revenues is made clear in Section 7, Clause 1, which provides: "All bills for raising revenue shall originate in the House of Representatives; but the Senate may propose or concur with amendments as on other bills," and in Section 8, Clause 1, which provides: "The Congress shall have the power to lay and collect taxes . . ." However, the crux of congressional responsibility in fiscal control and budgeting is set forth in Section 9, Clause 7:

> No money shall be drawn from the Treasury, but in consequence of appropriations made by law; and a regular statement and account of the receipts and expenditures of all public money shall be published from time to time.

Though not explicitly stated, this last provision is generally understood to mean that the House of Representatives shall have the sole power to initiate appropriations bills since such bills are within the interpretation given to the phrase "bills for raising revenue" found in Section 7. The constitutional meaning of this delegation of authority has never been seriously questioned since Alexander Hamilton, the first Secretary of the Treasury, explained its intent as follows:

> The design of the Constitution in this provision was, as I conceive, to secure these important ends,—that the *purpose*, the *limit*, and the *fund* of every expenditure should be ascertained by a previous law. The public security is complete in this particular, if no money can be expended, but for an *object*, to an *extent*, and *out of a fund*, which the laws have prescribed.

It is upon this understanding of expenditure control that Congress exercises its fiscal responsibility to the Nation through the congressional budget process. As traditionally defined, the congressional budget process is a mechanism for allocating the federal government's financial resources among alternative programs and purposes. Since such an allocation of financial resources necessitates choosing among alternative uses of public monies, the congressional budget process is essentially an economic decision-making process, political in nature. It requires Congress to evaluate the uses for the taxpayer's dollars, as proposed in the President's budget, and to make decisions, via the voting of expenditures, as to whether, for example, a dollar is best spent for defense or for education. Thus, expenditure decisions determine what tack government spending shall take and are thereby explicitly or implicitly responsive to and determinative of national goals and purposes.[2]

In making such decisions, Representatives and Senators, as representatives of their particular districts and states and as national legislators, speak for a variety of interests and must reconcile these interests in determining how best to allocate federal funds. As political scientist Aaron Wildavsky points out, the crucial aspect of congressional budgeting is

> whose preferences are to prevail in disputes about which activities are to be carried on and to what degree, in light of limited resources.[3]

To aid in resolving this question, Congress has created an elaborate system of machinery and rules under which it operates and by which it translates its preferences into meaningful political decisions on the budget.

The expenditure of funds for the carrying on of the federal government's activities and programs is the heart and end result of the congressional budget process, a process which also encompasses and necessitates the raising of revenues to make funds available for expenditures. The major participants in the congressional budget process will be examined here, emphasizing the role of each actor in the main stages of the budget process, with an eye toward budgetary and fiscal reform.

Participants in the Budget Process

To understand fully the congressional budget process, one must examine it in the context of the overall problem of federal budgeting. Three phases are readily discernible in this larger process: (1) the preparation and submission of the executive budget by the President, (2) legislative action on the budget by Congress, and (3) execution and review of the enacted budget.

A. THE ROLE OF THE EXECUTIVE

The Budget and Accounting Act of 1921 established the present national budget system and gave the President plenary authority in the preparation of the budget. Title II of the 1921 Act provides that the President shall submit to Congress at the beginning of each session a federal budget summarizing and detailing estimates of the projected federal budget expenditures, appropriations and receipts for the coming fiscal year, expenditures and receipts from the previous fiscal year, and estimated expenditures and receipts for the current fiscal year.

To aid the President in the enormous and arduous task of preparing the budget, provision was made for a Bureau of the Budget (BOB) in Section 207 of the 1921 Act. The BOB was charged with the administrative duty of compiling the budget and was vested with the power to assemble, correlate, revise, reduce, or increase departmental and agency estimates. Originally placed within the Department of the Treasury, the BOB was transferred by Executive Order to the Office of the President in 1939. At the head of the Bureau is a Director appointed by and responsible to the President.

The BOB functions as a source of information as to what the President may expect from the executive departments and agencies in the way of budget estimates. Considering the propensity of executive agencies to ask for more than they can get, it also functions as a "blood-letting" device to trim agency estimates. Under Section 209 of the Act, the BOB is authorized to make detailed studies of the various agencies to determine what changes should be made in (1) existing organization, activities, and business methods, (2) appropriations, (3) assignment of particular services or activities, and (4) grouping of services within the agency in question.

Although the BOB is required to submit requested information to the revenue and appropriations committees of Congress, it is apparent that it functions solely as an arm of the executive branch. To balance the role of the President and the BOB in preparing the budget, Title III of the Budgeting and Accounting Act provided for the establishment of a General Accounting Office (GAO) to be headed by a Comptroller General of the United States. Responsible only to Congress, the Comptroller General is appointed by the President with the advice and consent of the Senate to a nonrenewable 15-year term. (The appointment of the Director of the BOB does not require congressional assent.)

The GAO was intended to be the fiscal representative of Congress, and was empowered independently to audit the financial transactions of the federal government and to transmit reports of such audits to Congress. To this end, Congress gave to the GAO wide investigatory power under Section 312 of the 1921 Act to inquire into all matters concerning the receipt, disbursement, and use of public funds and to make recommendations to Congress concerning necessary legislation. Section 312 also empowered the GAO to carry out such investigations as the House and Senate committees on finance may recommend and to require all agency heads to furnish such information as the GAO might request concerning the powers, activities, financial transactions, and business methods of government offices. Under Section 309 the GAO may prescribe accounting procedures for government departments.[4]

Nevertheless, despite these broad powers, the GAO has not entirely lived up to expectations. Passed during a Republican administration after having been vetoed by President Wilson in 1920, the Budget and Accounting Act of 1921 was intended by its drafters to put federal budgeting on a business basis.[5] The General Accounting Office, it was hoped, would serve to counter-balance the BOB: GAO was supposed to play not only an active post-audit role in reviewing budget expenditures, but also to serve a valuable pre-audit function by aiding Congress in initiating budget policy. As M.I.T. political scientist John S. Saloma III notes in an excellent study of the congressional budget process:

> The GAO was created . . . as part of the budgetary reforms of 1921, both to assist Congress in the post-examination or review of budgetary expenditures and to serve as a counterweight to the Bureau of the Budget in the executive branch. The broad investigating and reporting authority vested in the GAO by section 312 of the Budget and Accounting Act encompassed both pre- and post-examination of the budget. However, Congress has never developed a pre-audit budgetary role for the GAO.[6]

The reasons behind Congress' failure to develop a pre-audit role for GAO, and the consequent relegation of the GAO to a post-audit capacity, will be examined later. Suffice it to say for the moment that this failure has had the debilitating effect of sapping congressional initiative in budgetary matters, thus reducing Congress' power of budget control in contrast to that of the President.

This imbalance of power is also manifested in other ways. It is apparent from the structure of the executive branch that Congress is at an inherent organizational disadvantage in dealing with budgetary matters. Simply having plenary authority in the formulation of the budget makes the President's job incomparably easier. The President's budget decisions, while made with the advice of the Director of the Budget and after consulting with various department heads, are solely his own and require no majority consensus among his advisors. On the other hand, the 535 elected Members of Congress represent divergent economic, geographical, and social interests (and are split between a 100-Member Senate and a 435-Member House into two separate and virtually autonomous legislative bodies). The individual Congressman, in examining the budget and acting on fiscal legislation, must be responsible not only for the overall welfare of the Nation but also for the needs of his district. Thus, the fact that the final decision of "who gets what"—the allocation of federal funds as determined by Congress through a majority decision—leads necessarily to compromises, accommodations, and some degree of irrationality in dealing with the budget.

Nonetheless, in truth, the executive may be far less capable of weighing equitably and accurately the diverse interests than is the Congress. However, under the guise of increased efficiency in deciding how the budget dollar should be spent, Congress tends to approve the President's budget requests in a perfunctory manner. This is particularly true when the same political party controls both Congress and the White House.

In examining its present role, Congress must recognize that the real threat to congressional fiscal power lies not so much in executive usurpation as in Congress' failure to exploit its own potential.

B. THE BUDGET AND CONGRESS

The congressional budget process is best discussed functionally in terms of the committee framework through which Congress exercises its fiscal control. Ideally, this process may be broken down into five identifiable stages: (1) authorization, (2) appropriation, (3) revenue, (4) economic analysis and policy coordination, and (5) budget review.[7] Each stage is dominated by certain of Congress' legislative, appropriations, or finance committees and operates within a system of rules, explicit and implicit.

Authorization. A basic characteristic of the congressional budget process, and essential to any understanding of expenditure control, is the distinction between authorizations and appropriations. This distinction is set out in the Rules of the House of Representatives. Rule XI, Clause 2, stipulates that:

> No appropriation shall be reported in any general appropriation bill, or be in order as an amendment thereto, for any expenditure not previously authorized by law. . . .

A similar rule obtains in the Senate. In effect, these rules state that no appropriations shall be made without prior authorization by law, thereby providing "double insurance" in the control of expenditures. Not only are expenditures forbidden by Congress unless "in consequence of appropriations made by law," but such appropriations must be preceded by legislation "authorizing" the expenditures in question.

Authorization is thus the "birth stage" of government spending.[8] The legislative or authorizations committees of Congress—e.g., Armed Services, Banking and Currency, Public Works Committees—create the activities and programs which must later be funded through appropriations; they make the basic policy decisions concerning the types of activities and programs government should undertake. This is usually accomplished by the enactment of substantive legislation creating the activity or program in question and authorizing the appropriation of funds for such an activity or function.

In addition, these legislative committees of Congress also determine whether existing programs or activities shall be continued, expanded, or canceled. This is done by passing authorizations limited in time, thus requiring that the activity or program be reviewed by its jurisdictional committee before it can be continued. Frequently, authorizations are made annually, thus requiring a department or agency to come before the legislative committees of Congress every year if they are to have their activities or programs continued. This may be time-consuming for the departments or agencies involved, and can be particularly burdensome to the committees, whose time must also be devoted to studying basic policy questions raised in the creating of new programs.

Another point that should be noted is that the legislative committees often have little regard for the overall cost of government activities and programs since such projects are rarely fully financed at their inception and, indeed, their total cost may be unknown. This is particularly true of costly "pork barrel" public works projects, the expense of which may not be considered by weighing one program against another in terms of dollar alternatives and policy considerations. In addition, concern is rarely exhibited by the legislative committees for the taxes needed to pay for the programs authorized, this matter being left for the appropriations and revenue committees to settle among themselves.

In discussing the distinction between authorizations and appropriations, it must be kept in mind that while appropriations cannot be made without prior authorizations, the reverse is not always true. As some types of substantive legislation may also include funding authority, this "automatically" requires the appropriations committees of Congress to liquidate such prior commitments through a later appropriation of funds. Liquidation takes place, as a simple formality, when the agency incurring the obligation requests an "appropriation to liquidate contract authorization." This type of procedure is sometimes referred to as "backdoor spending" and is particularly evident in the financing of military procurement programs and federal housing programs. These and similar types of authorizations thus have the effect of making many expenditures immune from effective control by the appropriations committees of Congress. The granting of funding authority in substantive legislation forces the appropriations committees to fund programs which they might otherwise be reluctant to approve but which they are afforded no opportunity to effectively review.

Appropriations. In the *authorization* of activities and programs the Congress sets the ceiling for the amount of funds that may be appropriated; *appropriations* finance the functions of government. While the appropriations committees may not exceed the funding limit set by the legislative committees, they are under no obligation to appropriate all or any part of the funds for authorized activities and programs.

Through their enactments, the appropriations committees of Congress give the departments and agencies of government the authority to incur obligations and to make expenditures. Generally, three basic types of appropriations are employed by the appropriations committees in financing the functions of government. These are:

1. Regular or "lump sum" appropriations, definite in amount but varying as to date of expiration—e.g., one-year appropriations normally used for current expenditures, with authority expiring at the end of one fiscal year; multiple-ye arappropriations, normally used for nonrecurring expenditures, with authority expiring at the end of a specified time period; and no-year appropriations, mostly used for defense or continuing public works projects and available for an indefinite period of time.

2. Current indefinite appropriations, indefinite in amount but having a specified purpose, often used for covering deficits such as those incurred by the Post Office Department. Such appropriations being indefinite in amount

are relatively immune from effective control by the appropriations committees.

3. Permanent, or "open ended," appropriations, automatically making funds available each year without action by the appropriations committees of Congress. For example, continuing expenditures in payment of the national debt are funded by this means. Like the current indefinite appropriation, this type of appropriation is also immune from control by the appropriations committees of Congress.

The Appropriations Process

The appropriations process formally begins with the reception of the President's budget message by Congress and the transmittal of the proposed federal budget to the House of Representatives. Once received by the House, the budget is referred to the House Committee on Appropriations and divided among its 12 subcommittees on a departmental or agency basis—Agriculture, District of Columbia, Foreign Aid, Treasury and Post Office, etc. These subcommittees then hold "executive" sessions (closed hearings)[9] on the various budget items within the purview of their responsibility, taking testimony from department heads, the BOB and other interested parties, and finally drafting suitable appropriations measures.

After the appropriations bills are drafted by the subcommittees, the full committee meets and occasionally revises the various appropriations bills before reporting them to the House. Regular appropriations bills usually number about 20. In addition, there may be various non-regular appropriations bills—indefinite appropriations, appropriations to liquidate contract authorizations, etc. These regular and non-regular bills are often a maze of detail, containing numerous restrictions and limitations. For example, the enacted appropriations bills for 1960 covered 248 pages and totaled approximately 100,000 words.[10] Single appropriations bills have contained as many as 2,000 titles, although 350–400 is now average.[11]

Appropriations measures are considered in debate by the "Committee of the Whole House on the State of the Union" and then are reported to the full House in Congress assembled for final action. (This is somewhat *pro forma*, since the House will usually pass appropriations bills reported by the Committee of the Whole.) Once agreed to, the bills then go to the Senate.[12]

In the event of Senate amendments to the House version, the amended bill is referred to a conference committee made up of 10 to 20 members from both the House and Senate Appropriations Committees who meet and resolve the differences between the House and Senate measures. The compromise measure is then submitted to each house for final passage before being sent to the President for signing. With the President's signature on the enacted bill, the appropriations process is complete.

The House Appropriations Committee is the most prominent of the two appropriations committees of Congress. This prominence may be attributed to the general pre-eminence accorded the House in fiscal affairs by virtue of its constitutional authority to initiate revenue bills (Article I, Section 7) and, as a logical adjunct of this power, by virtue of its exclusive right to initiate appropriations measures. It is also a result of the Senate's structural inability to deal with the budget in the same detail as the House. The Senate, having 335 fewer members than the House, has a proportionately greater work load, and is thus no doubt less well equipped to deal effectively with the budget than the House. When one considers that the federal budget and its various appendices and summaries is well over 1500 pages, and that the record of the hearings in the House alone may run 25,000 pages or more, the enormity of the appropriations work load is obvious.

The House Appropriations Committee is composed of 50 Members and has a staff of about equal number. By contrast, the Senate Appropriations Committee is composed of only 26 of that body's Members, all of whom also serve on other Senate committees, and has a staff of 30. Unable to match the House in manpower and beset with a greater per capita work load and larger responsibilities, the Senate Appropriations Committee has been content to function more or less as a "court of appeals and last resort" for departments or agencies who have had their budget requests cut by the House Appropriations Committee.[13]

In general, decisions of the House Appropriations Committee are accorded a high degree of respect by the Congress, as witnessed by the fact that its recommendations (i.e., committee reports) are accepted by the House 90 per cent of the time.[14] This high percentage of House approval for the work of the Committee may be accounted for in terms of the concept of specialization of function and the norm of reciprocity, both of which reflect a second basic characteristic of the congressional budget process—decentralization of decision-making.[15]

To insure "double control" of expenditures, the House and Senate have established a functional division between the authorization and appropriations processes. To pass effectively upon the authorization and appropriations legislation coming before the Congress, the House and Senate have also resolved themselves into committees and subcommittees, thus decentralizing the process of decision-making. Each committee or subcommittee takes on a "specialized" informational function, becoming, as it were, "experts" in various fields of legislation. This is particularly true of the House Appropriations Committee with its 12 highly specialized subcommittees, each of which works with complex legislation, further complicated by the need for difficult fiscal analysis.

As a result, certain norms of parliamentary behavior have arisen with regard to the decisions of the Committee and its subcommittees (and are seen, perhaps to a lesser extent, in the work of other committees). The most obvious pattern is one which is often referred to as "reciprocity"—seen in the manner in which the rank and file Members of Congress will respect committee and subcommittee decisions with the expectation that they will receive similar respect for the decisions of the committee or subcommittee on which they serve. This attitude, interacting with the concept of specialization of function, seems to say, in effect, that a committee or subcommittee best knows its own work and, except for politically partisan issues, committee decisions should be left undisturbed. Reciprocity tends to limit meaningful debate on major issues of fiscal policy raised in the allocation of federal funds. It does, however, lead to stability and parliamentary harmony in the consideration of bills. Professor Richard Fenno describes this behavioral process in the following terms:

> Conflict . . . is minimized by the deference traditionally accorded to the recommendation of the subcommittee which has specialized in the area, has worked hard, and has "the facts." "It's a matter of 'You respect my work and I'll respect yours!'" It's frowned upon if you offer an amendment in the full committee if you aren't on the subcommittee. It's considered presumptuous to pose as an expert if you aren't on the subcommittee.[16]

The major decisions regarding the budget involve comparisons among different departments or agencies as to how funds can best be apportioned. Such decisions involving "cross-agency" or "cross-program" comparisons are impossible under the present system of appropriations, yet these are the crucial decisions that have to be made if savings are to be effected and, perhaps more importantly, if Congress is to play an active role in the making of national and fiscal policy.

Decisions as to whether to cut the defense budget or the education budget, for example, are essentially policy decisions. They involve the setting of priorities among alternative programs and alternative uses of the taxpayer's dollar. Congress must determine, for example, whether a dollar is best spent for education or defense, mindful that a dollar expended for a $2.8 billion education program goes a longer way toward meeting program needs than does a dollar expended for a $60.5 billion defense program (1967 budget figure). Such a decision calls for an evaluation of national goals and purposes. Is defense or education the nation's greater need?

Often unable to make such crucial policy decisions, the appropriations committees sometimes concern themselves with less important matters which are more easily decided.

A second argument flows in reverse: that in making budget decisions, the appropriations committees of Congress may deliberately or inadvertently make policy decisions which are the legitimate prerogatives of the legislative committees which authorized the funds. In some instances there is a disregard for the issue involved or the economic consequences of their decisions.

This is seen in the manner in which budget reductions are made. While it is part of the job of the appropriations committees of Congress to make budget reductions, the committees, in an effort to effect economy in departmental and agency operations, often resort to "meat ax" cuts, broadly slashing agency requests, rather than examining and reducing budget requests on a program-by-program or item-by-item basis. Large budget cuts also frequently reflect the frustrations of the appropriations committees in examining the budget.

Well equipped organizationally to deal in detail with the agency requests, the subcommittees often lack sufficient time or staff to undertake a more detailed examination of budget requests. (This is sometimes referred to as the "scalpel" technique.) To compensate for this inability, they adopt the cruder but more efficient "meat ax" approach. In the process, they may inadvertently make important budget decisions, unaware of their impact on over-all fiscal policy. Trimming a million dollars off the top of the education budget may be more justified than lopping off $500 million from the defense budget, but the committees at present cannot make such comparisons.

Another criticism of expenditure control via budget reductions is that the actual total reduction in the budget is rather insignificant, rarely more than 5 per cent. Many so-called "reductions" are nothing more than "paper cuts" which have no effect on actual expenditures. Thus, while a subcommittee may under-fund certain programs which an agency is obligated to carry out, the agency may often be advised to seek supplemental appropriations at the beginning of the next session. Also, reductions made by the House are often restored by the Senate. Hence, such *pro forma* budget-cutting techniques result in many departments and agencies artificially inflating their budget requests, which has a circuitous or spiraling effect on the appropriations process: the more the departmental and agency requests are cut, the greater the spread between initial requests and actual needs.

Effective expenditure control is predicated on adequate budget information. Unfortunately, information is not always equally available to all committee members. This is partially the result of the seniority system. Veteran committee Members, by virtue of tenure alone, can make greater demands on committee staff time and usually have better access to vital or "inside" budget information. Moreover, since information is power in budgetary matters, senior Members, themselves surrounded with the top professional staff of the committee, may be reluctant to hire additional staff to afford a greater dispersal of information. This is more or less a matter of perspective. As Saloma puts it:

> The individuals in the position to do most about staffing the committee have a virtual monopoly of the staff—and are much less apt to see a need for increased staff. Junior members—who may include a sizeable number of "activists" or "legislative technicians"—feel the need for staff assistance more acutely but lack the power to obtain it.[17]

It should be apparent that the workings of the seniority system and the norm of reciprocity sometimes result in major budget changes being made by a relatively few Members of the committees with the greatest seniority and the best budget information. Such changes may not always be indicative of the majority sentiment on the committee. In addition, budget decisions are also political decisions and are thus amenable to considerations other than efficiency and economy in the allocation of federal funds. Of course, the interaction of the concepts of specialization and reciprocity also tends to result in subcommittee decisions which are rarely subjected to extensive debate during the consideration of appropriations bills.

Finally, effective expenditure control is hindered by the fact that a large portion of the budget, including most nondefense programs, consists of certain fixed or uncontrollable obligations—contract authorizations and similar "back door" spending measures, permanent appropriations, etc.— which have been funded on a continuing or permanent basis. Professor Murray Weidenbaum, in an authoritative study for the American Enterprise Institute, found that only 58 per cent of the 1964 budget requests were subject to effective control via the appropriations process.[18] The remaining 42 per cent—including 77 per cent of all nondefense spending—is beyond the control of the appropriations committees of Congress.[19] This is largely the result of funding authority being contained in substantive, rather than appropriations, measures. In his definitive work on federal budgeting, Professor Weidenbaum notes that such legislation is often the work of committees more concerned with enacting programs than with paying for them:

> The bulk of the expenditures for the civilian, welfare agencies is authorized virtually automatically as a result of the basic, continuing commitments contained in statutes generally written by and reported out by committees of the Congress concerned with the individual program or group being benefited rather than with the state of federal finances.[20]

Many of these uncontrollable expenditures may have no relationship to the real needs of federal spending. In some cases, they are simply illogical. As an example, Weidenbaum cites the fact that, by law

> . . . visitor fees at Yellowstone National Park are used automatically to finance educational expenses of dependents of park personnel, while visitor fees at Grand Teton National Park are used for payments to the State of Wyoming, in effect, in lieu of taxes. The rationale for the special treatment is, to put it mildly, somewhat obscure.[21]

These and other uncontrollable expenditures are referred to by Weidenbaum as the "built-in" rigidities of the budget system.[22] As such they restrict effective congressional use of the budget dollar—a dollar which might be effectively allocated were it amenable to control by the appropriations committees of Congress.

Oversight of Administration

A secondary function of the appropriations committees, related to allocation of funds, is legislative oversight of administration as a check on executive authority. It has already been shown how the legislative committees exercise oversight of the executive departments and agencies by reviewing program plans and passing upon the merits of initiating new programs and continuing old programs. This same type of oversight is exercised by the appropriations subcommittees with regard to departmental and agency budget requests. However, oversight is not necessarily confined to the once-a-year examination of budget requests; appropriations subcommittees expect to be kept informed of departmental and agency operations throughout the entire year and in some cases to be consulted prior to the making of departmental decisions.[23]

Oversight is manifested in several ways: the subcommittee may ask that an agency conduct inquiries and make periodic reports regarding certain matters; the subcommittee may criticize or issue instructions to an agency or department through committee reports or orally.[24] Of course, oversight is also performed in the examination of departmental and agency budget requests. Thus subcommittees may often cut appropriations in an effort to improve departmental or agency performance. As an alternative, subcommittees often seek to limit the authority of departments and agencies by the use of restrictive provisions in appropriations bills. This latter practice accounts for much of the detail and complexity found in appropriations bills.

Through these various means of oversight the appropriations subcommittees are able to control many of the administrative aspects of departmental and agency programs, although more often than not they dwell on administrative trivia which could better be left to the legislative committees responsible for the enactment and periodic review of the program in question.

In summary, the appropriations process suffers from a number of structural and functional defects which prevent it from performing as a mechanism for economically and efficiently allocating funds among the programs previously authorized by Congress:

1. The characteristic of decentralization, as reflected in the specialization of function and the norm of reciprocity, fragmentizes the appropriations process, resulting in several virtually autonomous subcommittees whose work is rarely questioned extensively in full committee or on the House floor.

2. The appropriations subcommittees are unable to examine departmental or agency budget requests in terms of the alternative use of the budget dollar.

3. In examining budget requests and making budget reductions, subcommittees may inadvertently make policy decisions although they may be unaware of the economic consequences.

4. The impact of budget reductions is difficult to calculate; most large reductions are restored in the Senate or by later supplemental or deficiency appropriations; reductions made for the current fiscal year may not affect current expenditures, due to carry-over expenditures.

5. Many programs that need examining are immune from effective review and control by the appropriations committees because of funding authority being contained in substantive legislation.

6. In the performance of the secondary function of legislative oversight, the appropriations subcommittees often concern themselves with administrative minutiae rather than program achievement.

Other Stages in the Budget Process

Revenue. Although the primary emphasis in this study is on the expenditure side of the budget equation, since spending is the area of primary importance to fiscal control, the revenue side of the equation is of equal importance if the system is to function effectively. Article I, Section 7, of the Constitution provides: "All bills for raising revenue shall originate in the House of Representatives." The committee responsible for initiating such revenue legislation is the House Committee on Ways and Means. Like the House Appropriations Committee *vis-à-vis* the Senate Appropriations Committee, the House Ways and Means Committee is pre-eminent over its counterpart in the Senate— the Senate Finance Committee.

Ideally, the House Ways and Means Committee and Senate Finance Committee are supposed to assure that Congress provides tax revenue equal to the amount that the executive department spends in any fiscal year. However, as with the appropriations committees, the work of these two revenue committees falls short of its ideal. Estimating the amount of revenue that the government will need to carry on its programs is not an easy task. Many long-term programs (particularly public work projects), are not fully financed at the authorization stage, and their total cost may be unknown. Further, since the raising of revenues is sensitive to public income, which may depend on such relatively uncontrollable events as wars, droughts, business recessions, etc., revenues are often less than expenditures, resulting in an unbalanced budget. Also, because many expenditures flow through uncontrollable trust fund accounts for Social Security, highway construction, etc., rather than through regular budgetary accounts, the possibility of equalizing revenues and expenditures is further diminished.

On the expenditure side of the budget equation, it has been shown how the authorizations and appropriations committees of the House and Senate function almost entirely independently of one another. It is not surprising, therefore, that expenditures are rarely considered in the light of revenues. However, some semblance of coordination and concern for over-all policy does exist among the revenue committees of Congress as a result of the work of the Joint Committee on Internal Revenue Taxation.

This Committee, made up of five Members each from the House Ways and Means and Senate Finance Committees, was established in 1926 by a concurrent resolution of both Houses of Congress and was empowered to investigate the operation and effect of federal internal revenue taxation. The Committee serves to pull together the major revenue issues raised in the President's budget, giving an over-all view of such issues to the revenue committees of Congress. This results in a closer working relation between the House and Senate with regard to revenue matters. The chief advantage of the Committee is that it provides joint staffing for the revenue committees, which effects a more integrated consideration of revenues. As shall be seen, other attempts at an integrated or consolidated consideration of appropriations, via the legislative budget and the omnibus appropriations bill, have failed.

Economic Analysis and Policy Coordination. In the economic analysis and policy coordination stage of the budget, an effort is made to effect a joint consideration of the President's Economic Report through the work of the Joint Economic Committee, established in 1946. While this Committee (composed of eight Members each from the House and Senate) does not have a formal relationship to the legislative, appropriations, or revenue committees of Congress, it does serve to inform Congress of the policy issues raised by the President's Economic Report and the impact of the budget upon the nation's economy.

Expenditure Review. The final stage of the congressional budget process is the expenditure review. Actually, this stage of the congressional budget process may be considered as part of the execution phase, since expenditure review takes place after Congress has completed its appropriations and is concerned principally with the manner in which the Executive carries out the programs which the Congress has authorized and funded.[25]

Most of the work at the expenditure review stage is intended to be performed by the House and Senate Government Operations Committees. These Committees are empowered to review agency expenditures and investigate agency performance as well as recommend action by the legislative and appropriations committees of Congress. Originally established in 1922 as the Committees on Expenditures in the Executive Department, the Government Operations Committees are regarded as the "watchdog" committees of Congress since they serve as a means of providing continual oversight of executive departments and agencies.

Working closely with the Government Operations Committees in their "watchdog" capacity is the GAO. Its frequent reports—several hundred a year—are relied on extensively by the Government Operations Committees in conducting their investigations and making recommendations.[26] The Government Operations Committees have conducted a number of investigations based on GAO reports of irregularities or abuses by government agencies. However, by and large, such reports go virtually unnoticed by Congress and rarely result in legislative action. Nevertheless, these reports do result occasionally in administrative changes within the executive branch.

Another committee in the expenditure review stage of the budget process, although it plays a somewhat less important role, is the Joint Committee on Reduction of Non-Essential Expenditures, established in 1941. Its function is to consider all government expenditures and to recommend elimination of those expenditures it considers to be nonessential. While it may investigate over-all departmental and agency operations, as well as consider the President's budget, the Committee rarely devotes its attention to policy-oriented considerations. Composed of six Members from each House, the Committee is unique in that the Secretary of the Treasury and the Director of the BOB sit as members. It is unique also in that it rarely meets.

A Thirteen-Point Program for Budgetary and Fiscal Reform

Despite the attempted reforms of 1946,* congressional budget procedures remain much the same as they were forty years ago.[27] During this period, we have witnessed startling changes in the executive branch and even the judiciary; however, the Congress still struggles to give an appearance of assuming its constitutional responsibilities with respect to fiscal and budgetary matters when in actuality it has surrendered much of this role to the executive branch.

Reform is clearly needed; all commentators seem to agree on that. The real question is, what kind? This paper has discussed congressional budgeting in terms of certain limitations and has recognized characteristics distinctive of the congressional budget process. These include: (a) the division between the authorization and appropriations functions of Congress; (b) decentralization as exemplified by the congressional committee system and based on the recognized norms of reciprocity and specialization of function; and (c) the institutional roles played in the budget process by the major actors in the federal system—the Executive and the BOB, and Congress and the GAO. Particular emphasis has been given the role of the House Appropriations Committee. Other structural features besides the above-mentioned characteristics have been recognized as limitations on reform. These include the inviolable four-way division of power and authority among the major fiscal committees of Congress (House and Senate Appropriations, and House Ways and Means and Senate Finance), and the constitutional pre-eminence of the House in initiating revenue and appropriations measures, with primary importance being accorded the latter function.

It is also apparent that if reforms are to be acceptable to Congress, they should not reach too far beyond the precedent of past reforms but should build upon them. For example, it has been shown that reforms along the line of the legislative budget concept and joint committee proposals have received relatively wide endorsement from Congress (but not necessarily the appropriations committees), while the omnibus appropriations bill was condemned by a majority of the rank and file members after their initial experience with it in 1950.

As previously defined, the congressional process, in the ideal, is nothing more than a mechanism for allocating federal funds—through the political process of law-making—among alternative programs and purposes. The goals

* Past reforms are discussed in an appendix to this chapter.

of the congressional budget process are much like those of any business budget to the extent that Congress is concerned that the allocation of funds must be accomplished with *sufficient control to insure that programs and projects will be economically and efficiently carried out*. This implies, as a second goal, the need *for sound budget procedures or expenditure control based on adequate information*. However, unlike a business, Congress can control both expenditures and revenues and must also *debate and decide major fiscal policy issues* concerning such expenditures and revenues, as well as other matters of national concern. Finally, it is vested with the job of *overseeing or checking the authority of the executive branch* of government in the execution of the enacted budget. With these goals in mind, and cognizant of the limitations upon them inherent in the functioning of the congressional budget process, a plan of fiscal and budgetary reform may now be discussed.

The criticism most often leveled at the congressional budget process is that Congress lacks the organizational machinery and coordination for dealing with budgetary matters. It is charged that Congress at no time considers the budget as a whole—expenditures are not weighed against revenues. Furthermore, in making appropriations, Congress does not examine the national importance of one program in relation to another. It is charged that fiscal priorities are based more upon political expediency than upon the public need. Certainly, Congress cannot allocate federal funds efficiently and economically when it lacks the fiscal machinery to answer the basic question of whether or not an extra dollar would be more wisely spent on program A or on program B—on defense or on education, to use on oft-cited example.[28]

Thus, the major difficulty confronting Congress in its basic task of allocating funds is how to enhance the ability of Congress to evaluate alternative uses of funds. One means of solving this problem, as recognized in a recent report of the Council on Economic Development (CED), is to provide for wider partisan debate on fiscal policy and to examine the proposed budget as a whole.[29]

As has been shown, the decentralized consideration of the budget by the fiscal committees and subcommittees of Congress is inimical to any over-all view of the budget in terms of policy. Commenting on the lack of an integrated budget review, Dr. George B. Galloway rightly summed up the problem when he stated:

> In short, the fiscal machinery of Congress is fragmented and dispersive. The tax committees tend to be tax minded; and the spending committees are tempted to be expenditure minded. The Joint Committee on the Budget provided for by section 138 of the Legislative Reorganization Act of 1946 might have been budget minded, but for various reasons it has failed to function as planned and is no longer active.

> Under these circumstances, it is evident that the existing fiscal machinery of Congress is not now such as to give that body an overall coordinated view of Federal fiscal policy.[30]

1. Joint Committee on the Budget

To aid Congress in making its budget decisions, it is suggested that a modified Joint Committee on the Budget be established. Based upon the earlier Joint Committee proposals passed by the Senate to carry out the intent of Section 138 of the 1946 Act, this Committee would have similar objectives and purposes. It would be empowered to review carefully and fully executive budget requests, recommend some system of priorities with regard to demands on federal revenue, consider an over-all maximum of federal spending, and otherwise build a mechanism for the development of a legislative budget in contrast to an executive budget with which Congress has struggled in the past. Such a joint committee plan is embodied in H.R. 37 sponsored by the author (and similar bills) introduced in the 89th Congress.

Several departures from earlier proposals should be noted. For instance, H.R. 37 provides for a Joint Committee composed of 36 Members (rather than 102), with the House being represented by 21 Members and the Senate by 15 Members including representation from the House Committees on Appropriations, Ways and Means, and Government Operations. The Senate Members are selected from the Senate Appropriations, Finance, and Government Operations Committees. Unlike many previous joint budget committee proposals, this would have the advantage of a membership from the Government Operations Committees of Congress. In addition, it would enlist the service of the GAO in a pre-audit capacity by requiring that it provide analytical reports on proposed agency budgets. *Therefore, it is recommended that Congress establish a modified Joint Legislative Committee on the Budget.*

2. Budget Information Service

In support of the functions of this Committee, Congress needs some type of Budget Information Service to give the Joint Committee and other members of the House and Senate current budget information. This Service would also encourage wider and more informed policy debates on budget matters. As Congress moves through the various stages of budget consideration, it gets only a glimpse of the budget, frozen at each particular stage into voluminous hearings, committee reports, GAO reports, and articles in the *Congressional Record*. What Congress needs is a continual and summarizing view of budget activities in Congress, perhaps available on a day-to-day basis, and taking into account congressional action on the budget up to the moment that the report is issued. This needed information would be purely factual and thus would not require extensive staff services. However, attention should be given to the introduction of analytical computer technology in dealing with budget information in order to make it more current, more comprehensive, and more accurate. A recent study of Congress made by Arthur D. Little, management consultants, revealed that:

. . . the use of high-speed computers to facilitate the work of Congress and its committees is almost nonexistent. The very nature of some analytical problems of Congress calls for flexible manipulation of massive data into many different arrangements to serve many different purposes. Only with large-scale computers can this be done thoroughly and economically.[31]

These findings are expecially applicable to Congress' consideration of the budget. The appropriations committees of Congress, in particular, are called upon to make difficult economic comparisons with regard to alternative uses of funds. Part of the problem is not having proper machinery with which to do this job. The other part of the problem is not having sufficient information to make the comparisons expected of them. One is the function of the other.

Such analytical information could be used to good advantage in conjunction with other budget documents such as hearings, committee reports, GAO findings, etc., which are more factually oriented in terms of expenditure analysis than over-all policy and program considerations. *Therefore, it is recommended that Congress provide a computerized Budget Information Service to give the Joint Committee on the Budget and the other members of the House and Senate current and accurate budget information, and that the facilities and staff of such a Budget Information Service be located within the Library of Congress.*

3. Improving the Presentation of the Budget—Use of a Planning–Programming–Budgeting System

If fuller policy debates and broader budget examination are to be accomplished, attention must also be given to reforming the budget document itself. The budget should be presented on a program basis, similar to the planning–programming–budgeting system under which the executive branch now requires its departments and agencies to submit their budgets. This sort of budget presentation, in the words of the CED:

. . . focuses on alternative means for attaining objectives, and permits continuous comparison of results achieved with costs incurred. It provides a rational approach in relating means to ends and is a tool for sharpening managerial judgment in planning and decision-making. [2]

This type of approach is necessary if Congress is to consider alternative uses of funds in terms of policy ramifications. It would allow the Congress, and particularly the fiscal committees of Congress, to familiarize themselves with the policy bases on which the budget was submitted and the real reasons why agency reductions were made by the BOB or the President prior to submitting the budget to Congress. As it stands now, Congress sees the agency requests in the total budget after the real "bloodletting" has taken place.

The reasons and economic assumptions underlying such agency reductions by the BOB are, in many cases, unknown or unascertainable.

Such a program presentation of the budget should be made in conjunction with program classification schedules indexed so that appropriations requests could still be made on an agency basis, according to function.

While many items in the budget are accompanied by schedules showing the objects of expenditures in a standard classification—personnel, office equipment, construction materials, etc.—the budget document contains no summary of such schedules showing the demands made by each function or each department for personnel, contractual services, etc. These summaries are available in separate form several months after the budget has been presented, but there is no indication of the extent to which one object of expenditure may be substituted for another; that is, equipment for personnel, services of other agencies in place of additional personnel, etc. The presentation of the budget on a program basis, cross-indexed according to function, will eliminate such defects from the budget document. *Therefore, it is recommended that the federal budget be presented on a programming–planning–budgeting basis (cross-indexed according to function) similar to that presently employed by the executive branch of the government.*

4. Rescheduling of the Budget

Wider debate in matters of fiscal policy and greater control and comprehension of the budget as a whole may be accomplished by a rescheduling of the budget process. As a result of a multitude of annual authorizations which confront Congress at the beginning of each session, appropriations often extend well beyond the beginning of the fiscal year (July 1). This lag between the beginning of the fiscal year and passage of appropriations often delays the start of departmental programs and is almost totally unnecessary.

One means of alleviating this problem is to reduce the number of annual appropriations. Another is to revise the fiscal year so that it coincides with the calendar year. At the minimum, Congress will have to accept the year-round session, with periodic recesses for campaigning or vacations, if it is to have sufficient time to review and act upon the President's budget. *Therefore, it is recommended that Congress adopt the year-round session (with scheduled recesses) and revise the fiscal year to coincide with the calendar year.*

5. Limiting the Use of Annual Authorizations to Short-term Programs

Authorization represents the birth stage of substantive legislation. It is the point at which Congress, through its legislative committees, can most actively exercise control over how the budget dollar will be allocated. It is at this stage of the budget process that new programs are proposed and old programs examined, and funding authorization approved or disapproved. Unfortunately, Congress does not sufficiently concern itself with the broad policy issues found at this stage, all too often showing overt and undue concern with the time-consuming details involved in reviewing annual authorizations. This sometimes results in the delay of appropriations and the stagnation of government programs.

Many long-term programs have short-term authorizations, requiring agency heads to come before the legislative committees of Congress each year to ask for funds for the continuation of various projects already in progress. Such constant review of government programs through annual authorizations exhausts committee time that could otherwise be spent considering new authorizations or reviewing permanent authorizations, which are more significant in terms of broad-range policy. Any control over agency activities can best be left to the appropriations committees, which should examine expenditures annually, and the Government Operations Committees, which maintain continual surveillance of agency performance. *Therefore, it is recommended that the use of annual authorizations be limited to short-term programs and that permanent or long-term authorizations be used wherever possible.*

6. "Price-tagging" Authorizations

Another problem area with regard to authorizations arises as a result of long-term programs being authorized without full knowledge of their total costs. This is particularly true in the case of continuing public works projects, which may be passed without adequate regard for alternative uses of funds. The adoption of two recommendations by the Congress will check the tendency of authorization committees to impose new committments when annually reviewing authorizations and will curb irresponsible "pork barrel" legislation practices, which often have an inflationary effect on the economy. *Therefore, it is recommended that every new authorization carry a "price tag" giving the total cost of the program or maximum annual cost and that such programs be completed with the funds initially authorized.*

7. Reducing "Fixed" Budgetary Commitments

The appropriations process, that is, the funding of the programs which which the legislative committees have authorized, is the one point where Congress exerts its most direct control over the allocation of funds. However, as has been shown from Weidenbaum's study, 42 per cent of all government spending—almost all non-defense spending—is immune from congressional control through the appropriations process. This results from certain "built-in rigidities"—that is, (a) permanent appropriations, (b) continuing public works projects, and (c) "back door" spending schemes—contained in substantive legislation and beyond the control of the appropriations committees of Congress. Many commitments of this type may have no relation to federal spending needs. They hinder effective control of the budget dollar by tying up funds that could be allocated to more important uses were they subject to control by the appropriations committees. *Therefore, it is recommended that Congress re-examine its statutory or "fixed" budgetary commitments in the light of changing conditions and needs, with an eye toward eliminating permanent commitments wherever possible or making such commitments subject to review and control by the appropriations committees of Congress.*

8. *Joint Appropriations Committee Hearings*

In addition to establishing a Joint Committee on the Budget, other reforms are needed in order to develop a closer working relationship between the appropriations committees of the House and Senate. The decentralized manner in which the budget is handled prevents such a close relationship. It would seem desirable to adopt some joint rules which would be applicable to both bodies and which might result in more harmony between the House and Senate. The usefulness of joint committees of the House and Senate has long been recognized in various areas of common interest. The Joint Committees on Economics, Internal Revenue Taxation, Printing, Defense Production, and others have gained general acceptance. Consideration might also be given to possible joint hearings of the appropriations committees of the House and Senate early in the year.

The advantages of joint hearings are obvious. They effect a savings in time by avoiding duplication of testimony and also make for a more comprehensive review of the budget. Such hearings need not be extensive. Their purpose would be to set the tone and establish a direction for later and more complete hearings by the separate appropriations committees and their subcommittees. To this end, it is advisable that such hearings cover only major policy areas and that testimony be taken only from those who are in a position to reflect the policy of the executive department heads, agency administrators, etc. In a similar recommendation, the CED suggested that such hearings relate solely to the functional and program aspects of the budget, and that a "strong professional staff" be employed by the two full committees in holding such hearings.[33] *Therefore, it is recommended that the House and Senate Appropriations Committees hold joint hearings at the beginning of each session, to hear testimony from department heads and agency administra-*

tors, including the Director of the Budget, regarding over-all fiscal policy and budget programming, and that such professional and clerical staff as necessary be provided.

9. Revising Appropriations Procedure and Organization on a Functional Basis

Another reform, also suggested by the CED and others, is that appropriations be made on a functional and program basis, rather than on an "item of expense" basis, so as to coincide with the submission of the final budget and agency budgets on the planning–programming–budgeting basis. In addition, as a check against extensive fragmentation of the budget process, the House and Senate subcommittees should be reorganized on a functional (as opposed to an agency) basis.[34] This would provide for almost complete coordination of all levels of the executive and congressional budget processes on a program budget basis. *Therefore, it is recommended that appropriations be made according to program or function, instead of an object of expense, and that the procedure and organization of the appropriations subcommittees of Congress be revised accordingly.*

10. Increasing the Staffs of the Appropriations Committees

Additional "housekeeping" reforms are needed by the appropriations committees of Congress. One problem that cuts across all areas of congressional concern, but is particularly seen with regard to the appropriations committees of Congress, is the matter of staffing. The staff assistance available to the appropriations committees in examining a $112 billion budget is no match for the staff assistance rendered the President by the BOB and executive departments of the budget. It would be ludicrous to believe that the appropriations committee staffs must match the executive department's staff man for man in order to do an effective job in considering the budget. The appropriations committees need not concern themselves with the mass of detail found in the President's budget but should instead concentrate on the broader policy questions implicit in the President's choice of programs. To accomplish this, however, they need greater professional help and the use of analytical information provided by the GAO and a computerized Budget Information Service. *Therefore, it is recommended that the staffs of the appropriations committees of Congress be increased and that such committees and staffs be provided with, and make full use of, reports and analytical information supplied by the GAO and a Budget Information Service.*

11. Restricting the Use of Executive Sessions by House Appropriations Subcommittees

Further "housekeeping" reform should be made with regard to the use of executive sessions (closed hearings) by the House appropriations subcommittees. This type of proceeding does not allow the public or other Members of Congress access to testimony until after it is published several months following the committee hearings. This is too late for use by other Members of Congress, including those on the Senate Appropriations Committee who may have already elicited testimony from witnesses which duplicates that which was previously given in closed session to the House appropriations subcommittees. In addition, decisions made behind closed doors may not always reflect the best interests of the public. An open door at committee hearings tends to insure that decisions are made with due regard for the public interest by holding the decision-makers up to public opinion and leaving the subject matter open to public debate. *Therefore, it is recommended that the use of executive sessions by the House appropriations subcommittees be limited to hearings where national security is involved.*)

12. Improving the "Legislative Oversight" Function of the Government Operations Committee— Additional Minority Staff

An area of much needed budgetary reform is that of legislative oversight and expenditure review. Oversight may be accomplished in three ways: (1) through Congress' power of authorization; (2) through its power of appropriations; and (3) through its investigatory power, which is an adjunct to both the authorization and appropriations functions. The formal task of legislative oversight is carried out by the Government Operations Committee, which is empowered by Congress to receive reports and audits from the GAO and to conduct government-wide investigations of departmental and agency operations based on such reports. It is also the job of the Government Operations Committee to recommend action to the authorizations and appropriations committees of Congress. There are, however, certain impediments to the effective operation of oversight and expenditure review by the Government Operations Committee.

The Government Operations Committee is woefully understaffed on the minority side. The ratio of majority to minority personnel presently stands at about 56 to 3. Such understaffing of the minority defeats the purpose of a committee which is intended to serve the "watchdog" function of overseeing and reviewing the activities and finances of the executive branch of government. It is important that the minority membership of such a committee be well staffed, particularly when the majority party in Congress is also the party in power in the White House. Without adequate staffing, the minority is unable to obtain sufficient information to enable it to play its part in testing the appropriate exercise of authority by the Executive. This leaves the functioning of government open to the excesses which may arise through majority party collusion between the legislative and executive branches of government. An articulate, constructive, and informed opposition contributes significantly to the quality of government and the vitality of the two-party system. *Therefore, it is recommended that the inequities of minority staffing on the Government Operations Committee be corrected.*

13. *Enhancing the Place of the GAO in the Congressional Budget Process—Including a Pre-audit Role*

The Government Operations Committee, in conjunction with the GAO, also functions in an expenditure review capacity in examining departmental and agency performance. However, it is apparent that the GAO has failed to keep abreast of the BOB in dealing with the budget. It has been noted how the drafters of the 1921 reforms wished to see the GAO actively participating in the consideration of the proposed budget. Congress has failed to develop a pre-audit role for the GAO. Even the GAO's well-publicized post-audit role of expenditure review produces relatively meager results. The GAO does serve a valuable function in examining expenditures of the previous fiscal year through an auditing of government accounts; but, as the Little report emphasizes,

> . . . auditing does not test the validity and consequence of plans, programs, and policies. It does not illuminate discussions in these areas or project the consequences of alternative courses of action.[35]

Similarly, the CED has found the reports and audits of the GAO to be "narrowly focused," providing "only spot-check evidence, in strictly monetary terms," unconcerned with program and policy approaches to the budget. This should be remedied, particularly if the federal budget is to be put on a planning–programming basis.

Another criticism often made of the GAO is that its Director is a political appointee of the President, with the confirmation of the Senate. Because of the nature of the roles played by the Executive and Congress in budget matters, the GAO should have a Director appointed by and solely responsible to the legislative branch. *Therefore, it is recommended that the GAO be made to play a wider and more active role in the congressional budget process by examining expenditures and conducting audits with full regard for the policy issues raised by the alternative use of funds, and that a pre-audit role be developed by the GAO (as provided for in the Joint Committee on the Budget); in addition, it is recommended that the GAO be headed by a Director appointed by and solely responsible to the Congress.*

REFERENCES

1. U.S. Congress, Senate, Government Operations Committee staff, *Financial Management in the Federal Government*, 87th Cong., 1st Sess., 1961, p. 3.

2. Weidenbaum, Murray L., *Federal Budgeting: The Choice of Government Programs*, Washington, American Enterprise Institute, 1964, pp. 56–66.

3. Wildavsky, Aaron, *Toward a Radical Incrementalism: A Proposal to Aid Congress in Reform of the Budgetary Process*, AEI Series on "Congress: The First Branch of Government," Washington, American Enterprise Institute, 1965, p. 3.

4. In addition, Congress has seen fit from time to time to expand the authority and activities of the GAO. This is evident in the Government Corporation Control Act of 1945, the Federal Property and Administrative Services Act of 1949, the Post Office Financial Control Act of 1950, and the Budget and Accounting Procedures Act of 1950.

5. Saloma, John S., III, *The Responsible Use of Power: A Critical Analysis of the Congressional Budgetary Process*, Washington, American Enterprise Institute, 1964, p. 8.

6. *Ibid.*, p. 38.

7. *Ibid.*, p. 14.

8. Weidenbaum, *op. cit.*, p. 25.

9. The rationale for executive sessions is that the work of the subcommittees requires frank discussion and therefore the publicity of open hearings would be inimical to the candor necessary for the efficient conduct of subcommittee business. Of course, where matters of national security may be involved, executive sessions are mandatory.

10. Harris, Joseph P., *Congressional Control of Administration*, Washington, The Brookings Institution, 1964, pp. 106, 92.

11. Burkhead, Jesse, *Government Spending*, New York, John Wiley & Sons, Inc., 1956, p. 316.

12. Senate procedure with respect to appropriations bills is much the same as that followed in the House, only less extensive. All appropriations bills received by the Senate are referred to the Senate Appropriations Committee whose subcommittees hold further hearings, and take additional testimony. Unlike the House hearings, the Senate subcommittee hearings are open to the public. The full Committee takes action on the measures presented to it by the subcommittees, sometimes making amendments to the House version, and reports such bills to the Senate. The Senate considers the House bills and any amendments offered in committee or on the floor of the Senate. These measures are then voted upon and sent to the President for his signature.

13. The Senate Appropriations Committee prides itself on the quality rather than the quantity of its committee work, looking somewhat askance at the propensity of the House to make large budget reductions. The Senate Appropriations Committee, according to Wildavsky, views itself as playing the lesser but more noble role of the "responsible legislator who sees to it that the irrepressible lower House does not do too much damage either to constituency or to national interests." (Wildavsky, *op. cit.*, p. 12.)

On the other hand, the House Appropriations Committee regards itself as less of a budget slashing ogre and more as a "guardian of the Treasury." (*Ibid.*, p. 11.) While the House Appropriations Committee does have a penchant for cutting departmental and agency budgets and succeeds in doing so 77.2 per cent of the time, in terms of aggregate amounts, the total reduction of the budget is comparatively small. (*Ibid.*, p. 12, citing figures compiled by Richard F. Fenno, Jr., "The House Appropriations Committee as a Political System: The Problem of Integration," American Political Science Review, LVI (1962), p. 312.) Arthur Smithies, author of *The Budgetary Process in the United States* (New York: McGraw-Hill Book Company, Inc., 1964), p. 140, asserts that: "A bona fide cut in the President's appropriation request of as much as 5 per cent, even by a hostile Congress, is the exception rather than the rule."

14. Wildavsky, *op. cit.*, p. 10.
15. Saloma, *op. cit.*, p. 17.
16. *Ibid.*, citing Fenno, *op. cit.*, p. 316.
17. Saloma, *op. cit.*, p. 53.
18. Weidenbaum, *op. cit.*, p. 83.
19. *Ibid.*
20. *Ibid.*, pp. 83–84.
21. Weidenbaum, Murray L., "More Effective Control Over Government Spending," St. Louis University, 1965, p. 3, mimeographed.
22. Weidenbaum, *Federal Budgeting*, p. 39ff.
23. Harris, *op. cit.*, p. 83.
24. *Ibid.*, p. 89.
25. Since Congress' only role in the execution phase of the budget is with regard to legislative oversight of the executive branch and the auditing of expenditures, no consideration will be given to other aspects involved in the formal execution of the enacted budget.
26. GAO audits and reports are also available to the other committees of Congress.
27. Smithies, *op. cit.*, p. 131.
28. Weidenbaum, *Federal Budgeting*, p. 85.
29. Committee for Economic Development, *Budgeting for National Objectives*, a statement by the Research and Policy Committee (New York: The Committee for Economic Development, 1966), pp. 42–43.
30. U.S. Congress, *Financial Management*, etc., *op. cit.*, p. 50.
31. Little, Arthur D., Inc., *Management Study of the U.S. Congress*, Commissioned by NBC News for the special televised report, "Congress Needs Help," Nov. 24, 1965, p. 27.
32. CED, *op. cit.*, p. 34.
33. CED, *op. cit.*, pp. 46–47.
34. *Ibid.*, p. 47.
35. Little, *op. cit.*, pp. 23–24.

PAUL FINDLEY, M.C.
20th District, Illinois

LOBBYING

by Paul Findley, M.C.*

Lobbying is essential to good government, and one of our most pressing needs today is for more lobbying—not less.

The term "lobbying" derives from the practice of persons, individually or collectively, waiting in the lobbies of legislative halls to arrest the attention of lawmakers and influence their decisions on legislative matters. Ever since the first government took unto itself, or was granted, the right to bestow, buy, sell, or seize property, the lobbyist has sought to influence the decision-maker. The practice of lobbying is as old as government, and it is neither exclusive with democratic systems nor confined to the legislative branch within democratic government. Lobbying occurs whenever and wherever the opportunity exists for individuals, acting on their own behalf or on behalf of others, to petition the decision-maker with respect to the passage, defeat, or administration of a law, an ordinance, an edict, or other determination. In the United States lobbying occurs at all levels of government and may be found in most large organizations.

To most Americans the typical mental image of a Congressional lobbyist is one of a florid-faced, loudly dressed character in possession of a fat cigar, a bulging wallet, and an evil intent. His *modus operandi* is assumed to be the successful employment of wine, women, and song. In actuality, the most skillful professional lobbyists are conservatively dressed, ordinary-looking individuals who are adept at assembling information and getting it into the hands of lawmakers. Many of them are objective, honest, and provide assistance and information with no strings attached.

* Former newspaperman Findley is a Member of the House Agriculture committee, chairman of the House Republican Task Force on NATO, and former member of the Education and Labor Committee. He was first elected to Congress in 1960 and prepresnts the 20th District of Illinois.

Lobbying is essentially the method by which individuals or groups make their interests known to legislators. To characterize all lobbying as "evil" is as ridiculous as the attempt to dismiss politics as "a dirty game." Neither is intrinsically good or bad; both are necessary adjuncts to the democratic process.

For purposes of the Federal Lobbying Act, all substantial attempts to influence legislation for pay or for any consideration constitute lobbying. The United States Supreme Court has interpreted lobbying as being direct communication with Members of Congress on pending or proposed federal legislation.[1] The Act applies "to any persons (except a political committee as defined in the Federal Practices Act, and duly organized state or local committees of a political party), who by himself, or through any agent or employee or other persons in any manner whatsoever, directly or indirectly, solicits, collects, or receives money or any other things of value to be used principally to aid, or the principal purpose of which person is to aid, in the accomplishment of any of the following purposes: (a) The passage or defeat of any legislation by the Congress of the United States; (b) To influence, directly or indirectly, the passage or defeat of any legislation by the Congress of the United States."[2]

The term "person" includes an individual, partnership, committee (as excepted), association, corporation, and any other organization or group of persons. The term "legislation" means bills, resolutions, amendments, nominations, and other matters pending or proposed in either house of Congress and includes any other matter which may be the subject of action by either house.

Until 1946 there was no federal control or regulation of lobbying. In that year Congress passed a bundle of reforms following extensive hearings and study by a joint committee on the organization of Congress (the LaFollette-Monroney Committee of 1945–46). One of the reforms sought to regulate lobbying. The Supreme Court has explained the objectives of the Lobbying Act in the following language:

Present-day legislative complexities are such that individual Members of Congress cannot be expected to explore the myriad pressures to which they are regularly subjected. Yet full realization of the American ideal of government by elected representatives depends to no small extent on their ability to properly evaluate such pressures. Otherwise the voice of the people may all too easily be drowned out by the voice of special interest groups seeking favored treatment while masquerading as proponents of the public weal. This is the evil that the Lobbying Act was designed to help prevent. . . . Congress has not sought to prohibit these pressures. It has merely provided for a modicum of information from those who for hire attempt to influence legislation or who collect special funds for that purpose . . .[3]

Essentially, what the Federal Lobbying Act sought to do was to make the names and amounts expended by paid lobbyists a matter of public record. As my colleague Don Rumsfeld explains, "We generally have two courses of action around here. We can pass a law, or we can call in the reporters." The law passed by Congress in 1946 was not intended to prevent or even deter lobbying. The simple motive of the Act was to allow the public to know who the paid lobbyists were by requiring them to register as such and to report their expenditures. Following are some of the things the Act does *not* do:

1. It does not curtail the right of free speech or freedom of the press or the right of petition.

2. It has no application to the publishers of newspapers, magazines, or other publications acting in the regular course of business.

3. It has no application to persons who appear openly and frankly before the committees of Congress and engage in no other activities to influence legislation.

4. It does not require any reports of any persons or organizations now required to report under the provisions of the present Corrupt Practices Act.

5. It does not apply in any manner to persons who appear voluntarily without compensation.

6. It does not apply to organizations formed for other purposes whose efforts to influence legislation are merely incidental to the purposes for which formed.[4]

The last point, unfortunately, is the Act's downfall. The provision that the Act applies only to those organizations "the principle purpose of which" is to influence legislation is a loophole big enough to drive a Mack truck through.

Many of the largest and most active lobbying groups in Washington (*e.g.*, the National Association of Manufacturers) are not registered because they claim that their principal purpose is to be a national organization, not a lobby group. Charitable groups like to mix it up in Washington, too. Under law they run the risk of losing their tax-exempt status if they are caught lobbying. So what do they do? They merely form other organizations, comprised of leaders of various groups, and these special-purpose, special-interest groups lobby merrily above the law.

What we have on the books today is a law that requires registration of lobbyists and reports of receipts and expenditures in connection with attempts made, directly or indirectly, to influence legislation. The Act does not curb or regulate these attempts in any manner; it merely requires public disclosure of lobbying efforts and identification of those engaged in them. Violation of the law is a misdeameanor, punishable by a fine of not more than $4,000 and/or imprisonment of not more than 12 months. (In addition, anyone caught violating the Lobby Act cannot lobby again for three years. If he does so and is caught, the penalties can go up to a fine of $10,000 and 5 years in a Federal penitentiary.)

The trouble with the Act is that it is loosely worded. The words "direct communication with Congress" do not appear in it. The Act refers to influence exerted "directly or indirectly," which brings up a host of questions. For instance, is making a talk a "contribution?" If so, when is one "retained" for the purpose of influencing the "passage or defeat of any legislation?"

In a dissent to the landmark Harriss case, Justice William O. Douglas asked if the Act applied in the following cases:

1. When one addresses a trade union for repeal of a labor law;
2. When a manufacturer's association runs ads in papers for a sales tax;
3. When a farm group undertakes to raise money for an education program to be conducted in newspapers, magazines, and on radio and television, showing the need for revision of our attitudes on world trade;
4. When a group of oil companies puts agents in the nation's capital to sound the alarm at hostile legislation, to exert influence on Congress to defeat it, to work on the Hill for passage of laws favorable to the oil interests;
5. When a business, labor, farm, religious, social, racial, or other group which raises money to contact people with the requests that they write their Congressman to get a law repealed or modified, to get a proposed law passed, or themselves to propose a law.

The Court has generally ruled that activities such as (1), (2), and (3) are not violations of the Act, or even covered by the Act. Such activities as (4) and (5) are covered by the Act because they concern Congress directly. Douglas says that the other activities are also pressure on Congress, although they do not involve direct contact and should be covered by the Act.

The difficulty in enacting and enforcing a tough lobbying law stems from the First Amendment to the Constitution which provides that

> Congress shall make no law . . . abridging the freedom of speech, or of the press; or the right of people . . . to petition the Government for redress of grievances.

Can an individual (or group) say that he is being hurt by a bad law and merely acting under his constitutional right in demanding a change in the law? Can Congress require that everyone register as a lobbyist before writing an article, making a speech, filing an advertisement, appearing on radio or television, or writing a letter seeking to influence existing, pending, or proposed legislation? Just how much right does Congress have to designate who can present what kind of appeal for changes in legislation?

The First Amendment is a broad one, and as Justice Robert H. Jackson noted in a lobby case, "Of course their conflicting claims and propaganda are confusing, annoying, and at times, no doubt, deceiving and corrupting. But we may not forget that our Constitutional system is to allow the greatest freedom of access to Congress, so that the people may press for their selfish interests with Congress acting as arbiter of their demands and conflicts."

As millions of dollars continue to be spent to lobby Congress, Members must wrestle with the problem of how to assure honesty in lobbying while protecting the constitutional right of every citizen to have access to his Representative. It's a tough problem. Elizabeth Yadlosky, Legislative Attorney in the American Law Division of the Library of Congress, sums it up this way:

Since most legislators cannot be specialists in every type of problem which comes before Congress, the detailed and specialized type of information which a lobbyist may offer can be of great value provided it is honestly presented. Most expressions of opinion appearing in the public press are to the effect that lobbying in itself is not an evil but is a necessary and important ingredient of democracy. Indeed, nearly every citizen is engaged in one way or another in trying to influence public opinion, that bedrock of legislation. It is not lobbying as such, but the how of it, the who of it, and the financing of it that properly concerns Congress and the public.

As noted, the loose wording of the present law permits many lobby in-interests to dodge compliance by simply stating that influencing Congress is not their *chief* function. Other groups spend "general" funds instead of monies collected and earmarked for the specific purpose of influencing Congress. But to add insult to injury, the present law fails to designate anyone to investigate the honesty of lobby registration statements or to enforce reporting provisions! In the first 17 years of the lobby law's existence, only four cases were prosecuted, and only one of them resulted in a conviction for violation. Today, the lobby law is more the butt of jokes than it is a buttress of the public interest.

The fact that reports of lobby expenditures totaled more than $10 million in 1954 but had fallen to $4 million by 1964 indicates that more groups are finding ways to side-step the present law. Obviously, the hundreds of new office buildings in Washington are being occupied by representatives of business, labor, trade associations, and other groups. They are spending millions of dollars to "keep a man in Washington" to look after their legislative and executive-administrative interests.

For the most part their interests are narrow. Few champion broad public interests. Taxpayers and consumers as such are not effectively organized.

It is therefore not with the amount of lobbying per se that I am concerned. Rather, my concern is with the imbalance of lobbying, with the failure of many lobbyists to register and report accurately their expenditures, and with the special treatment which has been given to one category of lobbyists—those representing foreign sugar interests.

One of these days some bright, alert, and aggressive people will, I hope, put together lobbying organizations to represent taxpayers and consumers. In the meantime, through default on the part of the Democrats, if for no other reason, the Republican Party must attempt to fill this need. The middle- and low-middle income groups comprise the vast majority of the population. Effective lobbying has enabled the very high and the very low income groups to get favored treatment in Washington, and this, of course, has put the squeeze on those in the center. They must have better champions in the future.

The handling of sugar legislation in 1965 showed tragically the pre-eminence of special interests in Capitol Hill lobbying, the need for more effective lobbying for the broad interests of taxpayers and consumers, and the need for at least two Congressional committees to review policies for receiving lobbyists for foreign interests.

The Sugar Act, in effect, forces American homemakers to pay a $700 million a year premium for the sugar they use. A system of quotas, licenses, controls, import fees, direct payments and excise fees are combined to give certain foreign interests favored treatment, protect favored local growers, guarantee profits for refiners, and deny to consumers the advantage of competitive markets.

The bill became law because consumers and taxpayers had no effective lobby on Capitol Hill, while the narrow special interests were represented skillfully.

Lobbyists for foreign interests had the advantage of special treatment by the Senate Finance Committee and the House Agriculture Committee. Other congressional committees—without exception, I believe—routinely refuse to hear representations made directly in behalf of foreign interests. They insist that all such statements and requests be channeled through diplomatic paths by way of the U.S. State Department. This rule should be made mandatory for all committees.

The Sugar Act also pointed up the vast lobbying impact of the executive branch and the need for better staffing for minority interests in Congress. To illustrate: during my battle against the sugar lobbyists, I called an official of the sugar division of the U.S. Department of Agriculture and asked him for assistance in drafting an amendment I had in mind. He replied politely but firmly that he was a part of the executive branch, and in view of the fact that the executive branch did not want the bill amended, I should look elsewhere for help. This meant, of course, that the vast research and technical resources of the Department of Agriculture were closed to Congressmen critical of the bill. The denial of help was especially ironic because four months earlier the Johnson Administration had taken a different view of the bill and at that time favored an amendment similar to the one I wanted to construct.

Within proper limits and bounds the executive branch should lobby for its legislative objectives, just as narrow special interests can be expected to do their best in self-protection.

Needed are a curb on lobbying for foreign interests, better disclosure rules for all lobbyists, and above all, more lobbying—not less—for Mr. and Mrs. Average American, the neglected people who work for a living, carry most of the tax load, and get no Treasury checks.

REFERENCES

1. United States v. Harriss, 347 U.S. 612, 620 (1954).
2. 60 Stat. 306; 2 USC 266.
3. United States v. Harriss, 347 US 612, 625 (1954).
4. Report of the House Committee on Education and Labor, 80th Congress, 1st Session.

ANCHER NELSEN, M.C.
2nd District, Minnesota

LOBBYING BY THE ADMINISTRATION

*by Ancher Nelsen, M.C.**

When our country was young, it was considered at best improper and at worst unconstitutional for the Administration to "sponsor" detailed legislation introduced in Congress. As time progressed, it became merely unwise to admit that a growing number of bills were being drafted by the executive branch of the government. Now even the pretext has been dropped. The administration operates an institutionalized system for the drafting of policy legislation, and when one party controls both branches, it possesses the tools to almost insure its acceptance by Congress.

Within the Executive Office of the President, the Bureau of the Budget provides a central clearance system for the coordination of all the Administration's legislative affairs. The necessity for some such arrangement is obvious when one views the complexity of our federal bureaucracy. The President could not possibly be expected to keep tabs on the details affecting the expanding number of agencies. Thus, the Bureau of the Budget was established by the Budget and Accounting Act signed by President Harding on June 10, 1921. Under Presidents Harding, Coolidge, and Hoover, the Bureau reviewed the legislative proposals of the various departments only in regard to cost. It did not involve itself in the coordination and development of the programs. The main emphasis was on economy.

President Franklin Roosevelt expanded the functions of the Bureau to permit Presidential clearance of policy lines to be established by the legislation. Budget Circular 336, issued "by direction of the President" on December 21, 1935, required that all except private relief bills and all reports on pending legislation had to be reviewed by the Bureau "for consideration by the Presi-

* Mr. Nelsen represents the 2nd District of Minnesota. He was first elected to Congress in 1958 and currently serves on the House Committee on Interstate and Foreign Commerce and is ranking minority Member of the District of Columbia Committee.

dent" before going to the Congress.[1] When the proposals subsequently were sent to Congress, they were to include a statement as to "whether proposed legislation was or was not in accord with the President's program."[2] Oral testimony before Congressional committees was also to be required to run this gauntlet. Budget Circular 346, again issued "by direction of the President," on January 19, 1939, officially recognized the Bureau as the Presidential agent on all proposals. In 1948, the Bureau's functions were enormously increased with the decision that it would *not only review bills but also draft* Administration proposals.

The Bureau of the Budget is but one part of the Executive Office of the President. Also included are the White House Office, the Council of Economic Advisers, the National Security Council and its Central Intelligence Agency, the National Aeronautics and Space Council, the Office of Economic Opportunity, the Office of Emergency Planning, the Office of Science and Technology, and the Office of Special Representative for Trade Negotiations. There are approximately 140 titled positions listed under these offices, plus regional offices with large staffs. Together they have a budget of over $100 million a year.[3] Thus, the President has enormous resources, both in terms of money and of specialists closely surrounding him, to say nothing of the two and one-half million federal employees attached to the other civilian departments and agencies.

At this time, no issue will be taken with either the quantity of assistance available to the President or the quality or wisdom of any legislation authored and expounded by employees of the executive branch. The point that needs to be aired is whether these employees, and thus public money, are being utilized in such a way as to constitute improper expenditures. In short, is the Administration engaged in lobbying Congress with the tax monies Congress itself appropriates?

The evidence we have been able to compile points toward an affirmative answer. The executive branch does indeed engage in lobbying activities designed to put pressure on Congress to enact certain legislation. Congress has long recognized the awesome potential of the vast executive apparatus. When agencies created as tools to administer the laws are wheeled into the political firing line and used as weapons against dissent, the effect is devastating. Moreover, there is a specific statute governing the use of appropriated funds. Title 18, Section 1913, of the U.S. Code reads as follows:

Section 1913. LOBBYING WITH APPROPRIATED MONEYS. No parts of the money appropriated by an enactment of Congress shall, in the absence of express authorization by Congress, be used directly or indirectly to pay for any personal service, advertisement, telegram, telephone, letter, printed or written matter, or other device, intended or designed to influence in any manner a Member of Congress, to favor or oppose, by vote or otherwise, any legislation or appropriation by Congress, whether before or after the introduction of any bill or resolution proposing such legislation or appropriation: But this shall not prevent officers or employees of the U.S. or of its departments or agencies from communicating to Members of Congress on the request of any Member of Congress, through the proper channels requests for legislation or appropriations which they deem necessary for the efficient conduct of the public business.

Whoever . . . violates . . . this section, shall be fined not more than $500 or imprisoned not more than 1 year; or both . . .

In addition, Congress has attached to a number of appropriations bills a clause which almost invariably follows either of the following forms:

No part of any appropriation contained in the Act shall be used for publicity or propaganda purposes not authorized by the Congress.[4]

No part of any appropriation contained in this Act, or of the funds available for expenditure by any corporation or agency included in this Act, shall be used for publicity or propaganda purposes designed to support or defeat legislation pending before the Congress.[5]

The Senate Appropriations Committee went a step further when it wrote prohibitive language into the text of the Agriculture Appropriations Bill in 1963.

Provided further, That no part of the funds appropriated or made available under this Act shall be used, (1) to influence the vote in any referendum; (2) to influence agricultural legislation except as permitted in 18 USC 1913; or (3) for salaries or other expenses of members of county and community committees established pursuant to section 8(b) of the Soil Conservation and Domestic Allotment Act, as amended, for engaging in any activities other than advisory and supervisory duties and delegated program functions prescribed in administrative regulations.[6]

These explicit legal prohibitions have been and are being violated by the Administration. It should be made clear that this is not a blanket condemnation of lobbying by the Administration. Certainly, any Administration should be expected to use all legal means at its disposal to encourage acceptance of its programs. However, examples cited later in this chapter will show how "lobbying" can get out of bounds.

The Subtle Approach

The techniques of Administration lobbying can be roughly divided into two classes: (1) indirect lobbying, by means of appeals to the public to generate "grass roots" support for Administration programs; and (2) direct lobbying of Members of Congress themselves.

The most obvious form of indirect lobbying is the personal appeal by the President to the people. President Franklin Roosevelt brought this lobbying activity to a polished status with his nationwide "fireside chats." One of President Eisenhower's television appearances was designed to secure public support for the Landrum-Griffin Act. Presidents Kennedy and Johnson have used the radio and television media extensively to generate public support of

Administration proposals. The implication, of course, is that the people will then lobby their Congressmen in behalf of certain legislation desired by the Administration. However, there are subtler and more questionable forms of indirect lobbying, and the practice is by no means an overnight phenomenon.

On December 31, 1948, the Subcommittee on Publicity and Propaganda of the Committee on Expenditures in the Executive Departments, in its final report to the House, cited many instances of unlawful and improper activities in this area.[7] The Subcommittee found that most of the violations cited were committed by personnel not connected with the regular agency publicity offices. The policies were formulated in Washington, but the actions were carried out by the field offices—those closest to and most trusted by the people. The actions were "designed to mislead the public and bring pressure on and discredit the Congress."[8]

The Subcommittee reported a tremendous drive organized by several agencies to drum up support for President Truman's national health program. Officials of the Public Health Service, Children's Bureau, Office of Education, Department of Agriculture, and the Social Security Board were found to have set up "health workshops" financed with federal funds unquestionably designed to create favorable public sentiment for the Administration's plan.[9] The committee report quoted a letter dated December 10, 1945, from Thomas Parran, then Surgeon General of the U.S. Public Health Service, to all field representatives and staff operatives throughout the country, saying:

Every officer of the Public Health Service will wish to familiarize himself with the President's message and will be guided by its provisions when making any public statements likely to be interpreted as representing the official views of the Public Health Service.[10]

Additionally, the committee found that during appearances at these workshops only the Administration's viewpoint was presented. During the hearings held by the Committee, Dr. Herman Hilleboe, then Assistant Attorney General, was asked by Chairman Forest A. Harness if the literature presented at the "workshops" was limited to pro-Administration material. Dr. Hilleboe answered: "We would naturally give emphasis to that, because that is why we are in government. Otherwise, we should get out of government."[11] Harry J. Becker, health consultant in the U.S. Children's Bureau, made several speeches around the country in favor of the Truman plan. When asked if he had presented both sides of the question, Mr. Becker replied: "I don't know what you mean by 'both sides.' "[12]

In the same vein, the Committee held hearings on June 20 and July 16, 1947, to investigate propaganda initiated by the War Department to stimulate public pressure on Congress to create universal military training. The Committee found that the Department had employed service personnel and even civilians hired for the specific purpose of convincing Congress that there was great public demand for UMT through the use of citizens committees, women's groups, radio panels, pamphlets, motion pictures, by radio, newspapers, and other means.[13]

Concerning a movie showing the UMT project and Fort Knox, it was disclosed that the War Department had spent at least $41,600 and that

a close and careful examination and analysis of the scenario shows the most subtle of propaganda techniques as developed by the motion-picture industry in past years.[14]

The Department of Agriculture also came under fire around this time in connection with alleged activities of certain employees to arouse farmers against Congress because the House had reduced the funds of several of the Department's agencies. Public hearings were held on December 4, 1947. As a result of the investigation, the Committee found that

many AAA county committeemen were prevailed upon by key officials in the Production and Marketing Administration to conduct a subtle program of propagandizing their farm members by predicting dire consequences to follow, and either implying or suggesting outright that protests be made to their Representatives and Senators in Washington.[15]

The Department of Agriculture quickly sent warnings to its field representatives reporting the Committee's action and cautioning against future pressure attempts.

In summary, the Committee warned that "the greatest and most effective lobby in the Nation today is that conducted by Federal administrative agencies."[16] Two million Federal employees, it pointed out, comprise a "very effective field army" in a campaign to influence Congress.[17] The employees are strategically located in all states, and it is to be assumed that they are loyal to their Washington superiors and will follow almost any ordered line.

As early as 1948, then, Congress was warned by one of its own committees that

While most of the lobbying activity by federal employees is aimed at specific legislation to increase the power and appropriations of specific departments and agencies, the overall effect is further encroachment upon the rights and liberties of individual citizens. . . . The problem presents an increasing threat to our present system of government, inasmuch as any legislator who attempts to oppose legislation advocated by federally-inspired pressure groups for what he conceives to be the greater national good, is increasingly victimized by each expansion of the Federal Government and the number of the employees. . . . The public is being conditioned by its own Government to demand more and more subsidies, guaranties, and outright grants, and to defeat any Member of Congress who dares to raise his voice in protest.[18]

The White House Regional Conferences

In November, 1961, the Administration sponsored and financed a series of "White House Conferences" in Chicago, Cleveland, Detroit, St. Louis,

Nashville, New York City, Seattle, Philadelphia, San Francisco, Los Angeles, Madison, and Denver. The Conferences were widely publicized as seminars to provide information concerning federal programs. In announcing the Conferences, President Kennedy declared:

> . . . we have arranged to have representatives of the various agencies and departments of Government travel through some of the major cities of the United States to talk to the informed and interested citizens on the problems that our people are facing and on those governmental actions which might assist our country to move forward.[19]

It sounded nice. However, the Conferences had hardly begun when other voices were heard. A small item on page 129 of *The New York Times*, November 14, 1961, served notice that:

> The Colorado Republican State Central Committee, in a full-page advertisement in a Denver newspaper, charged today that "the Democratic high command" was "using your tax money to finance this partisan political rally, to offer the official alibis for their failure to follow through on many campaign promises and to try to drum up the popular support that now is lacking for the New Frontier programs."

The charge of the Republican State Central Committee of Colorado, although an obvious partisan attack, is nevertheless reinforced by a look at the proceedings of some of the Conferences in other cities.

Item—On November 8, 1961, in Chicago, Dr. Robert C. Weaver, then Administrator of the Housing and Home Finance Agency, stated that while there could be Federal participation without Federal control, he thought there should be more Federal control to maintain adequate standards.[20]

Item—In St. Louis on the same day, Secretary of Commerce Luther Hodges was pushing the Administration's policies in regard to foreign competition for world markets. "We must give the President adequate authority to negotiate mutual reductions of trade barriers with other countries," he said, characterizing opponents of the Administration stand as "those who deliberately confuse the American concept of promoting the general welfare with the idea of a welfare state."[21]

The Conferences were defended with the assertion that since the discussions were "open," both sides of the issues would be presented. Even on the face of it, this argument falls flat. Who presented the other side? Certainly the public officials did not. The "other side" was presented by private citizens *who had been cleared for participation.*

Item—In Nashville, Dr. Joseph W. Johnson, Jr., of Chattanooga, the Speaker of the House of Delegates of the Tennessee State Medical Association, was finally chosen to participate in the discussion on Medicare after another physician, Dr. Charles C. Trebue, IV, of Nashville, the immediate past president of the State Medical Association, *had been rejected.* Trebue, it should be pointed out, had earlier testified against Medicare before a Congressional committee.[22]

Perhaps the most curious statements uttered during these "information forums" were those by Abraham J. Ribicoff, then Secretary of Health, Education and Welfare. In New York, he said he saw "no real solution until the Federal Government assumes its proper role in the financing of American education,"[23] and the next day urged the audience to "please stay with the President and work and fight to support his program."[24] (During the latter session, the listeners were given blue postcards with which they were instructed to inform the President of their support for Medicare.) In Los Angeles, Ribicoff remarked that since most state governments were dominated by rural elements, the city schools would have to rely on the Federal Government.[25]

It took ten members of the House Government Operations Committee most of 1962 to obtain data on how much departmental funds were spent on these road shows. In a letter to Joseph Campbell, the Comptroller General of the United States, they requested a complete accounting of the expenditures. By May 28, 1962, Mr. Campbell had requested such information from thirty agencies. However, the Committee members did not receive the complete report until January 28, 1963. Part of the delay was due to the fact that all agencies had to submit their reports to the White House for final clearance. The Comptroller did not verify the figures presented, but based on information reported by the agencies, the estimated cost of the White House Regional Conferences was $232,140.[26] There is reason to believe that the actual figure was much higher, but without the cooperation of the White House, the Committee members could go no further.

A brief review by the Comptroller General of the legal questions involved in the Conferences resulted in this weak opinion:

> . . . we cannot say that the conferences constituted publicity or propaganda . . . even though some of the speeches made at the Conferences by cabinet officers and their assistants may have contained statements urging support of legislative proposals by the Administration.[27]

While he could find no authority in statutes providing for the expenditure of federal tax funds for the Conferences, in his opinion there was absolutely nothing wrong in using such funds since no statute specifically prohibited expenditures for White House Regional Conferences!

The cycle was completed when Mr. Campbell revealed that since Section 1913 of Title 18 is criminal in nature, the enforcement of that section "would be for determination in the first instance by the Department of Justice,"[28] one of the departments which participated in the Conferences!

The Department of Agriculture

The ineffective enforcement of Section 1913 in regard to the Conferences has apparently encouraged the departments and agencies to send more of their salesmen into the hinterlands. In the Department of Agriculture alone, employee travel expenses since 1961 have been averaging almost $14 million more per year than during the eight years prior to 1961.[29] (There is more documented evidence revealing flagrant lobbying practices by this department than any other, perhaps due to the stubborn determination of the American farmer not to be coerced or propagandized.)

On April 3, 1963, Under Secretary of Agriculture Charles S. Murphy spoke before the National Federation of Grain Cooperatives in Washington, D.C. Part of that speech dealt with the Congressionally established wheat referendum to be held on May 21 of that year. The Department was required to provide information on both sides of the question before the referendum. Nevertheless, the Murphy speech was mailed by the Department to all ASC committees to be circulated among the voting farmers before May 21. At one point in the speech, Murphy exclaimed: "How anyone claiming to speak for the farmer could oppose a 'Yes' vote in this referendum I do not understand."[30]

The letter threatened that the farmers would lose $700 million in income if they failed to support the referendum. Frightful memories of depression days and "Hoover Wagons" were insidiously recalled, the contention being that a vote against the referendum was a vote for the return to the early Thirties. Murphy also attacked the large farm organization which was advocating the defeat of the referendum.

Also at stake in this referendum may be the future of a particular farm organization. . . . It seems to me that any farm organization taking this position is bound to lose no matter what the outcome of the referendum. If the referendum carries, the loss of face and prestige is obvious. On the other hand, if the referendum loses, the result for the farm organization responsible could be much worse.[31]

That the referendum was rejected by the farmers and that the farm organization referred to is still going strong are somewhat reassuring facts, but the primary lesson to be learned by this shabby episode is that the Federal agencies have gained the courage to openly violate Section 1913, Title 18, of the law.

An equally unsubtle and even more dangerous attempt to influence the outcome of the referendum was the directive sent out by Ray Fitzgerald, Deputy Administrator for State and County Operations of the Agriculture Stabilization and Conservation Service, to all local ASC committeemen.[32] Fitzgerald directed the committeemen to obtain prime time on all the local television and radio facilities to push for a "Yes" vote. These "public service" programs included appearances by local and state ASC committees and special taped or filmed performances by Secretary Orville Freeman, ASC Administrator Horace Godfrey, and Associate Administrator Edwin Jaenke. The most intriguing aspect of the plot was the method the committeemen were to use to obtain the prime time. The directive noted that radio and television have special advantages in their timeliness and broad availability to rural people. It continued:

An additional advantage is that broadcasting stations have a special obligation to the public which does not exist in the case of publications.

This obligation was defined as

the presentation of public service information—especially in the field of agriculture.

The directive went on:

This is spelled out in federal licensing laws. These stations must renew their operating licenses every three years, and they want to make a good record in public service programming because this is a factor in renewal.

The stations provide these programs in return for two special favors granted by the Government:

(1) exclusive use of a broadcast frequency, and (2) the policy of the Government not to establish federally operated stations in competition with stations being operated commercially.

While this is not the place to debate the propriety of such a regulation, the evidence fully supports the charge that a blatant attempt was made to blackmail stations into cooperation by threatening them with the loss of their licenses.

The directive continued:

The program was developed, and the referendum provided, by an Act of Congress. This is the same Congress under whose laws commercial radio and TV stations are permitted to operate.

Thus, Fitzgerald suggested by innuendo, Congress would like to see a "Yes" vote on the referendum.

Obviously, if Congress had wanted a "Yes" vote on the wheat program, it would have acted directly through substantive law instead of taking the referendum route!

In November, 1963, I received a letter from a newly elected ASCS community committeeman. The letter related the orientation program which committeemen must undergo by direction of the ASCS. This gentleman attended a meeting and his observations of that meeting are as follows:

The meeting was almost entirely propaganda for continuation of Government farm programs. These (sic) included: (1) Introduction (on film) by Orville Freeman welcoming us to our new duties (as newly-elected committeemen) and mentioning a new diploma, recognizing our elections; (2) An outline of the organization of the U.S.D.A. with emphasis on local, state, regional, and Washington ASCS Administration and administrators; (3) Talk by Milton Maxwell, State chairman and a very personable gentleman, on new duties of the community committee; (4) Film on why we need Government controls in agriculture; (5) Slides giving production figures with emphasis on how much better things have been since 1960; (6) Explanation of the genesis of the feed grain program, how its effects have slowed (obvious conclusion: now more controls are needed) and how much more work has been thrown on high U.S.D.A. officials in Washington to persuade big city Congressmen to continue controls in spite of the adverse vote in the wheat referendum. . . . Now I ask, "Is it right to use our tax money to promulgate Government programs?" In other words, a huge sales program to spend our money is now being financed with more of our money. I would say that funds of the U.S.D.A. devoted to administration could be cut sharply with no appreciable loss in real function. . . . P.S.—The cost of these meetings in payments to committeemen is not small. Sixty community committeemen per county at $10 equals $600. For the United States, 2,200 counties at $600 equals $1,320,000.[33]

The letter shows that we still have a few people who have not swallowed the Madison Avenue approach to government.

"It's What's Happening, Baby"

Not all of the federal lobbying expenditures and pressures are used to promote proposed legislation. There is a large and continuing effort to arouse public sympathy for existing programs. One famous incident illustrates this. On June 28, 1965, the Office of Economic Opportunity sponsored a 90-minute television program in cooperation with the Columbia Broadcasting System to generate support and participation in the Job Corps training program. This marathon, entitled "It's What's Happening, Baby," presented a progression of rock-and-roll performers geared to appeal to the teenage audience interspersed with "commercials" advocating the Job Corps. CBS presented the program as a "public service" (bringing memories to some of the Fitzgerald directive). The Job Corps has come under continuing criticism since its formation, and the centers established remain largely unused. Nevertheless, at the time of the program, the OEO claimed that it had more than 275,000 applicants for the Job Corps and only 8,000 in the camps. Why, then, was it deemed necessary to advertise the program? Holmes Brown, OEO's top press agent and a former publicity man for the Ford Motor Company, offered this explanation: "It's like army recruiting or selling Ford cars; you want to keep pressure on your market."[34]

Congress did not appropriate money for the poverty program in order to sell still another government agency to the taxpayers. Congress passed the program, wisely or not, to answer a highly advertised need. If the program as presently constituted is failing to meet that need, then it should be changed by Congress. The money was not appropriated for the purpose of stemming criticism and enlarging a poorly conceived and poorly administered program through mass "public service" appeals.

Finally, the most widely used form of indirect federal lobbying is found in the thousands of government publications put out by the executive branch. Millions of pages are printed every year to publicize government programs. The most ambitious project of them all has just been published and sent to thousands of state and local governmental units in the form of a 400-page "mail order catalogue" of available federal programs. Ostensibly, its purpose is to inform; but will it not subtly generate widespread support for further federal programs? One is reminded of the prediction of Alexander de Toqueville that our Republic would last only until people discovered that they could vote themselves money out of the public treasury.

The Bold Approach

We turn now to direct executive lobbying techniques aimed at Congress and note that this less subtle but equally dangerous approach has been used in varying degrees since the formation of the Union. The methods can be roughly grouped into three categories: (1) efforts on the part of the President himself; (2) pressures and liaison exerted by the Executive Office of the President, and particularly the White House Office; and (3) activities of the liaison offices of the federal departments and agencies.

Direct Presidential lobbying may take many forms, from patronage appointments to prestigious social invitations. Even President Lincoln secured three crucial votes by promising federal appointments to three Members of the House.[35] (The votes were delivered and two appointments made, but Lincoln's assassination prevented the third appointment.) The Civil Service merit system has removed many of the President's plums, but some are still available. The Federal judgeships and excepted-service bureaucratic positions can still be manipulated at the President's pleasure. While such manipulation is disgusting to the idealist, it has largely been accepted as an inevitable aspect of an elective form of government. It is the degree to which Presidential appointment power may be used as an effective weapon for executive lobbying of the legislative branch that Congress must watch.

The following excerpt from a recent interview with Lawrence F. O'Brien sheds some light on President Johnson's lobbying techniques:

Q. Do the President's social events at the White House help?

A. Very much so.

Q. Are invitations to the wives of Congressmen to be guests in the living quarters of the White House helpful, too?

A. It has had a great impact, and I think it's all part and parcel of President Johnson's attempt to further refine and broaden this basic concept of individual contact and rapport. The freshmen in this Congress have been invited to the White House on at least three occasions so far since they were elected.

Q. Don't they come over, too, on bill-signing occasions?

A. That's right. And, as you know, we've had briefings for the Members of Congress.

Q. How much contact does the President himself have, individually, with Senators and Congressmen?

A. The President has regular and continuing contact with the Democratic leadership on a day-to-day basis; with the Republican leadership on appropriate occasions. He has a great deal of contact with key members of Congress, the chairmen of committees and subcommittees. Beyond that, however, he has many occasions for individual and small-group contact. There could be signing ceremonies, briefings, social occasions—a variety of contact. The President will, on occasion, telephone members of Congress.

Q. Is all that organized?

A. To some extent, yes—but the situation at the moment can dictate any call or contact.

Q. The President seems to go up to the Capitol more frequently than any other President within memory. Does this help, too?

A. Of course it does. He has the great advantage of knowing most of these people intimately. They are old friends, old associates, and it becomes an occasion when there is a great deal of warmth, a great deal of banter—a very friendly occasion.[36]

Every President since Franklin Roosevelt has used Presidential liaison offices to bridge the gap between the White House and the Congress. Roosevelt used Tommy Corcoran and other White House intimates to influence Members of Congress on an informal basis. President Truman was the first President officially to assign an aide specifically to handle his liaison with Congress. President Eisenhower enlarged this modest beginning and magnified its effectiveness manyfold by appointing General Wilton B. Persons, one of the most adept Pentagon lobbyists in the business, as his chief legislative liaison man. When Persons was elevated to chief of staff of the White House Office, he was replaced by Bryce Harlow, a former Republican counsel for the House Armed Services Committee, who brought the art of Congressional persuasion to its highest point to that date.

Today there seems little gap left to bridge. White House liaison men can be seen wandering the Congressional corridors—convincing, trading, cajoling, promising, delivering, nose-counting—on almost any given day. In the first session of the 89th Congress, when a close vote appeared in the making, it was not an uncommon sight to find the White House corps lined up so solidly that Members of Congress had to elbow their way into the Chamber. Beware of Greeks bearing gifts, as the phrase goes; liaison officials are usually prepared to offer anything from dams to post offices, judgeships to Job Corps camps, defense bases, invitations to the White House for dinner, or you-name-it.

The "credit" for the most highly organized operation must go to Lawrence F. O'Brien, the present Postmaster General, who was appointed Chief of Legislative Affairs by President Kennedy in 1961. Although his title has changed, O'Brien is apparently to retain his interest in Capitol Hill by order of President Johnson. The following excerpt from an interview with O'Brien in *Nation's Business*, April, 1965, explains the basic structure of the "O'Brien System:"

The top legislative officers of departments and agencies—about 40 of them— meet periodically as a team with Mr. O'Brien to review the Administration's program for Congress. They discuss how it is moving, difficulties that have arisen or lie ahead, how they may be overcome, how prospects for passage can be improved. Every Monday morning, Mr. O'Brien's office receives from every department and agency a written report on the status of legislation for which they are responsible and the contacts they had with Congress the previous week. These are reviewed by Mr. O'Brien and his staff and consolidated into a single report, which includes their own views, and given to President Johnson on Monday evening for study and use in connection with his regular Tuesday breakfast meeting with Congressional leaders. "In the four years since this program began, White House contacts with Members of Congress have increased 300 per cent. We try to keep it a team effort, everybody working for the Administration's entire program—day in and day out, not just during crises. Agency heads and their aides have two responsibilities, really, day-to-day accountability for programs in which they're particularly interested, and promotion of the President's total program at all times. When we get into a crisis, we bring 40 legislative officers into the act and all pull together.[37]

President Johnson strongly supports the executive-legislative liaison system. He has repeatedly told his Cabinet that he considers a federal department's legislative liaison officer second in importance only to the Cabinet member himself, saying: "If we are to get our legislative program through [Congress], you must have heavyweights in these jobs—people with political sensitivity and substantive knowledge of your programs. I expect them to keep you thoroughly informed of the situation affecting your programs on the Hill, and, in turn, I expect you to keep me informed at all times."[38]

Congressional liaison offices with the federal departments and agencies are a comparatively recent innovation. The Department of Defense established the first such office shortly after World War II. The process was completed in 1963, when the Department of the Interior established its office. The liaison services provided by the staffs of these offices are complicated and intertwined, linking the Cabinet members, the Congress, the Bureau of the Budget, the White House Office, and other departments and agencies as well as internal bureaus and offices. In terms of personnel and costs involved in direct congressional liaison, in fiscal year 1963 there were 737 people employed in the departments and agencies with a budget of nearly $8 million.[39] With the growth of government services, we can logically assume that these figures have increased since 1963. It should also be noted that these figures would be considerably higher if all Congressional assistance costs were available. The State Department admits this in the following statement:

> In addition to the personnel in the department directly involved full time in preparing and providing information to the Congress, many employees throughout the department spend varying amounts of time preparing informational material for the Congress; nearly all of the responses to congressional inquiries and material for presentation are prepared by the relevant or functional specialists. However, it is impossible to identify these individuals in terms of the hours so spent and their salary costs.[40]

Obviously, some informational services to Congress are legitimate. The liaison offices serve as focal points for congressional inquiries and constituent requests. However, under the "O'Brien System," the word "information" has been stretched beyond reason. The current lobbying campaign in the Office of Economic Opportunity is a good illustration of this. The current lobbying campaign in the Office of Economic Opportunity is a good illustration of this. In describing a top-secret, four-page memorandum submitted to Poverty Chief R. Sargent Shriver by OEO's chief lobbyist, William G. Phillips, columnists Rowland Evans and Robert Novak summed up the liaison policies of OEO in this quote from the memo:

> It is not excessive to state that no work has more importance during the current session than that work which supports OEO's position on the Hill.[41]

Summary

Although lobbying by the Administration has been greatly refined and intensified in recent years, with understandably more effective results, even direct pressures applied to Congress have not escaped some conspicuous bipartisan backfires. Senator Wayne Morse (D., Ore.), fired off this blast during a recent debate on the foreign aid program:

> No amount of systematic briefing of Senate aides by officials of AID, and no amount of slick footwork by a bloated AID Congressional Relations Office can hide the transparent and obvious difficulties of the AID program.[42]

The term "arm twisting" was applied to Administration lobbying practices by Democratic Representative Otis G. Pike when he remarked during the debate on a farm bill that his arm ached "from the twisting it has taken."[43]

The centralized structure of the Administration's activities reveals itself often to Congressmen when one department or agency is found lobbying vigorously for another's legislation. One angered recipient of this type of pressure exclaimed:

> If the Agriculture Department wants to send a guy who knows about the farm bill, I don't give damn what his title is. But a Post Office guy wanted to talk to me about it, and I refused to accept him as an emissary.[44]

Another backfire result of strong Administration lobbying is to be seen in the number of normally administration-oriented Congressmen who have discovered that it is often profitable to use a potential "No" vote in order to bargain for Administration favors. As one Democratic Representative put it, "I know guys who are *looking* for places to break with them."[45]

When we look at the legislative history of the first session of the 89th Congress, it is obvious that these instances of rebellion were the voices of a tiny minority. Also, no attempt is made here to judge the merits of the specific legislation, proposals, and programs. But the legislative history clearly shows that the concept of an effective check and balance system has been under attack.

Item—No public hearings were allowed on the complex, three-layer Medicare Act.

Item—Only one House amendment and no Senate amendments were allowed on the $1.3 billion-a-year Elementary and Secondary Education Act.

Item—The bill to provide aid to Appalachia was approved by the Senate Public Works Committee after only two days of hearings, shutting off waiting witnesses. (The same committee held only a one-day hearing on the Water Pollution Control Act.)

Item—There were no amendments allowed and a bare minimum of debate in the House on the crucial question of repealing Section 14(b) of the Taft-Hartley Act.

The ease with which the Administration pushed through its legislative program last year disturbed even the Senate Majority Leader, the Honorable Mike Mansfield. In a telephone interview with columnist Arthur Krock, Sen. Mansfield reflected:

> We have passed a lot of major bills at this session, some of them very hastily, and they stand in extreme need of a going-over for loopholes, rough corners, and particularly for an assessment of current and ultimate cost in the framework of our capacity to meet it.[46]

Lester Milbrath has defined lobbying as

> the stimulation and transmission of a communication, by someone other than a citizen acting on his own behalf, directed to a governmental decision-maker with the hope of influencing his decision.[47]

Through the expert use of the four P's—Personnel, Pamphlets, Propaganda, and Pressure—the executive branch has transformed its legal prerogative to convince public opinion into a possibly illegal attempt to mold public acceptance for its policies. Some would have us believe that this is a progressive step, in line with the growing appreciation of the trained program specialist in our technical world. We must remember, however, that our government deals with people, and in so doing it must be designed to protect the rights of all people.

Program specialists suffer from what Thorstein Veblen termed "trained incapacity." In their association with other specialists in their own fields, they develop a set of values which often overlooks significant aspects of human reality. This is especially dangerous in government. In an efficiently administered bureaucracy, there is a tendency for the supervisors to accept without question the findings of their own specialists and, in turn, for their specialists to arrange their findings according to what they think the supervisors want. In this process, there is a definite lack of consideration of the human element.

I am not condemning or even suggesting that the specialists are always wrong. I am advocating that it is the responsibility of Congress to question the conclusions of the specialists to make sure that they relate their fundamental assumptions to actual human problems. Lewis Dexter has written that the real problem of democracy is as much, or more, to find solutions which are acceptable to many different groups, rather than simply to respond to alleged majority demands of the judgment of the specialists.[48]

The criminal statute covering lobbying by the executive branch is clear enough, and the penalties for violation are equally clear and present. The dilemma is that the responsibility for enforcing the statute rests with the Justice Department, an arm of the executive branch!

In these times of Administration-generated concensus, it is urgently necessary that Congress enact legislation to provide for a more effective, independent method of enforcing the law governing lobbying of the people's representatives by the *administrative* arm of their federal government.

REFERENCES

1. National Emergency Council, "Proceedings of the Twenty-Eighth Meeting," Dec. 17, 1935, National Archives, pp. 14–23.
2. *Ibid.*
3. Heren, Louis, "The King's Men: A British View of the White House," *Harper's Magazine*, February, 1965, p. 110.
4. Public Law 88–245: Departments of State, Justice, and Commerce, the Judiciary, and Related Agencies Appropriation Act of 1964. Title VII, Section 701. Dec. 30, 1963.
5. Public Law 88–215: Independent Offices Appropriation Act of 1964. Title III, Section 301. Dec. 19, 1963.
6. Public Law 88–250: Department of Agriculture and Related Agencies Appropriation Act of 1964. Title I, Agricultural Stabilization and Conservation Service—Expenses. Dec. 30, 1963.
7. U.S. 80th Congress, House Report No. 2474. Final Report of the Subcommittee on Publicity and Propaganda, Twenty-third Intermediate Report of the Committee on Expenditures in the Executive Departments, Dec. 31, 1948.
8. *Ibid.*, p. 2.
9. U.S. 80th Congress, House Report No. 786. July 2, 1947.
10. U.S. 80th Congress, House Report No. 2474, p. 3.
11. *Ibid.*
12. *Ibid.*, p. 4.
13. *Ibid.*, p. 5.
14. *Ibid.*
15. *Ibid.*
16. *Ibid.*, p. 7.
17. According to the Joint Committee on Reduction of Nonessential Federal Expenditures, the federal civilian employment total for October 1965 was 2,528,696. This figure does not include the State and local officials who administer federal programs but who are officially listed on State and local payrolls. U.S. 89th Congress, Senate Committee Print No. 261.
18. U.S. 80th Congress, House Report No. 2474, p. 8.
19. *The New York Times*, Nov. 8, 1961, p. L21.
20. *The New York Times*, Nov. 9, 1961, p. L23.
21. *Ibid.*, p. L16.
22. *The New York Times*, Nov. 10, 1961, p. L22.
23. *The New York Times*, Nov. 17, 1961, p. L37.
24. *The New York Times*, Nov. 18, 1961, p. L26.

25. *The New York Times*, Nov. 21, 1961, p. L34.
26. Special report on the "Estimated Cost of White House Regional Conferences," by the Comptroller General of the United States. From the files of the Government Operations Committee of the House of Representatives.
27. Letter from the Comptroller General to Congressman Robert P. Griffin, Nov. 8, 1962. Letter numbered B–147578. From the files of the Government Operations Committee, House, p. 6.
28. *Ibid.*, p. 5.
29. "Obligations for Travel, Fiscal Years 1942–1963." Prepared by the Office of Budget and Finance of the Division of Budgetary and Financial Reports, Jan. 17, 1954: "Fiscal Years 1954–1958." Prepared by the Office of Budget and Finance of the Division of Budgetary and Financial Reporting, Jan. 23, 1957. "Fiscal Years 1957–1966." Prepared by the Office of Budget and Finance of the Division of Accounting Policies and Systems, Jan. 25, 1965.
30. *Congressional Record*, Appendix, May 23, 1963, p. A3301.
31. *Ibid.*
32. Bailey, Charles W., "USDA Accused of Pressuring Broadcasters," *Congressional Record*, June 6, 1963, pp. 9816, 9817. Richard Wilson, "Arm Twisting on a High Level," *Congressional Record*, June 19, 1963, pp. 10566, 19567.
33. *Congressional Record*, Dec. 16. 1963, p. 23587.
34. Steele, Jack, "Who Dreamed Up 'Depraved' TV Show Used to Lure Teenagers into Poverty Programs?" *Washington Daily News*, June 30, 1965.
35. MacNeil, Neil, *Forge of Democracy*, New York, David McKay Company, Inc., 1963. pp. 246–47.
36. "From White House to Capitol . . . How Things Get Done," *U.S. News and World Report*, Sept. 20, 1965, p. 71.
37. "Lyndon's Lobbyists: How They Get What He Wants," *Nation's Business*, April 1965, p. 98.
38. *Nation's Business, op. cit.*, p. 38.
39. Data in the files of the Chairman, Subcommittee on Foreign Operations and Government Information, House Committee on Government Operations.
40. *Ibid.*
41. Evans, Rowland, and Robert Novak, "The Poverty Lobby," *Washington Post*, Feb. 1, 1965, p. A13.
42. *Business Week, op. cit.*, p. 91.
43. Greenfield, Meg, "Why Are You Calling Me, Son?" *The Reporter*, Aug. 16, 1962, p. 29.
44. *Ibid.*, p. 30.
45. *Ibid.*
46. Krock, Arthur, "Second Look at Great Society Urged," *Wilmington Morning News*, Sept. 22, 1965, p. 23.
47. Milbrath, Lester W., *The Washington Lobbyists*, Chicago, Rand McNally & Co., 1962, p. 8.
48. Dexter, Lewis Anthony, " 'Check and Balance' Today: What Does It Mean for Congress and Congressmen?" in *Congress: The First Branch of Government*, American Enterprise Institute, 1966.

ROBERT H. MICHEL, M.C.
18th District, Illinois

REORGANIZATION OF THE COMMITTEES ON GOVERNMENT OPERATIONS AND MINORITY CONTROL OF INVESTIGATION

by Robert H. Michel, M.C.*

The President of the United States is the sole executive authority in the United States. The Constitution vests the executive power in him, with little guidance as to the manner of its exercise other than that he shall take care that the laws be faithfully executed. As Commander-in-Chief of the Armed Forces, he can order the military forces of the United States virtually anywhere he chooses. For example, the substantial increase of military forces in Vietnam was carried through within the powers invested in the Presidency. Similarly, the decision to intervene in Korea was the President's.

In contrast, the political leadership of the Soviet Union is divided. As Chairman of the Council of Ministers, Kosygin is the formal head of the Soviet Government and thus exercises all the formal authority inherent in that office. As General Secretary of the CPSU, Brezhnev is head of the Soviet Communist Party, which is the real source of political power in the Soviet system. And as a member of the Politburo, Kosygin shares in this power. Under present conditions both sources of power, governmental and political, complement one another, but it is unlikely that either the Soviet Premier or General Secretary could act independently on a crucial question, for example, making a military commitment in the same manner as the President of the United States, who commands sole executive authority.

* A Member of the House Committee on Appropriations, Mr. Michel was first elected to Congress in 1956 and has served on the Government Operations Committee. He represents the 18th Congressional District of Illinois and served as administrative assistant to his precedessor in office.

[Mr. Michel's article was delivered as a speech on the Floor of the House April .25, 1966.—Ed.]

In the American constitutional system it is extraordinarily difficult to remove a President before his 4-year term of office ends. The most significant attempt of this sort, the impeachment of President Andrew Johnson, failed. Thus, except for death or virtually total disability, the President can exercise his authority for four years and even eight if re-elected.

Tenure of office for the political leader is not necessarily a guarantee in the Soviet political system, except during the Stalin years of totalitarianism. Within a few months after assuming Stalin's mantle, Malenkov was divested of his authority as General Secretary of the CPSU, retaining only the Premiership of the Government. In February, 1955, Malenkov was forced to resign from this office to be replaced by Bulganin. Khrushchev retained the position of General Secretary of the Party. In July, 1957, Bulganin was removed, and Khrushchev assumed both positions as Premier of the Government and First Secretary of the Party. But even in this position his power was limited by various political forces acting within the Soviet political system. Some scholars have referred to Khrushchev's leadership not as a dictatorship but rather as a collegial leadership in which he played a major role. Of course, Khrushchev himself was removed from both offices in October 1964. And there are no assurances that Brezhnev and Kosygin will hold their posts for two, three, four, or any determined number of years.

Thus, by virtue of having a constitutional tenure of four years and perhaps even eight, it could be said that the President has an advantage in exercising the power he holds over that of the present Soviet political leasership. This power has been building up for over 30 years; so that the omnipotent executive has become the nation's greatest spender of its taxpayers' money in all its peacetime history. The Chief Executive concerns himself with the air we breathe and the water we drink, with junkyards and with beauty—not to mention building houses for us, planning our cities, and reclaiming blighted areas. All of these things require money—tax money. Moreover, attention to these matters leaves the executive short on time to defend the nation against its enemies and to conduct its foreign affairs, which are the primary duties laid upon him by the Constitution.

Very recent events demonstrate dramatically the growing power of the executive. The *New York Herald Tribune* of November 9, 1965, reported:

> There is a more fundamental issue in the President's crackdown on aluminum than his use of the stockpile for purposes clearly beyond the intent of Congress in authorizing its creation. Mr. Johnson has moved his Administration into the business of administering industrial prices . . . The proper extent of the government's coercive powers is . . . of much greater significance than whether the price of aluminum should be a half-cent higher or a quarter-cent lower. Mr. Johnson is concerned over inflation, and rightly so (though not sufficiently concerned to balance his own budget) . . .
>
> We have a far better mechanism than Presidential judgment for determining "justified" price levels; the forces of a free market . . . In the short run, prices may go higher than they should; in the long run, they could hardly be sustained

in a competitive market . . . The President has every right to "state the public interest," as he himself might put it; but when he begins trotting out the Federal arsenal of economic weapons, he risks launching a dangerous spiral of his own—a spiral of coercion that is not easily stopped.

The matters covered by the executive directly affect the daily lives of millions of people. There is no question that big government has been getting bigger as well as more intrusive.

Minimal effective checks on executive power require that: (1) each individual whose interests are directly affected by government action shall, if he wishes, have a meaningful day in court (not necessarily a court of law). If before a congressional committee, he should be allowed to present his case upon the assumption that someone with real authority will in good faith seriously consider his statement; (2) the congressional committee should be independent and objective—free from external direction by party or executive officials; and (3) the congressional committee should reveal to the public the facts presented and the details of procedure, thus avoiding either arbitrary departures from general rules or unfair application of general rules.

Committee decisions are accepted in part because they are supported and enforced by the power of the Congress. They are also accepted because they are regarded as fair and just in their own right and are viewed as the product of a legislative body which is regarded as serving a common need and indispensable function in our society.

There are certain attributes which we usually look for in determining the fairness and justice of a committee decision in its own right, as far as procedure is concerned. We are more willing to attribute these qualities to judgments arrived at (1) manifestly on the basis of the weight of testimony; (2) after all parties brought forward by both the majority and minority[1] have had a chance to present their case fully; (3) undominated by the special interest of the chairman in the outcome of the investigation; or (4) not on the initiative of the chairman, but at the request of the minority.

Committee decisions often depart widely from these standards for what are deemed compelling reasons. Thereby, committees may forfeit public confidence in their fairness and justice and rely for acceptance instead upon public respect for Congress.

For example, committee members may rely partly on information and arguments presented by the Administration without holding a full hearing for presentation of conflicting views. Chairmen may consent to committee action only after pressure from the news media and even then may have a special interest in the outcome.

Such factors greatly weaken the moral force, so to speak, of committee decisions. But the possibility of investigation by the government operations committees under minority control, in those cases where these conditions are present, may do much to restore the moral force otherwise lacking and thus secure public acceptance of the fairness and justice of congressional actions.

The existence of minority control would be a constant reminder to the official that excessive actions risk legislative inquiry and reversal. It would be a constant source of assurance and security to the individual citizen that he has a forceful method of vindicating his rights against the executive before an independent tribunal.

If the executive process is part and parcel of a necessary delegation of power to government officials to enable them to handle adequately the problems of modern society, then congressional review seems essential to insure that this power be exercised conscientiously, within the minimum demands of procedural fair play, without the requirement of a judicially determinable violation of constitutional or statutory rights. The delegation of discretionary powers to the minority party in Congress is neither new nor foreign to a congressional "rule of law." What is novel is the enormous amount of discretion entrusted to modern executive officials.

Rule XI, section 691, 8(c)(2), of the House of Representatives, states that the Committee on Government Operations "shall have the duty of studying the operation of Government activities at all levels with a view to determining its economy and efficiency." Control of the Executive has long been one of the main functions of the Congress. For example, from 1789 to 1925 there were upwards of 300 congressional investigations of executive conduct. Since Congress has yielded more and more authority to the executive, I feel it must seek ways of insuring that the executive carries out Congress' intentions. For that reason, I introduced H.R. 9252 to provide—(See Appendix III for full text.)

> . . . that the majority of the membership (including the chairman) of the Committee on Government Operations of the Senate and House of Representatives, respectively, shall be composed of members of a major political party other than the political party of which the President of the United States is a member.

The requirement that the chairman be a Member of the minority party would not permit the chairman to play the part of an autocrat with impunity since the chairman and the committee would have to depend upon the whole House or Senate for legislative acceptance of their proposals. But it would tend to give the chairman a spirit of independence and freedom to criticize the operations of the executive.

Quite often a minority Member will have information which it would be in the public interest to disclose in the press; a newsman will recognize this but will be reluctant to use the information which does not have an "official stamp". H.R. 9252 would provide an official minority outlet to the news media.

Although I have been unable to find any legislative precedents for H.R. 9252, there certainly are many precedents for minority control of investigations—the most famous being the minority investigation of the Teapot Dome scandal. In 1923, the executive and both houses of Congress were under the control of Republicans, but Senator Thomas J. Walsh, Democrat of Montana, was prevailed upon to take command of the Public Lands Committee to investigate improprieties surrounding the leasing of the Teapot Dome oil reserve.

The most recent instance occurred when Senator Harry Byrd was permitted to retain his chairmanship of the Joint Committee on Reduction of Nonessential Federal Expenditures in the Republican 80th and 83rd Congresses, although the executive was not Republican in the 80th Congress. Also, in the 63rd Congress, when the Senate had 72 standing committees, 51 Democrats, and a one-committee-chairmanship rule, 21 committees were perforce chaired by Republicans.[2]

It is true that in the early days of the House, and at least up through 1898 in the Senate, some standing (and select) committees had majorities on them from the minority party or were chaired by a Member of the minority party, but to our knowledge the resolutions or rules creating them did not specify such a result. It usually occurred because the committees were relatively minor in nature, or because distinction was given to a Member with long service in a particular area.

In his *Forge of Democracy*, Neil MacNeil (p. 157) states:

> Down until the Civil War, in fact, it was not unusual for the Speaker to give political control of some of the less important House committees to the political minority and even appoint minority stalwarts to be chairmen of them. John Quincy Adams, for example, normally chaired a House committee, no matter which party controlled the House.

McConachie, *supra*, records that as a result of committee elections in the Senate in 1816, the Finance Committee came under minority control, and the Chairman of the Senate Committee on Commerce and Manufactures was a Member of the minority (p. 275). He also records that the Chairman of the Senate Committee on Pensions in 1845 was a Member of the minority (p. 282), and that in the early days of the House, some committee chairmen were from the minority (p. 139). Samuel Randall, of Pennsylvania, a Democrat and Speaker during the 44th and 45th Congresses (1876, 1878), was Chairman of the House Committee on Public Expenditures (a minor committee) in the Republican controlled Congress of 1883 (p. 140).

In 1898, of 59 Senate committees in a Republican-controlled Senate, 11 were chaired by Democrats and 2 by Populists (p. 293).

In all such instances, to our knowledge, however, these situations occurred from factors other than specific resolutions and rules specifying minority control or minority chairmen. We thus have been unable to find any precedents for H.R. 9252 as a considered and definite policy of Congress.

Minority parties have formed their own *ad hoc* committees on an informal basis, such as the Republican Congressional Food Study Committee, which was created in 1943. It consisted of 44 or 45 Members of the Republican

Party in the House, under the chairmanship of the Honorable Thomas Jenkins of Ohio,[3] but it had no official sanction or authority.

Of course, when the Presidency has been in control of one party and one or both houses of Congress have been in control of the other party, congressional committees will be created of majorities in the party not of the President, but such situations are the result of politics and not of determined policy.

The provisions in the House rules relating to selection of committees are found in Rule X:

1. There shall be elected by the House, at the commencement of each Congress, the following standing committees: . . .
2. The Speaker shall appoint all select and conference committees which shall be ordered by the House from time to time.
3. At the commencement of each Congress, the House shall elect as chairman of each standing committee one of the members thereof; . . .

The provisions in the Senate rules relating to selection of committees are found in Rule XXIV:

1. In the appointment of the standing committees, the Senate, unless otherwise ordered, shall proceed to ballot to appoint severally the chairman of each committee, and then, by one ballot, the other members necessary to complete the same. A majority of the whole number of votes given shall be necessary to the choice of a chairman of a standing committee, but a plurality of votes shall elect the other members thereof. All other committees shall be appointed by ballot, unless otherwise ordered, and a plurality of votes shall appoint.

Taken literally, the rules of both houses do not prohibit the selection of committees controlled by a minority as long as the consensus in both Chambers is in agreement with such a prospect.

Secondly, the concepts of separation of powers and checks and balances support the thesis that the committee in each house charged primarily with oversight of the expenditure of funds by the executive branch and the efficient operation of that branch should be in the control of the party opposite to the President's. The swing of power away from Congress to the executive, the vast authorization of administrative powers by Congress to the executive branch, the huge growth of that branch, the great enlargement of the policy and legislation proposing functions of the executive, and the consequent need for a thorough oversight by Congress are conditions which support H.R. 9252.

Perhaps the major function of Congress today is oversight of the sprawling administrative structure; this function is necessarily diminished when the party of the President and the majority party in Congress (and thus the majority on every committee) is one and the same.[4]

The most certain way to assure that funds are being expended by the administrative agencies in accordance with law, that waste and misfeasance will be ferreted out, is to place general authority regarding oversight of expenditures and efficiency in committees where the party opposite to that of the President is given control. It is the most certain way that the Congress and the public will be fully informed, that the public welfare is receiving maximum benefit, and that "whitewashing" will be eliminated.

The principle behind the bill was expressed by John Stuart Mill, in his *Representative Government* (Everyman Edition, page 239):

Instead of the function of governing, for which it is radically unfit, the proper office of a representative assembly is to watch and control the Government; to throw the light of publicity on its acts; to compel a full exposition and justification of all of them which anyone considers questionable; to censure them if found condemnable; and, if the men who compose the Government abuse their trust or fulfill it in a manner which conflicts with the deliberate sense of the Nation, to expel them from office, and either expressly or virtually appoint their sucecssors.

Joseph P. Harris, in his *Congressional Control of Administration*, (1964) (pp. 292–293), states:

Congressional investigations of administration, and especially of charges of mismanagement or misconduct of executive officers, are seldom free of partisanship. Many result in divided reports, the members of one party absolving the executive officers of any serious blame for shortcomings, and those of the other party finding them guilty of misconduct or incompetence as charged. This obvious partisanship seriously impairs the utility of the inquiry except as a weapon of party warfare; the public is more likely to be confused than informed by such conflicting findings.

Lindsay Rogers, in *The American Senate*, (1926) (p. 202), states:

. . . party control in the House of Representatives is now so strong as to shut off that body from embarrassing inquiries into Executive performances. Only when the majority of the House and the President belong to different political parties do the latter's agents suffer any scrutiny. This, for example, was the case during Mr. Wilson's last 2 years. Then 51 congressional investigations were in progress. But when a President has a Congress of his own political faith, inquisitions are not so frequent, their institution by the House of Representatives is extremely rare, and Senate majorities are not anxious to act.

Dr. George Galloway, in his *The Investigative Function of Congress*, (supra, page 59) states:

In the final analysis, therefore, investigation may be viewed as the legitimate function and duty of a political party. It would appear to be part of its duty to reveal the errors, shortcomings, and misdeeds of the representatives of the other party in office.

He then lists some of the purposes of the investigative function (pp. 64–65).

It is a safeguard against imbecilities as well as corruption. It is the American method of achieving ministerial responsibility without reducing power. It is one of the checks in a system of checks and balances. . . .

. . . it is a substitute for a system of administrative courts needed to protect the citizen from the arbitrary action of subordinate officials.

. . . it is a security against the misuse of opportunity. There is always the danger that public positions will become places of profit, that office will be employed as a means of private plunder.

But, he reports (pp. 66–67):

. . . in order to secure the appointment of a committee of investigation, the support of a majority of those present in the Chamber is necessary, which is difficult to obtain when both the majority of the House and the Executive belong to the same party. The administration leaders will resort to every parliamentary stratagem to avert the danger. Many inquiries are proposed which fail to receive the support of the Rules Committee or the House and consequently fall through. Others are authorized but never reach completion. . . .

Possible examples of such consequences in recent years might include the TFX investigation, the Bobby Baker investigation, the failure to investigate alleged pressure put upon federal employees to contribute to Democratic "Galas," and the considerable activity of the Legislative Oversight Subcommittee of the House Interstate and Foreign Commerce Committee during the Eisenhower years as contrasted with its relative inactivity since 1961.

As Dr. Galloway points out in his book *Congress and Parliament:*

The use of committes of inquiry by legislative bodies dates back to the practice of the British House of Commons in the seventeenth century. The Commons used them in disputed election cases as early as the end of the sixteenth century, and as an aid in the legislative process after 1688. Later, the inquisitorial power was assumed by the American colonial assemblies, which modeled themselves after the House of Commons, and asserted the same privileges. The practice of the Continental Congress and of the state legislatures in the period following the Revolution furnished further evidence of the heritage of this device by U.S. legislatures. Likewise, the Federal Congress after 1789 assumed that the legislative power implied the use of committees of inquiry with power to send for persons and papers.

The British still have devices for the efficient and expeditious conduct of investigations that Congress could well copy. Since 1861, the select committee of Public Accounts of the House of Commons has been a critic of Treasury administration, and by reporting its findings to the Commons has fastened financial responsibility on the executive. Secondly, about half of the time of the House of Commons during a normal session is devoted to the criticism of government policy and administration, and is largely controlled by the opposition.

The select committee on Public Accounts has 15 members and is chaired by a member of the opposition. The financial control exercised by the Accounts Committee is both retrospective and deterrent. As Basil Chubb states:

Select committees cannot, of course, ensure efficiency and economy; only the efforts of the administration itself can do that. But they are sufficient to assure the House of Commons that its wishes are carried out, that government is conducted honestly and faithfully, and that where business is not transacted efficiently there is a fair chance that notice will be taken. . . . Active select committees, criticizing and appraising the conduct of public business, have a powerful effect at once deterrent and stimulating, and they go as far as it is possible to go under our present system of government to enable the House of Commons to see that it gets twenty shillings' worth of goods for every pound it spends.[5]

Like our own Committee on Government Operations, the Accounts Committee is effective largely because it has at its disposal the reports and investigations of the Comptroller and Auditor General. Also like our Government Operations Committee, the Accounts Committee is not concerned with financial policy (which is reserved for our Appropriations Committee), but rather with insuring that government expenditure conforms with the orders of the House of Commons and that public business is conducted faithfully and economically.

However, unlike our present Government Operations Committee, the Accounts Committee is always chaired by the opposition. Therefore, the Accounts Committee would receive and examine the reports of the Comptroller and Auditor General and would submit such recommendations as it saw fit in connection with such reports, a function not always performed by our government operations committees with respect to reports of our Comptroller General.

With respect to the second point, Dr. Galloway asserts:

As it works in the English Parliament, question-time has several beneficial results. It keeps the ministry alert to the temper of the Commons and keeps the civil service on its toes. It provides a safety valve for the daily escape of parliamentary steam that might otherwise accumulate and explode in sensational investigations. It directs the attention of the Cabinet to inconsistent or conflicting departmental policies and programs and to instances of administrative inefficiency or private grievance.[6]

I am reluctant to suggest the creation of special investigating committees and would leave the performance of the investigative function of Congress to its standing committees. I believe that H.R. 9252, without the need for any additional specific language, provides for the effective devices just discussed: (1) more significant use of the reports of the Comptroller General and, (2) public discussion of government policy and administration, thereby eliminating executive secrecy.

I also favor codes of fair conduct voluntarily adopted by congressional committees and codes of fair play mandatory upon all congressional investigating groups by statute or standing order.

One must be realistic about the current chances for adoption of any one or more of the many proposals for congressional reform including: "resident agents for Congress," "joint committee on legislative-executive relations," "automated information systems," use of "congressional specialists," "institutional devices for improved congressional intelligence," establishment of "oversight calendars" pertaining to oversight of the Administration, and many other fine recommendations.

And what I propose in H.R. 9252 is a long, long way from ever getting a favorable vote with the present complexion of the Congress.

Hearings before the Joint Committee on the Organization of Congress were held in 1945, and many alarms for reform sounded at that time are still ringing over 20 years later. Dr. W. Y. Elliott, professor of Political Science at Harvard, then Vice Chairman of the War Production Board, testified on June 26 of that year that there had been some improvement over the early days of President Franklin Roosevelt's first administration, but "there is still in my judgment need for the closest legislative scrutiny of the actions taken by the executive and administrative agencies of the Government."

Dr. Elliott pointed out that the operation of committees through the service of hearings is a method of getting *ex post facto* accountability of the administrative agencies—a problem that is still with us today. Reorganization of the committees on government operations, as I have outlined, will, by its nature, prevent errors at the formative stages, both of legislation and of administrative policy.

Dr. Elliott reminded the Committee

> that legislative and representative government is on trial the world over as to its ability to survive in a period when crises are recurrent and when often the very safety of the Nation or its economic stability may be involved as much by delay as by ill-considered decisions.

He also emphasized:

> The Committee on Appropriations of the House reviews the budget of every part of the Government. But it cannot in the nature of things do more than express the views of the committee as to the functions being performed. The power of the purse is always an ultimate power in the legislative body and a very useful one.[7]

The fundamental purpose of H.R. 9252 is to assure that funds are being expended by the administrative agencies in accordance with law and that waste and misfeasance will not go undetected. With the swing of power away from the Congress to the executive, the vast authorization of administrative powers by the Congress to the executive, the huge growth of the executive, and the great enlargement of the policy and legislative proposing functions of the executive, the need for thorough and persistent oversight by the Congress of administrative activities is heightened. The interest of good government demands determined, persistent, and independent examination into and evaluation of the manner in which the executive branch is carrying out the legislative mandates under which it operates. The function of critically analyzing executive use of legislative authority and the transactions which flow therefrom is one of the most important responsibilities the legislative branch must fulfill. Fulfillment of this responsibility is essential to an informed citizenry, the very touchstone of our democratic processes. With the majority party in Congress the same as the party of the President, thereby giving rise, under present procedures, to each committee being chaired by a member of the President's party and having a majority of its members of the same political party, it is only realistic to recognize that a climate exists in which the important oversight function of the Congress is subject to political pressures inimical to the necessity for full disclosure and critical scrutiny of executive actions.

My bill proposes to assure more aggressive inquiry by the Congress into executive actions through removing the political compatibility between membership of the key oversight committees of both houses and the executive. I believe the proposals contained in the bill—that the chairmanship and majority membership of the House and Senate committees on Government Operations be comprised of Members of a major political party other than that of the President—would provide the most direct and efficient way to assure that inappropriate political considerations will not obtrude upon the oversight function.

I realize that the matter of how any committee of the Senate and House is to be organized is one peculiarly within the provisions of each particular Congress to resolve unless a constitutional amendment is enacted. I am also well aware of the fact that the problems which we are attempting to overcome are ones which are rooted in the political processes of our governmental structure.

Therefore, I think it is important to point out that the various proposals for congressional reform are not the only means available for minimizing the degree to which the oversight functions of the Congress are subject to political persuasions.

It is in the very interest of obtaining the independent examination and evaluation of executive activities, which are essential to the proper functioning of our governmental processes, that the Congress in 1921 established the General Accounting Office. The General Accounting Office was created as an independent agency in the legislative branch and is headed by the Comptroller General of the United States under a 15-year appointment. The Comptroller General is not subject to removal except for cause and he may not be reappointed for a second term. The office functions as an agent of the Congress. As an arm of the Congress, one of the main functions of the General Accounting Office is in the area of great concern which led me to introduce my bill—to assure the conduct of administrative agency programs in accordance with law and to detect waste and misfeasance where they occur. In executing this important function the General Accounting Office has consistently been guided by the principal that its effectiveness depends upon a reputation for independence of action and objectivity of view. Not only has it remained completely free from political influence, but I believe that it is constantly alert to the dangers of being placed in a position where its actions and decisions could be construed as being motivated by political considerations.

There is no need to detail the extent to which the General Accounting Office is responsive to the undertaking of examinations and investigations at the request of the Congress, its committees and its individual members. Nor is it necessary to detail the valuable work undertaken by that office upon its own initiative in carrying out its statutory responsibilities. A cursory review of the annual reports of the Comptroller General and the direct contacts members of both houses have had with the office would make obvious the fact that the General Accounting Office is a valuable tool toward accomplishment of the objectives my bill is designed to attain. For example, during the 88th Congress, the Comptroller General of the United States submitted a total of 668 audit reports and other communications to the Congress on fiscal and related operations of the Government. During the 1st Session of the 89th Congress there were 75 different references in the *Congressional Record* relating to use by minority members of General Accounting Office reports and recommendations. Hearings conducted by the various congressional committees are replete with references to findings of the General Accounting Office.

Reports of the General Accounting Office are available for whatever use the minority will make of them. These reports and responses to inquiries from Members of the Congress contain objective views with respect to the issues covered therein and recommendations for corrective actions indicated. If the minority concludes that the subject of a General Accounting Office report or any other subject indicates a need for further investigation, within the purview of that Office as a nonpartisan, nonpolitical agency of the Congress, it is free to bring that matter to the attention of the Comptroller General with a request that he furnish advice on his findings.

A heightened appreciation by all the minority Members of the valuable assistance available to them through the services of the General Accounting Office, together with an increased utilization of those services to help bring to light matters relating to Government operations and expenditures, might go a long way toward obviating any immediate need for committee membership realignments as put forth in my bill.

However, in the final analysis, I believe that a reasonable man would agree that it is a fact that the substance of our desires cannot, in reality, be completely achieved through greater minority use of the General Accounting Office. It would not appear, particularly from some of the examples to which I have referred, that the assistance the Government Accounting Office could render in such situations would be sufficient to accomplish our purposes.

The efforts of the General Accounting Office are no substitute for investigation by congressional committees. The General Accounting Office has no power of subpoena: it is not organized and does not operate in the context of conducting hearings for the taking of testimony regarding factual matters which might be in dispute. To say that the efforts of the General Accounting Office are not a substitute for H.R. 9252 is not to say, of course, that the General Accounting Office cannot be of considerable use to minority Members of a committee who desire to obtain information.

Obviously, no need would exist for H.R. 9252 if one or both houses were controlled by the major party other than the President's. This is probably the best argument for the enactment of H.R. 9252 and the most realistic as far as presenting this to the Congress for a vote.

Since 1858 there have been 16 instances of one or both house of Congress controlled by the President's opposition party:

Congress	President
86th	R—Eisenhower
85th	R—Eisenhower
84th	R—Eisenhower
80th	D—Truman
72nd	R—Hoover
66th	D—Wilson
62nd	R—Taft
54th	D—Cleveland
52nd	R—B. Harrison
50th	D—Cleveland
49th	D—Cleveland
48th	R—Arthur
46th	R—Hayes
45th	R—Hayes
44th	R—Grant
36th	D—Buchanan

The effect of opposition control of one or both houses goes far beyond the provisions in H.R. 9252 and surely the nation has been the better for the checks and balances in our history. In fact, notwithstanding the statements by some political scientists that the magisterial and doctrinaire years between the 72nd and 80th Congresses did irreparable harm to our system of government, any one or all 16 instances cited above could very well have saved this nation from executive dictatorship. Some form of opposition control should not be left to chance.

As Lord Acton said, "Power tends to corrupt; absolute power corrupts absolutely." We pointed out in the beginning that a President whose party controls both houses of the Congress has, in some respects, more power than that of the present Soviet political leadership. Caesar took in hand the army, the empire, and the opposition. "All is Caesar's"; there was no opportunity for what we would call legislative oversight. Thus, the birth of executive dictatorship was the beginning of the decline and fall of the Roman Empire.

Our three-branch system of government has helped to prevent a dictatorship from arising in our nation. The deterrent to dictatorship would be strengthened by the existence and operation, on a regular basis within the legislative branch, of minority control of the investigations and reports of the powerful committees on government operations.

REFERENCES

1. The word "minority" will refer to the major minority party when both Houses of Congress are controlled by the same major party as that of the President, unless otherwise indicated.

2. A search through Hinds' and Cannon's *Precedents of the House of Representatives*, as well as Haynes' volumes on the U.S. Senate, and other volumes on Congress, including *Congressional Committees*, L. G. McConachie (1898); *The Jeffersonians*, Leonard White (1954); *Government by Investigation*, Alan Barth (1955); *Congressional Investigating Committees*, Marshall E. Dimock (1929); *Congressional Control of Administration*, Joseph P. Harris (1964); *The History of Legislative Methods in the Period Before 1825*, Ralph V. Harlow (1917); *The American Senate*, Lindsay Rogers (1926); *History of the House of Representatives*, George B. Galloway (1961); *Forge of Democracy*, Neil MacNeil (1963); *Party Government in the House of Representatives*, Paul D. Hasbrouck (1927); *Congressional Investigations*, Ernest J. Eberling (1928); *The Investigative Function of Congress*, George B. Galloway, 21 American Political Science Review, 47 (1927); *Legislative Procedure*, Robert Luce (1922); The United States Senate, 1787–1801, Senate Document 64, 87th Congress, 1st Session, uncovered no instances of the adoption of a bill such as H. R. 9252. All resolutions providing for investigations by standing or select committees that are produced in Hinds's and Cannon's Precedents merely provide for committees of a specified number, and in a rare instance, during the 1920's, a specification that the select Senate committee be composed of three members of the majority (Republicans) including one "progressive" Republican and two members of the minority (Democrats). Cannon's, *Precedents of the House of Representatives*, vol. VI, par. 364.

    The general rule, particularly over the last hundred years, seems to have been committee representation in accordance with party strength in both Houses. *Ibid*, vol. VIII, pars. 2184, 2187, 2188. Hinds' *Precedents of the House of Representatives*, vol. IV, pars. 4467, 4477, 4478, 4551.

3. 90 *Congressional Record*, A3454–A3458.

4. Note the comment by George B. Galloway in *History of the House of Representatives* (p. 185): "Today 'legislative oversight' has become a, if not the, principal activity of the standing committees of both Houses."

5. *Congress and Parliament* by Dr. George B. Galloway, National Planning Association, November 1955, p. 82.

6. *Ibid*, p. 74.

7. *Organization of Congress;* hearings before the Joint Committee on the Organization of Congress; 79th Congress, First Session; pursuant to H. Con. Res. 18; Part 4, June 26, 1945; U.S. Government Printing Office; Lib. of Cong. JK 1061 .A48 1945; pp. 951–973.

PART 3
Toward More Efficiency
and a Better Image

WILLIAM L. SPRINGER, M.C.
22nd District, Illinois

CONGRESSIONAL PAGES:
THEIR WORK AND SCHOOLING

by William L. Springer, M.C.*

Imagine in this year of 1966 an employer who—

Hires 14- and 15-year-old boys.

Brings them from distant homes to a big city.

Limits their schooling to three hours a day.

Makes them work a minimum of eight, and occasionally 12 or even 14 hours a day.

And leaves them unsupervised the rest of the time, free to sleep where they can find a room, eat what they please, and study whenever they can find the time; free also, should they desire, to roam a crime-infested metropolis.

Impossible, you say, in this age of child labor laws? Perhaps in the 19th century London that Charles Dickens wrote about, but not in modern Washington?

Unfortunately, it is not at all impossible when the employer is the Congress of the United States and the employees are pages of the Senate and House of Representatives.

It's true that the average congressional page bears scant resemblance to Dickens's Oliver Twist. Oliver was very poor. By comparison our pages are well-heeled members of the affluent society. Beginning pages are paid at the annual rate of $4,766, are stepped up to $5,077 after one year, and to $5,232 after two years. Not bad for teen-agers, particularly when it is considered that 34.1 million Americans are estimated to live in families with poverty-level incomes—less than $3,100 a year for a family of four.

* Mr. Springer is ranking minority Member of the House Committee on Interstate and Foreign Commerce and second ranking minority Member of the District of Columbia Committee. He was first elected to Congress in 1950 and represents the 22nd District of Illinois.

Nevertheless, despite its generosity as a paymaster, Congress is a hard taskmaster. It makes demands on these boys that federal law and the laws of most states wouldn't countenance from a private employer.

Most pages work from 10 A.M. to 5 P.M. Monday through Friday and from 9 A.M. until noon on Saturday. When a session lasts until past 5 o'clock, the pages stay until the House adjourns. The House Select Committee on the Education and Welfare of Congressional Pages, created by the 88th Congress, found that pages average 40 or more hours of work a week.[1] Senate pages work longer hours than House pages because of the more numerous night sessions.

The pages' school day beings at 6:30 A.M. and for most of them is over at 9:45. Most pages have classes in four subjects. A few have a fifth classroom period which lasts until 10:30. Classes are held in makeshift quarters on the third floor of the Library of Congress. There is a 15-minute break at 8 o'clock each morning, presumably for breakfast. It has been noted, however, that for many of the boys it is more a coke-and-candy break than anything else.

The Federal Fair Labor Standards Act prohibits the employment of 14- and 15-year-old children for more than three hours on a school day, for more than 18 hours during any school week, and for night work after 7 P.M.

These limitations on child labor imposed on employers engaged in interstate commerce do not apply to Congress. But surely Congress has a moral obligation to maintain standards at least as high as those it prescribed for private industry almost 30 years ago.

As part of its study, the Select Committee put this question to the U.S. Department of Labor's Bureau of Labor Standards: In how many states would it be legal for boys of 14 and 15 to go to school in the morning, and then work eight hours a day in general employment? The Bureau's reply is worth printing here in full:

In the first place, this could not be done because of the limitation set for hours in school plus hours of work in:

Alabama	Illinois	New York
Alaska	Kentucky	North Carolina
California	Louisiana	Ohio
Colorado	Maine	Pennsylvania
Florida	Maryland	Puerto Rico
Georgia	Michigan	Tennessee
Hawaii	New Jersey	Utah
		Washington

After eliminating these 21 States and Puerto Rico there is another group of States that prohibits nightwork of children under 16 after 7 P.M. (sometimes after 6 P.M.). Normally, if a boy went to school in the morning, he would hardly be able to start work before 12 o'clock—more probably 1 o'clock. If he started at 12 or later, he could not work in any of these additional States:

Arizona	Missouri (except on nights
Arkansas	preceding school days)
Delaware	New Hampshire
District of Columbia	New Mexico
Indiana	North Dakota
Iowa	Oklahoma
Kansas	Oregon (except on special permit)
Massachusetts	Rhode Island
Minnesota	Vermont
Mississippi	Virginia
	Wyoming

In 4 States, the boys could do this if they started at 12 o'clock and worked straight through, but they would not be permitted to work beyond 8 o'clock—Nebraska, South Carolina, West Virginia, and Wisconsin (9 P.M. on nights preceding nonschool days).

Connecticut sets a minimum age of 16 for practically all employment and so has been omitted from consideration as to nightwork.

This leaves 5 States in which boys of 14 and 15 could legally work 8 hours in the afternoon and evening. These States set a nightwork limitation of 9 or 10 P.M. or have no nightwork limitation:

Idaho	Nevada
Montana	South Dakota
	Texas

Since a half day of school would normally run till at least 11:30 A.M., we are not going into the possibility of boys getting out of school at 10:30 A.M. or earlier. In fact, the information given above is predicated on the assumption that first of all the States would allow boys of 14 and 15 to go to school only half days. This would probably not be permitted in any State.[2]

Thus, it is doubtful that a private employer could get by in any State with the kind of work-study program which has been required of our 14- and 15-year-old pages.

As far as House pages are concerned, the powers that be evidently have seen the light. They have restricted page appointments, effective January, 1966, to 11th and 12th grade students. To be eligible for an appointment a boy must have at least a "C" average. He also must maintain a "C" or better average while attending the Page School. Although there still is no minimum age, a boy usually will be 16 by the time he reaches the 11th grade.

While the new rules are pretty much in line with the Select Committee's recommendations, it must be emphasized that they apply only to House employees. Ninth and 10th graders still were on the job in the Senate at the beginning of the 89th Congress' second session on January 10, 1966, and even in the House the bar against lower grade youngsters was relaxed to allow Congressmen to fulfill commitments made before the rule was announced.

The Senate traditionally has shown a preference for younger boys, having a maximum age for pages of 17, while there is no age maximum in the House. Of the 98 boys who attended the Capitol Page School during the 1963–64 school year, 12 were 14 years old, 28 were 15, 36 were 16, 16 were 17 and six were 18. Sixteen of the boys were in the ninth grade, 31 in the 10th, 29 in the 11th and 22 in the 12th.[3]

Although the action taken by the House Administration Committee and the Democratic Patronage Committee in restricting page appointments to upper classmen and insisting that they meet satisfactory scholastic standards are important steps in the right direction, they fall considerably short of meeting some of the Select Committee's most telling objections to the present system.

The Select Committee made two alternative proposals. One was based on retention of high school pages, the other on a program for college students. If we are to continue employing high-school-age youngsters, the Select Committee said they should be selected on a nondiscriminatory basis without regard to race, religion, or sex; that no page may be appointed for longer than one calendar year or for a shorter time than one semester, and that consideration be given to increasing the number of pages so that each page could be given a longer classroom schedule and a shorter work assignment.

While there is no indication of any religious discrimination in the selection of pages, questions have been raised in the matters of race and sex. During the Select Committee's hearings, one of the Republican members, Congressman William S. Broomfield of Michigan, noted that no Negro had ever been employed as a page in either the House or Senate. "Is there any restriction to prohibit Negroes from serving as Capitol pages in the Congress?" he asked the Doorkeeper of the House of Representatives, William M. Miller, under whose supervision the House pages work.

"To the best of my knowledge, no sir, but none has been sent to our office," Mr. Miller replied.

I find it exceedingly strange that throughout all the years that the majority party has been in power in both Houses of Congress, years that have seen the enactment of epochal civil rights legislation supported by both parties, it was not until 1965 that the first Negro page was appointed. Appropriately, he came from Abraham Lincoln's home town, Springfield, Illinois, and was sponsored by Congressman Paul Findley, a Republican.

It should be emphasized here that the appointment of pages and other House employees is the prerogative of the majority party, which currently allows the minority to select six of the 50 pages serving the House. The six Republican pages are assigned to telephone duty in the GOP cloakroom. This duty involves answering congressional office calls for information about Floor activities, also relaying and taking of messages for House members. It is considered responsible work requiring more mature judgment than the errand-running and other chores given most pages. Telephone duty is assigned only to 16- or 17-year-old boys, so as a practical matter the Republican pages in recent years have all been in that age group. Except for the telephone pages, all other pages assigned to the Republican side of the House floor are selected by Democrats. If the fairer method of apportioning pages in ratio to a party's relative strength were used, Republicans would be entitled to name 16 or 17 of the pages serving the present House.

Another inconsistency between congressional preaching and congressional practice is the limitation of page appointments to youths of the male sex. Our passage of the Civil Rights Act of 1964, strictly forbidding discriminatory hiring practices based on sex, presaged a feminine invasion of many a hitherto male employment preserve. But not the page corps. As a father of three daughters, I can testify that young ladies are perfectly capable of running errands, taking telephone messages, and performing the various other activities expected of pages. Enrollment of girls in the Page School would cause no complications, the principal, Mr. Henry De Keyser, told the Select Committee. "In fact," he added, "I'm sure some of the boys would be delighted." The new regulations regarding the appointment of pages do not mention sex. However, one rule reads: "All pages are required to wear a dark blue suit (long trousers), white shirt, black tie, black socks and black shoes." That doesn't sound as if the hiring of any girls is contemplated.

For the first time the new regulations prescribe a minimum period for which a page may be appointed—30 days. We understand that some objections have been made to even this. It appears that some Congressmen have been in the habit of making appointments for as little as one week. Of the 98 boys enrolled in the Capitol Page School in 1963–64, 27 were there for less than a semester, 19 of whom served for 30 days.

"We have had, on the whole, unsatisfactory work at school from these 30-day pages," Principal De Keyser told the Committee. "Some of them . . . we never see. They do not bother to register at all. Most of them," he added, "look on this month's appointment as a glorified vacation." Since 30 days is hardly enough time for a boy to learn his way around the Capitol, the short-term pages also are of little use to their employers. Their supervisors testified that it takes most boys 90 to 120 days to adjust to the system.

I also regret that the new rules disregard the Select Committee's recommendation against employing any page for more than a year. During my 15 years in Congress I have become acquainted with many pages. The vast majority are boys of excellent character and habits. I believe, however, that the boy who tries to make a career out of being a page is making a mistake. Some career pages stay around long enough to learn too many angles. Bobby Baker served the Senate continuously from his arrival in 1942 as a 14-year-old page from Pickens, South Carolina, until his resignation 21 years later from his $19,612 a year post as secretary of the Senate Majority and chief figure in what is probably history's worst "conflict of interest" case involving a congressional employee.

The serious public implications of Baker's use of his privileged position to build a personal fortune overshadow the personal tragedy. That Baker betrayed the Senate's trust can hardly be questioned. But we must be concerned also with the extent to which the congressional page system contributed to Bobby Baker's delinquency.

In criticizing the present page system I intend no reflection on Principal De Keyser and his capable staff. Probably no other high school in Washington has as well qualified teachers as the Capitol Page School. The principal holds a doctorate in education from George Washington University, and all seven instructors have master's degrees. Within the limitations of the page system they do an excellent job. The school's small classes are another plus for students bright enough and self-disciplined enough to master the tough college preparatory course despite the distractions of a page's life. Graduates of the school have won national merit scholarships and have gone on to win scholastic honors in some of the nation's leading universities. But not all pages should be taking a college preparatory course. Educational authorities have pointed out that such a curriculum indicates the need for some selectivity of students as to intellectual capacity and attainment.[4] The Page School faculty has no control over the admission of students but must accept anyone with a page appointment. Dr. De Keyser testified that 20 per cent of the students did not meet the academic standards of the school.

Since 1947 the Page School has been operated by the District of Columbia Board of Education although no regular public school funds are used. Congress provides money for the Page School as part of the annual appropriation for the Legislative Branch. The budget for the 1965–66 school year was $85,712. Assuming a normal enrollment at any one time of 75–80 students, this amounts to more than $1,000 per student compared with a $700 per pupil expenditure in District of Columbia high schools.[5]

For many years before the D.C. school board took charge a private school for pages was conducted in the basement of the old Senate Office Building. The boys paid tuition fees. Pages have been employed as far back as the first Congress in 1789. They were called runners then. During the 27th Congress (1841–43) a Select Committee was appointed to ascertain whether the House was employing more boys "than the public good required." The problem then, according to the Committee's report, was that a Congressman whose sympathies were aroused by a destitute orphan would importune the Doorkeeper to put him on the payroll. The Committee recommended a definite limit on the number of pages. As a result of its inquiry the number was reduced from 12 to 8 and the pages' pay was raised from $1.50 to $2 a day.[6]

I have set down here my thoughts about the pages' long working hours, their short classroom schedules, and the pattern of discrimination that surrounds the present system. I am convinced that many, probably a majority, of my colleagues share most of these views. About another problem there is a unanimity of concern but a diversity of proposed solutions. It has been best defined by an evaluation committee of the Middle Atlantic States Association of Colleges and Secondary Schools in reporting on a study of the Capitol Page School in March, 1964. The committee's report contained this statement:

> It seems inconceivable to the members of this committee, all but one of whom are parents, that a 14- or 15-year-old boy should be turned loose in a large metropolis to find his own room, make his own arrangements for eating well-balanced and nourishing meals, engage in healthy and moral activities, and watch over his own physical and moral well-being. It is one thing for a page to live at home or in the home of his sponsor, where he can be a part of normal family living so necessary at this stage of growth. It is something else again to give these youngsters the great opportunity to be of direct service to their Government and at the same time deprive them of the basic protections to which they are entitled at this stage of their development. The Washington of today is a different city from that of 20 years ago.

To meet this problem, it has been proposed that Congress build a combination school and residence for pages on Capitol Hill. In the 88th Congress, committees of both the House and Senate reported bills authorizing up to $1½ million for such a purpose. That figure was based on estimates made a few years ago. The actual construction cost now undoubtedly would be much higher. If provision is made for coeducational facilities, the construction expense and the salaries of those who would be needed to supervise the pages would boost the cost still more. And we would still have the problem of high school students working longer hours than children of that age should work.

Instead, I strongly favor replacing our high-school-age pages with college students. I hope that this is one of the reforms that the Joint Committee on the Organization of the Congress will recommend this year.

At the same time, every taint of discrimination—whether based on sex, race, or politics—should be removed from the program. Selection of pages should be made by a nonpartisan committee of educators through a national competitive examination.

Such a program would have these advantages over the present system:

1. Congress no longer would be in a position of condoning its own use of child labor while condemning it for everyone else.
2. Mature college students would not require after-hours supervision.
3. There would be no need to build a costly school and residence.
4. The experience of being a page should prove more valuable to college students, particularly those majoring in government.
5. Meritorious students from all parts of the country can be helped to finance their college costs.

Congress already hires many college students in such capacities as elevator operators, policemen, folding room employees, and staff aides to individual Members and committees. They generally work set hours and sign up at Washington area colleges for day or night classes as their work schedules allow.

Converting our present page system into one involving college students does, of course, present some problems because of the long and uncertain working hours and early morning classes of our high-school pages. But these problems are not insuperable. One possible solution is to appoint more pages so that each will have a shorter work assignment. Another possibility is to limit page service to one year, which the student could consider in the nature of a sabbatical leave from classroom routine. He would be free to take any courses he could fit into his work schedule. But the emphasis would be on making his service to Congress in itself a valuable part of his educational experience. Following his page sabbatical he would be expected to resume his college course leading to a degree. This plan would, in my judgment, particularly appeal to political science majors as well as to those preparing for careers in other fields closely related to government and politics.

I mention these ideas for planning an educational program for college-age pages merely to show that it would be possible. Undoubtedly there are many other and better programs that could be developed once the basic decision is made to replace our high-school pages with college students. I am sure Congress would receive complete cooperation from all institutions of higher learning in the Washington area as well as from political scientists throughout the country in working out a satisfactory program.

REFERENCES

1. Report of the Select Committee on the Welfare and Education of Congressional Pages. House Report No. 1945, 88th Congress, 2nd Session, p. 2.
2. Hearing before the Select Committee on the Welfare and Education of Congressional Pages, pp. 58–59. U.S. Government Printing Office, 1965.
3. *Ibid.*, p. 55. Records of the Capitol Page School show that of 73 boys enrolled on June 3, 1965, 10 were in the 9th grade, 17 in the 10th, 31 in the 11th and 15 in the 12th. No age breakdown was available.
4. Report of the Evaluation Committee of the Middle States Association of Colleges and Secondary Schools after visit to Capitol Page School March 17–18, 1964.
5. The estimated per pupil operating cost of the Washington public schools in 1965–66 is $589 but this covers both elementary and high schools. The U.S. Office of Education informs me that $700 is a more realistic estimate for per student expenditures of the high schools alone.
6. House Report No. 30, 27th Congress, 2nd Session.

JOEL T. BROYHILL, M.C.
10th District, Virginia

REFORMS NEEDED IN HOUSE
PERSONNEL PROCEDURES

*by Joel T. Broyhill, M.C.**

Any honest attempt to shape a more efficient Congress must certainly include recommendations to end the cruel, costly, and to these adjectives I will add "ugly," political spoils system used in the employment of some 1,300 to 1,400 employees of the House of Representatives.

During the month of January following an election that changes the majority in the House, hundreds of competent, experienced employees of Congress are subject to immediate dismissal. I refer to the elevator operators, policemen, doorkeepers, publication distribution workers, pages, maintenance employees, and so on, who perform service functions for Congress and the public. These people are not in policy-making positions; they are not in a position to influence the welfare of either political party. They serve the majority well. They serve the minority equally well. They are primarily concerned with serving the public, with doing a good job, and earning funds for the support of their families.

The 10th Congressional District of Virginia, which I have the honor to represent, is adjacent to the District of Columbia. The Federal Government is our largest industry; approximately 80,000 of the people who reside in this district work for one of the three branches of the U.S. Government. I estimate that from one-third to one-half of the permanent and patronage employees of the House are my constituents, and because my year-round home is only eight miles from the Capitol, my congressional office in the Rayburn Building is

---

* Mr. Broyhill was first elected to Congress in 1952. He represents the 10th Congressional District of Virginia and serves on the Ways and Means and District of Columbia Committees of the House.

routinely open for business whether or not the Congress is in session. In thirteen years I have heard plenty of personnel problems.

From the standpoint of efficiency, the existence of a patronage system for the selection of non-policy employees is just nutty. Personnel management has been a standard tool of industry and business for many years. Congress itself recognized the importance of personnel management in the Executive Branch by establishing a career Civil Service for government employees. It is surely a fine piece of irony that we have created standing committees of Congress to legislate on improvement of the Civil Service in the Executive Branch while we continue to rely on an ancient system of patronage to dictate the selection of public servants within the Legislative Branch.

To the interruption of congressional activity with every change of control in the House must be added the grave injustice to the innocent, dedicated public servant who, in effect, has his head placed on the election block every two years. For example, there is on our rolls a man who has worked at his job here on the Hill for eleven years. He has a wife and seven children to support. From personal observation of his work I can certify that he is a capable, efficient employee, a genuinely courteous and able public servant. In November, 1964, his congressional sponsor was defeated. The following January the man was told by the patronage committee that unless another Member of the majority party agreed that the position could be charged to his patronage account, the employee would be separated at the end of the month. After two weeks of worry and anxious requests, the man fortunately found a new sponsor. However, if a new sponsor had not been found, the House would have lost a valuable employee with eleven years' experience and an excellent work record. Obviously, the employee would have lost a good deal more.

The tragedy of the situation is that the example cited above is commonplace. With 97½ per cent of the patronage jobs in the hands of the majority (as a small "courtesy," the patronage committee allots 32 positions to the minority party), it is obvious that 97½ per cent of these employees are in danger of losing their jobs at every congressional election. In fact, every time the majority in the House changes, hundreds of House employees are routinely separated from their jobs and most cruelly from their livelihoods. Applicants endorsed by the new majority are hired in a mad scramble, production dwindles with untrained employees, and those discharged often suffer a sustained loss of income during their search for new employment.

When I came to Congress in 1953, the majority in the House had changed to my party. Because my district is federally oriented, I received an unusually high number of applications for jobs in the House of Representatives. It was my practice to endorse all applicants who appeared to be good candidates regardless of their party affiliation. Many of them were hired. In the 1954 election, control of the House reverted to the other party, and I was quickly appraised of the fact that I was listed as the patron of 31 employees—22 in the folding room, 7 elevator operators, and 2 doorkeepers—when all of them came to me with dismissal notices the following January. Every one was fired within the month!

These were good employees. There was no bona fide reason for separating them. One I remember in particular was a law student just entering his last semester. He was so outstanding that he was given a direct commission as a first lieutenant for his military service. He then entered the general counsel's office of a federal agency and rose to the grade of GS-15. He is now successful in private practice.

Surely this is not only an outmoded method of personnel selection by a 20th-century Congress, but one which imposes severe penalties on a number of dedicated public servants and their families. Both parties are at fault; Congress and the people are the losers.

Let us examine the categories of employment in the House of Representatives. First, about 550 employees are appointed by the Patronage Committee, a function of the party holding the majority, and a committee on which no members of the minority party sit. The employees in this category work for the House as a whole and not for one political party. Their duties are completely nonpartisan in nature, and yet all of them, except for some policemen, may be fired when the majority changes. Worse, the job tenure of each individual employee in this category depends on the Member who nominated him to the Patronage Committee, which means that he is subject to dismissal in the event of the death or primary defeat of his sponsor even when party control is not changed. Obviously, it is patently impossible for him to feel that his security depends, as it properly should, upon the efficient performance of his duties. Moreover, when the hire-and-fire power of such employees rests with individual Members, it is next to impossible for the supervisors of these employees to be fully effective in *their* jobs.

The dependence of these employees upon their sponsoring Members also opens up the temptation for a Congressman to use House funds improperly to increase his staff allowance by demanding that his patronage appointee work part time, during official hours, in his congressional office. While there is no evidence to support a charge that most service employees are so abused, rumors are prevalent enough to suggest that the temptation is not always ignored.

Second, about 750 non-patronage employees work under the various political officers of the House, such as the Clerk, the Sergeant-at-Arms, the Doorkeeper, the Postmaster, and so forth. These department heads are changed when the majority changes, and new appointments and promotions are made with politics in mind. If a new majority is under pressure to place applicants, it is probable that dismissals will be made to create the needed vacancies. Again, job security is dependent upon electoral outcome.

Third, about 650 non-patronage employees work under non-political officers of the House such as the Architect of the Capitol and his Superintendent of House Office Buildings, the Coordinator of Information, the Legislative Counsel, and so on. A primitive form of merit system exists for some of these job holders, but it is limited and haphazardly applied.

Fourth, there are some 700 employees on the rolls of the standing, select, and joint committees of the House. Their tenure, in spite of the attempt of the Legislative Reorganization Act of 1946 to create a professional career staff for each of the committees, is solely dependent upon the chairman of the committee. In some cases, there is a clear division of staff between the majority and minority members of the committee, with the ranking minority member— by courtesy of the chairman—allowed to exercise discretion over hiring, firing, and promotion of minority employees. On a couple of committees, the hiring and firing of staff is done by action of the full committee without regard to political affiliation. On many committees, however, there is a disruptive turn-over whenever party control changes, and there may be such a shake-up even when the change is merely the passing of the chairmanship to the next ranking committee member of the same party.

Fifth, some 4,000 employees work in the offices of individual Congressmen.[1] Although not all Members use their full allowance for office staff, the increase of services offered by the Federal Government has caused a general enlargement of the staffs of most Members in order to handle the growing volume of "casework." The increasing impact of the Federal Government upon the daily lives of all Americans has also brought about an increase in the amount and variety of correspondence from citizens concerned about pending legislation.

The office staffs of Members of Congress must be large enough to handle these constituent problems and letters promptly, as a matter of service rightfully owed to the citizen. In light of the growing proportion of constituent services to his other responsibilities, most Congressmen are beginning to find that they have room on their staffs for only one or two employees who can be counted as either personal or political adherents. In practice, there is still a minimum of employee crossover between the political parties; most congressional staffers, whether in policy or clerical positions, are intensely loyal to their bosses, both personally and ideologically. Nor am I suggesting that loyalty to a Member's political beliefs is unimportant. However, it should be pointed out that with the increase in government services has come an increase in the proportion of a Congressman's staff that must be devoted to the expert handling of nonpolitical matters concerning the individual citizen. A growing cadre of professional "caseworkers" is the direct result of the growing federal influence over the daily lives of our citizens. A career class of employees of the House of Representatives is in the making; indeed, an increasing number of these people seek employment in other congressional offices upon the death, retirement, or defeat of their Members. They are fully capable of rendering expert assistance to another Member in handling constituent problems common to all congressional offices, and the need of incoming Members for this kind of expertise may be acute following such electoral upheavals as that of 1958, when one party lost 47 House seats.

At present no machinery exists for helping the experienced, trained staff of departing Members in their search for new jobs, or in helping freshmen Members find qualified applicants for their staffs beyond the limited activity of a Capitol Hill branch office of the U.S. Employment Service. Most of these people are professional Hill employees whose skills are to be found in handling problems common to every Congressman regardless of party affiliation.

Unfortunately, there are no set classifications or salaries for congressional office employees, which brings up a related problem in the existing set-up. A Member is free to pay an individual clerk any amount he wishes up to a basic salary of $7,500 ($20,578.39 gross), provided he does not exceed his total salary allowance. The result of this is a frustrating competition between Members to obtain the best secretaries, with the more competent of them sometimes offered higher salaries than their duties call for because some Members do not need a large staff and have excess salary allowance. Obviously, this must often mean that the best secretaries go to the Members who have the least need of them. It also means that each Member, in order to retain his best people, must pay them as much as possible, within the set limits, to prevent another Member from taking them by the offer of more money. A practical remedy for this situation, designed at once to eliminate the "bidding" which at present drives up salaries unrealistically and to give a continuing incentive to the employee, would be the establishment of specific positions with set salaries, along with the provision of a yearly experience increase. With the establishment of set standards, applicable to each office, career people could, when no promotion vacancy was available in their office, move by promotion to other offices as their skills increased and experience credits accumulated.

The Pay Rate Problem

There are 470 officials of the House of Representatives who have the authority to appoint employees and more than 2,000 rates of pay at which the salary of a new employee can be set. Some employees are paid on an hourly basis like Executive Branch wage board workers. The salaries of others must be individually fixed by law. A group of 500 to 600 employees were placed under a gross salary classification system in Public Law 88–652, effective October 13, 1964, but this is a small percentage of the total workers.

The entire pay rate jungle should be straightened out, of course, but particularly in need of modernization is the method by which salaries are determined for employees in the individual congressional offices. The "basic rate" method of determining clerk hire, established two decades ago, is in my judgment one of the most indefensible practices in the House of Representatives. The system was designed for the sole purpose of misrepresenting the true salaries received by staff employees of Members of Congress. Obviously, it looks much better in the papers back home to list an assistant's salary as "$7,500 base" rather than the $20,578.39 gross he actually gets! And any attempt to justify this misrepresentation on some other ground has got to fail. As Lincoln reasoned in the following story: "If you call a tail a leg, how many legs has a dog? Five? No, calling a tail a leg don't *make* it a leg." The practice is reprehensible, and Members worried about the bad public image of today's Congress would do well to begin the necessary housecleaning by abolishing the "basic rate" clerk hire system.

As seen below, the "basic rate" system is not only unethical; it is ridiculous. Since the system was established twenty years ago, subsequent cost of living and other increases have accumulated no fewer than twelve computations necessary to arrive at gross salary figures. If you don't have an up-to-date conversion chart handy, these are the steps through which you must go:

One:	20 per cent increase of first $1,200 10 per cent additional from $1,200 to $4,600 5 per cent further additional from $4,600 to $7,000
Two:	Add 14 per cent or a flat $250, whichever is the greater, but this increase must not exceed 25 per cent
Three:	Add 10 per cent
Four:	Add $330
Five:	Add 5 per cent
Six:	Add 10 per cent, but not more than $800 nor less than $300 a year
Seven:	Add 7½ per cent
Eight:	Add 10 per cent
Nine:	Add 7½ per cent
Ten:	Add 7 per cent
Eleven:	Add an amount equal to 3½ per centum of the gross rate of compensation (basic compensation plus additional compensation authorized by law) in effect immediately prior to the effective date of this section plus 1 per centum of such gross rate for each whole multiple, or part of a multiple, of $500 basic compensation.
Twelve:	Add 3.6 per cent[2]
Thirteen:	Add 2.9 per cent. (July 1, 1966.)

On January 12, 1966, I introduced H.R. 12004 (see Appendix), which would convert House Members' clerk hire and employee compensation paid therefrom to single per annum rates. In my view, a position unanimously endorsed by our Task Force on Congressional Reform, the public has a right to know exactly what salaries are being paid to the clerk hired by their Representatives. After all, let us remember that the taxpayers are footing the bill!

Conclusion

In addition to abolishing the "basic rate" pay system, I would recommend the following steps toward improving personnel procedures in the U.S. House of Representatives:

First, for House employees in the first four categories, we should eliminate entirely the political spoils system and establish in its place a full merit system for all except those in policy-level positions. Work records should be the sole basis for appointments, promotions, and dismissals.

Second, gross annual salaries and hourly rates should be the only two pay scales. Annual salaries might be in multiples of $60 to simplify bookkeeping procedures and radically reduce the number of different rates for which withholding and fringe benefit costs must be computed. In-grade pay increases could be established to compensate for additional skill brought by experience and training. This would encourage competent employees to remain when promotion opportunities are scarce, thus reducing the cost of training new employees.

Third, these matters should be supervised and coordinated by a central personnel office. Such an office could also assist freshmen Members in arranging interviews with prospective employees, obtaining references, furnishing shorthand, typing, and other tests, etc. A central personnel office should also help relocate employees who lose their positions through no fault of their own and arrange for their consideration in appropriate promotion opportunities.

Fourth, a task force under the supervision of the central personnel office should study each department in depth. Jobs should be classified in as many instances as possible (certainly, some elasticity in the organization of a Congressman's staff is not only desirable but necessary, in view of the differences in constituencies, committee assignments of Members, etc.), salaries set in line with private industry rates, and every possible non-political job brought under the merit system.

As a result of the patronage system, the maze of pay scales in the House, special resolutions authorizing additional committee employees, and month-to-month changes in the congressional offices, accurate figures in terms of numbers and categories of employees and funds expended are hard to come by. This fact alone militates for reform of personnel procedures in the U.S. House of Representatives.

A rough indication of the size of the problem, however, may be seen in the estimated appropriations as contained in testimony by the Clerk of the House for fiscal year 1966:[3]

Salaries, Officers, and employees of the House[4]	$ 9,880,625.00
Clerk hire allowance[5]	30,500,000.00
Office of the Coordinator of Information, salaries[6]	136,250.00
Joint Committee on Internal Revenue Taxation, staff[6]	390,000.00
	$40,906,875.00

Surely a payroll exceeding $40 million of the taxpayers' money should be justified in terms of efficiency and modern personnel procedures.

References

1. H. R. 855, which passed the House on May 26, 1966, provides for an increase in the basic clerk hire allowance of $7,000 per annum and authority for one additional clerk for each Member.
2. Records of the Disbursing Office, Clerk of the House of Representatives.
3. See Legislative Branch Appropriations for 1966, Hearings before a Subcommittee of the Committee on Appropriations, House of Representatives, 89th Congress, 1st Session.
4. Includes Office of the Chaplain ($15,000), Office of the Clerk of the House ($1,643,680), committee employees, *not* including investigative and other personnel than authorized staff for full committee (222 positions, total $3,800,000), Office of the Sergeant-at-Arms ($1,065,000), Office of the Doorkeeper ($1,620,-000), special and minority employees, offices of the majority and minority floor leaders, whips, and majority and minority caucus rooms ($402,230), and office of attending physician ($14,135), Office of the Postmaster ($512,000), Official Reporters of Debates and committee reporters ($511,720), and Office of the Legislative Counsel ($296,860). Total = $9,880,625.
5. Total estimate, Members and Resident Commissioner of Puerto Rico.
6. Included in the "Contingent Expenses of the House."

JOHN J. RHODES, M.C.
1st District Arizona

FLOOR PROCEDURE IN THE HOUSE OF REPRESENTATIVES

*by John J. Rhodes, M.C.**

All of the work of the House of Representatives points toward the time when the Membership meets on the Floor of the House for the purpose of enacting legislation. The work of the committees, the research and office work of the Members, the multifarious collateral efforts expended by employees of the House, all funnel toward that climax or series of climaxes which culminate in the enactment of legislation.

The procedures of the House should be aimed at (1) providing a full explanation and complete disclosure as to the provisions of a bill and the effect of its enactment on the government and the nation; (2) providing an orderly means whereby the majority works its will concerning legislation, *but also* (3) providing a means whereby the minority has ample opportunity to point out defects in a bill and to try to insert appropriate amendments, and (4) accomplishing all of this within a reasonable length of time.

Evolution of House Rules

In his Preface to Jefferson's *Manual and Rules of the House of Representatives*, 89th Congress, House Parliamentarian Lewis Deschler explains:

The parliamentary practice of the House of Representatives emanates from four sources: First, the Constitution of the United States; second, from Jefferson's *Manual;* third, from the rules adopted by the House itself from the beginning of its existence; and fourth, from the decisions of the Speaker of the House and from decisions of the Chairmen of the Committee of the Whole.

* Mr. Rhodes represents the 1st Congressional District of Arizona. He was first elected to Congress in 1952 and serves on the House Appropriations Committee. Mr. Rhodes has held a number of party leadership positions and is the present Chairman of the House Republican Policy Committee.

On April 13, 1789, the first House of Representatives adopted a short code of ten rules to govern the conduct of its business. Four of these rules, dealing with the duties of the Speaker, decorum and debate, bill procedure, and Committees of the Whole House, had been reported six days earlier by a select committee of eleven Members. The six additional rules related to committee service, leaves of absence, and the appointment of a standing Committee of Elections.

Thereafter, for nearly three-quarters of a century, the House gradually expanded the body of its rules by a process of accretion during each session of Congress.

In 1860, the House enacted the first sweeping revision of its rules, which by this date had grown to more than 150 in number. Most of the changes were technical in nature, combining subject matter for a reduction in the number, although some important restrictions were effected with respect to dilatory tactics.

By 1879, the number of rules had again increased, to 169. A committee of parliamentarians was appointed to sit during recess to review the matter and report a simplified code back to the House. In 1880, the House adopted a new code of 44 rules.

The new rules were hailed as a brilliant achievement in bringing order out of confusion, but various dilatory tactics remained. When Thomas Brackett Reed ascended the Speaker's chair in the 51st Congress, a determined minority could still frustrate the will of the majority by such devices as the "disappearing quorum," so called because Members, though actually present on the Floor, could simply refuse to vote.

In Reed's view, writes George Galloway, eminent historian of the House, "the business of an organism was to function, and the duty of a legislature was to legislate."[1] On January 29, 1890, a contested election case was brought to the Floor. The vote on consideration of the question was recorded as 161 in favor, 2 opposed, and 165 not voting. Quite obviously, this was less than a quorum, and the minority immediately engaged in its customary maneuver of objecting to the absence of a quorum. As described by Galloway:

> But when the objection of "no quorum" was raised, the Speaker directed the Clerk to record the names of those present and refusing to vote, and then he declared a quorum present and consideration of the election case in order. Immediately the House was in an uproar. Members poured into the aisles and denounced the Speaker as a "tyrant" and a "czar." The commotion continued for several hours amid scenes of unprecedented disorder. . . .[2]

But "Czar" Reed held firm, citing the Constitution, the practice of the English House of Commons, and the rules and precedents of the House of Representatives in support of his ruling. The following day he repeated the decision and this time declared that the Chair would henceforth ignore any motions and appeals clearly designed to force delay. Thus, within 24 hours, two of the most far-reaching decisions ever made from the Chair "finally doomed the dilatory tactics of a minority in the House to defeat."[3] Reed's rulings constituted a benchmark.

Shortly after the turn of the century, Rep. Joe Cannon of Illinois had assumed the Chair. Under the "Reed Rules" the Speaker's power had become second only to that of the nation's President; under Joe Cannon, that power became oppressive. The Speaker had almost unlimited discretion over which matters would come before the House. The Speaker sat as Chairman of the Committee on Rules, and he appointed the other standing committees of the House and designated their chairmen. The momentum of a growing discontent lay just under the surface; on March 16, 1910, it broke out in open rebellion.

Led by insurgent George Norris of Nebraska, a coalition of disgruntled Republicans and disaffected Democrats engineered a succession of moves that (1) enlarged the Rules Committee from 5 to 10 Members and prohibited the Speaker from sitting as a member thereon; (2) stripped the Speaker of his authority to appoint the other standing committees and their chairmen, and (3) restricted his power of recognition from the Chair. The Speaker was still the most important man in the House, but his role had been diminished. An era had ended.

Some further developments took place between 1910 and 1946, and the Legislative Reorganization Act of 1946 made sweeping changes in the Rules of the House with respect to the number, jurisdictions, and procedures of the standing committees. It is not my purpose here to provide a complete chronicle; I have merely pointed to some of the benchmarks in the evolution of present-day parliamentary procedure in the House of Representatives.

The Missing Link

While Deschler has called the Rules of the House

perhaps the most finely adjusted, scientifically balanced, and highly technical rules of any pariamentary body in the world,[4]

the reader should be aware of a very important missing link in the evolution: to wit, since 1936, there has been no printed addition to the monumental work of Asher Hinds and Clarence Cannon in compiling the *precedents* of the House.

As noted, the Rules of the House derive from four sources: from the Constitution, from Jefferson's *Manual*, from the rules adopted by the House itself from Congress to Congress, *and from the decisions of the Speakers of the House and of the Chairmen of the Committee of the Whole*. These decisions of the Speakers and Chairmen of the Committee of the Whole constitute the precedents of the House of Representatives, and incredibly enough, they have gone unpublished for thirty years! In effect, this places the House Parliamen-

tarian in a commanding, almost sole, position of authority to decide questions
of procedure, for without reference to the precedents of the last thirty years,
Members of the House are left to rush in "where angels fear to tread." This
is an unhealthy situation in a democracy, to say the least. Although be-
latedly, Congress has finally appropriated the money for the compilation to
be done.

How a Bill Reaches the Floor

Very briefly, a piece of legislation is introduced in the House by a Member dropping the bill in the hopper on the Clerk's desk. (This must be done
individually, for unlike the Senate, the House does not permit joint sponsorship of bills.) By direction of the Speaker, the bill is then referred to a standing or select committee.

The Chairman of the committee to which the bill has been referred may
further refer the bill to a subcommittee. The subcommittee, or the full committee, schedules hearings on the bill for the purpose of receiving testimony
of interested and expert witnesses. On most public bills, a sizeable amount
of staff work is involved.

When the committee is satisfied that it has heard from all of the witnesses
who need to be heard and that the proper amount of staff work has been done,
it goes into executive (closed) session for the purpose of "marking up" (*i.e.*,
drafting the final language) of the bill. Accompanied by a report, which may
include minority, supplemental, or additional views, the bill then goes to the
Rules Committee for terms of debate and on to the Floor by way of one of
the calendars of the House.

The House Calendars

There are five calendars which designate the business of the House,
namely: the Union, House, Private, Consent, and Discharge Calendars.

1. All bills raising revenue, general appropriation bills, and bills of a
business character directly or indirectly appropriating money or property are
referred to the Union Calendar. This is the calendar of the "Committee of
the Whole House on the State of the Union," which is simply a device for
expediting the business of the House and traces its origin to the English
Parliament.

The significant differences in the committee procedure as contrasted with that
of the House are: A quorum consists of 100 Members instead of a majority of the
House (which is 218); tellers[5] may be requested by 20 Members instead of by 44
(one-fifth of a majority of the House), the yea and nay vote may not be taken,
amendments may not be withdrawn or modified except with unanimous consent,
debate may be both general and under the five-minute rule for amendments, and
leave to extend remarks may be given only by unanimous consent since general
leaves may only be granted by the House.[6]

In other words, the Committee of the Whole, with the above-described differences in procedure, is the method by which the House readies legislation for a final verdict by the full House.

2. All bills of a public character not raising revenue nor directly or indirectly appropriating money or property are referred to the House Calendar. This is the ordinary calendar of the full House.

3. Legislation involving an individual's claim against the government, that is, a bill for the relief of some citizen to whom the government owes some reimbursement, etc., is placed on the Private Calendar.

4. Noncontroversial bills (*i.e.*, dealing with some relatively minor matter involving no great national issue) may be called up from what is called the Consent Calendar. These are bills which have already been printed on the House or Union Calendars; it is merely an expeditious procedure enabling the House to dispose of certain legislation with a minimum of effort. Consent Calendar days fall on the first and third Mondays of each month. The bills are read by title only and are passed by unanimous consent if no objection is heard. Each party appoints official objectors whose duty it is to monitor all legislation on the Consent Calendar and to object to any bill they feel should not be passed without debate. A single objection is enough to block the measure on first reading; if on second reading three or more Members object to the bill, it is stricken from the Consent Calendar and can only be restored in that session of Congress by unanimous consent.

5. The Discharge Calendar provides for consideration of a bill upon a motion signed by 218 Members, after the bill has been for thirty days in committee or seven days before the Rules Committee, to have the legislation brought to the Floor. Bills on the Discharge Calendar are privileged business and when called up on the second or fourth Monday of a month become the unfinished business of the House until final disposition.

The Discharge procedure is an extraordinary remedy against possible abuse by a legislative committee and as such is rarely resorted to. Indeed, most Members of the House are extremely reluctant to sign a discharge petition for the precise reason that it circumvents the legislative committee having responsibility for studying and reporting the bill.

Calendar Wednesday and the Rules Committee

To these five calendars may be added the procedure known as Calendar Wednesday, an extraordinary remedy available in the event of "abuse" by the Rules Committee. It is a seldom-used procedure, and perhaps for that reason there is a good deal of misunderstanding of how it works.

By way of a simple explanation, the present-day Rules Committee acts as a sort of traffic cop for the House, regulating the flow of legislation from the standing and select committees to the Floor. This was not always so, and the practice of granting special orders varies from Congress to Congress. However, since about 1910, most major bills are submitted to the Rules Committee for a decision on terms of debate and scheduling for floor action.

The range of the Rules Committee's jurisdiction over how and what may be done to any particular bill is very broad; as summed up by Floyd Riddick:

> These special orders may in effect suspend any of the rules of the House and prescribe a particular procedure for a certain duration of time.[7]

There are "open" rules, allowing a bill to be amended by the House, "closed" rules, which limit or prohibit amendments from the Floor, and a range of semi-open and semi-closed rules in between. In actual practice, most bills come to the Floor under the "five-minute" rule, under which general debate is closed in Committee of the Whole, with five minutes allotted to any Member proposing an amendment to the bill and five minutes allowed to a Member who wishes to speak in opposition to the amendment. The rule is contained in a resolution accompanying the bill, and the resolution itself is debatable under the "hour" rule, which is a Rule of the House (Rule XIV, paragraph 2). Theoretically, 435 Members could each demand an hour of debate on adoption of the resolution embodying the terms of debate for any bill reported by the Rules Committee. As a practical matter, debate is shut off by moving the previous question. The Member speaking may move the previous question at any time during his hour; in order for the debate to continue, it is necessary to vote down the previous question.

As with most bills reported by the Rules Committee, debate under Calendar Wednesday proceeds according to the five-minute rule. All debate must be confined to the subject matter of the bill, with the time equally divided between the proponents and opponents of the measure. In other words, Calendar Wednesday operates under the same general provisions as those which apply to most bills coming from the Rules Committee.

Some people have alleged that from time to time the Rules Committee has surpassed its traffic authority and succeeded in "bottling up" legislation by refusing to grant a rule, thereby preventing the bill from reaching the Floor. Actually, these instances have been rare, but Calendar Wednesday does exist as a safety measure in the event of such an occurrence. It was one of the precautionary procedures added to the 1910 bundle of reforms.

House Rule XXIV provides that on each Wednesday except during the last two weeks of the session:

> after the unfinished business has been disposed of, the Speaker shall call each standing committee in regular order, and then select committees, and each committee when named may call up for consideration any bill reported by it on a previous day and on the House Calendar.[8]

Whenever any committee shall have occupied one Wednesday, any unfinished business of that committee must wait until the other committees have been called in order and their business disposed of, unless the House shall determine otherwise by a two-thirds vote. Hence, Calendar Wednesday is neither as complicated nor as cumbersome as its detractors would suggest. It is rarely used for the reason that it is rarely necessary to bypass the now-common procedure of going through the Rules Committee.

The "21-day" Rule

Additionally, there is the precaution against "abuse" of the Rules Committee contained in the so-called "21-day" rule, reinstituted in the first session of the 89th Congress. This amendment to the Rules of the House provides that if the Committee on Rules shall adversely report, or fail to report within 21 calendar days after reference, any resolution pending before it which has been duly reported by one of the standing committees of the House, the Speaker may recognize the chairman or any Member of such committee for the purpose of calling up the bill for consideration by the House.[9]

However, this distinction between the two extraordinary procedures should be noted. While both are remedies against an unwarranted extension of authority by the Rules Committee, the calling up of bills under the 21-day rule is left to the discretion of the Speaker, whereas under Calendar Wednesday the power to call up a bill resides with the committee which reported the bill.

Suspension of the Rules

Bills may also be called up under Suspension of the Rules, a procedure permitted on two Mondays each month. Under this procedure, as with the 21-day rule, the decision is in the hands of the Speaker. His power of recognition is absolute. Bills called up under Suspension of the Rules, from any of the regular calendars, may not be divided, amended, postponed, tabled, reconsidered or recommitted, and must be passed by a two-thirds vote. The motions of individuals are given preference on the first Monday, of committees on the second. Debate is limited to forty minutes, 20 minutes to a side.

Suspension of the Rules is another of the House's extraordinary procedures and as such is very useful. Indeed, in frequency of use, it has become almost a regular procedure. However, there are grave risks involved in proceeding under Suspension of the Rules, and the matter deserves careful examination.

Quite often fifteen or more separate bills will be scheduled on a single day for consideration under Suspension of the Rules. Obviously, this puts a heavy burden on the individual Member if he is to do an adequate job of understanding the legislation upon which he is called to vote in such rapid succession. As a result, bills considered under Suspension of the Rules may be adopted with only a few Members having any real knowledge of their ramifications.

The Rules of the House should be changed to provide that only a certain number of bills may be called up each suspension day. However, it would probably be wise to have at least one suspension day each week so that this rather efficient method of enacting legislation could be utilized to the fullest extent, concomitant with giving each Member ample opportunity to understand each bill upon which he must vote.

As the name itself states, Suspension of the Rules bypasses the regular procedures of the House. Under ordinary processes, each bill coming to the Floor is accompanied by a report of the committee which handled the bill. These reports are of vital importance not only in serving notice to the full House that the measure has been carefully studied by the proper committee but in providing necessary background information for all Members in casting their votes. If a constitutional or interpretative question should later arise, the Supreme Court looks to the committee report in its attempt to determine the legislative intent.

Under Suspension of the Rules, a bill may be taken up whether or not it has even been referred to a committee. The Rules of the House should be amended to provide that every bill taken up under Suspension of the Rules be accompanied by a written report.

Most important, the Rules should be amended to provide for a clear definition of those matters which may be called up under this procedure. At present, only 20 minutes are allotted to each side for debate on a measure considered under Suspension of the Rules. This is hardly enough time to debate a complicated matter even if the bill in question is accompanied by a report. I would suggest that the following criteria govern the calling up of bills under Suspension of the Rules:

1. The bill should be relatively simple, that is, brief and not technically complex, the issue easily understood.

2. The bill should contain no matter involving long-range national policy, that is, it should have no major ramifications.

3. The bill should have no serious amendments in the offing.

Following are examples of bills which should *not* have been called up under Suspension of the Rules: H.R. 7042 (June 7, 1965) to amend the Federal Food, Drug, and Cosmetics Act for use of additives in confectionery; H.R. 3157 (same date) to amend the Railroad Retirement Act to increase spouses' annuities; H.R. 8030 (July 12, 1965) to discontinue the Postal Savings Plan; and H.R. 10238 (Sept. 20, 1965) regarding labor standards for persons employed by federal contractors.

The Loyal Opposition

With the exception of such instances as those referred to under Suspension of the Rules, most bills which are brought to the Floor of the House have been adequately studied. The time for general debate is fixed by the rule accompanying the bill and reflects the best judgment of the ranking Members of the appropriate committee in their recommendation to the Rules Committee concerning the time necessary for full discussion.

However, the same cannot be said for amendments. Theoretically, each Member of the House has five minutes to speak on any amendment offered. In practice, the majority can, by a majority vote, limit debate on "this amendment and all amendments thereto." This can result in a rampant majority denying sufficient time for the consideration of amendments. When debate is limited on a whole section or title of a bill by the imposition of a "gag" rule, it may indeed result in a complete lack of discussion of serious amendments which have been offered by Members.

A case in point occurred in the first session of the 89th Congress at the time the General Education Bill was up for debate. It was an open secret that the Administration had asked for passage of this bill without amendment. As a result, each amendment offered was met immediately by a motion offered by the Chairman of the Education and Labor Committee to limit debate. The bill was passed with a very minimum of time for debate and the defeat of all amendments to the bill, even though it was obvious to many Members that a number of these amendments should have been adopted.

A second case in point occurred with the passage of the so-called Highway Beautification Act of 1965. Here was the spectacle of a majority so intent on taking a passed bill to the White House for a party which the President had scheduled for that evening that it rode absolutely roughshod over all attempts at amendment. Similarly disposed in the opposite direction, a determined minority countered with a series of dilatory moves that kept the House in session—and the party waiting—until the weary hour of one o'clock in the morning! Result? A lot of frayed tempers and a bill poorer than the one which would have passed at 6 P.M. with proper consideration of the proposed amendments.

Conference Reports and the Hour Rule

Another phase in the enactment of legislation in which full disclosure is inhibited comes in the consideration of conference reports. When a conference report is presented, all time is controlled by the chairman of the conference committee, who is almost invariably the chairman of the legislative committee which presented the bill in the first place. The chairman may or may not yield time to the minority. Usually he does. There have been instances, however, and some in connection with quite important bills, in which the chairman of the conference committee either refused to yield any time to the minority or yielded them only such a small amount that an adequate explanation of the minority position was patently impossible.

It seems a matter of simple justice that the minority should be allotted half the time on conference reports, not by the grace of the majority yielding time, if it does, piecemeal, but as a matter of right. Since the minority is always given half the time during general debate on legislation, it is difficult to understand the rationale which accepts anything less in the matter of conference reports.

The "hour" rule dates from 1841 and applies to debate on a question of privilege as well as to debate on other questions. It should be amended to specify that one half hour be granted the opposition, with control of that time in their hands, on any question. Additionally, the minority should have an opportunity to include its views in the accompanying report.

Expediting Floor Procedure

In the interest of expediting Floor procedure—and the increasing demands on the time of Members call for some speeding up—the following changes in the Rules of the House might be considered:

1. The Rules should provide for a "live" quorum call and for a "pro forma" quorum call. The present Rules provide that once a quorum call is made, it must proceed through to final disposition. In fact, unless unanimous consent is given to "dispense with further proceedings under the call," the Sergeant-at-Arms is supposed to physically remove Members from their places of habitation, repose, or the like, and bring them bodily to the Floor. House Rule XV reads:

> In the absence of a quorum, 15 members, including the Speaker . . . shall be authorized to compel the attendance of absent members . . . and those for whom no sufficient excuse is made may . . . be sent for and arrested . . . and the House shall determine upon what condition they shall be discharged . . .

Neil MacNeil describes one particularly amusing incident—although I daresay it was not funny at the time—of the arrest of Members of the House in 1848. A vote was up, and the doors of the Hall had been locked and the Members sent for. One by one they were brought into the Well of the House to explain their absences. A Georgia Member explained that he had gone to the home of a friend whose child was dying, and was excused. In 1848 Members of the House received per diem salaries, and a Maryland Member proffered the argument that he was paid by the day, not by the night. He was *not* excused. A Member from Tennessee explained quite simply that he had gone to bed, "in accordance with the custom of all orderly men," and was promptly fined. Best of all, two Members sought to avoid this kind of humiliation by gaining access to the Chamber without arrest. One came in through a window, and the other, having gained access to one of the galleries, reached the Floor by sliding down one of the great marble pillars in the House![10]

In any event, today's quorum call is quite often used as a means of letting interested Members know that certain business is to be brought up next in order. In other words, it is a device used to allow the House to "shift gears" in a smooth manner. If this is the reason for a particular quorum call, then there is no good excuse for continuing the call after the interested Members have reported to the Floor. The pro forma quorum call would allow the call to be stopped at any point by unanimous consent of the Members present, and the device could save much time on the Floor, not to mention wear and tear on the Members.

2. At present any Member can require the entire *Journal* of the previous day's proceedings to be read. This can be extremely time-consuming, and consideration should be given to changing the Rules to provide that reading of the previous day's *Journal* be automatically dispensed with unless ten per cent of the Members present and voting demand that it be read.

3. It is a custom of long standing for Senate bills and messages from the President of the United States to be reported formally to the House by a clerk. In each such instance, it is necessary for the House to suspend its business to receive the report. If the House is in the Committee of the Whole, it is necessary for the Committee to rise and for the Speaker to resume the Chair. This is an archaism, and however courteous, is an unnecessary procedure. Senate bills and Presidential messages should be received automatically and proper disposition made of them without the formal trappings of a bygone age.

4. The practice of "qualifying to vote" should be ended. By custom, a Member who claims to have been in the Chamber and listening while the roll was being called but failed to hear his name may go to the well of the House and qualify to vote. This may seem a picayune matter, but because it involves a question of ethics, I think it deserves careful attention. The following colloquy between a freshmen Member (and graduate of West Point's rigid honor code) and the distinguished Chairman of the Joint Committee on the Organization of Congress last year serves to illustrate.

Rep. Callaway: When I first came here I was not aware of the rule, and I noticed Members frequently going to the Well to cast their vote at the end of the roll call. . . . the first time this happened to me when I was not present when my name was called, I did not go down to qualify because the rule very clearly states that I could not qualify. A number of people told me that everybody goes down to qualify, it is just done, and this is one of the rules that is not enforced. So while I say it may be trivial . . .

Senator Monroney quickly agreed, labeling the practice "an obsolete carryover from the old days," adding:

Apparently there was a reason for it before, but now with the business the Congress has (and) Members rushing to the Floor, missing their names on second roll call and having to quality and be dishonest, actually, about their qualification, (it) is most undesirable.

Rep. Callaway: That was my reason for bothering you with something so trivial.

Sen. Monroney: It is not trivial.[11]

As long as a Member reports to the Floor before a vote is announced, it is difficult to see why he should not be allowed to cast his vote. Indeed, the present practice—although it should be noted that most Members do not indulge in this sort of thing—gives rise to justifiable attacks on the ethical standards of Members of Congress.

5. Another archaism is the necessity for a Member to specifically reserve points of order in the event that committee reports are to be filed at a time the House is not in session. It is no secret that the minority has very little to do with the preparation of committee reports. However, the minority certainly has great interest in making sure that these reports are accurate and complete and that they comply with the Rules of the House. Points of order on conference reports should be automatically reserved by the Rules, and such points of order should be considered to have been presented in a timely fashion if they are presented during the consideration of the bill, either in the House or in the Committee of the Whole.

6. While the fiscal machinery of Congress and oversight are treated in other chapters of this book, I would recommend a change in the Rules of the House that has a bearing on both. It is one of the amazing results of the present Rules that funds which have been appropriated cannot by a subsequent Act be unappropriated. Because of this, there are rather large sums of money represented by appropriations for which the original purpose is no longer valid. Also, there are funds appropriated for purposes which should be re-examined by the Congress. The existing interpretation of the Rules deprives the Congress of a very important function in its role of legislative oversight, and this interpretation should be reconsidered.

7. Many Members are displeased over the apparent desire of the leadership of the House to leave Fridays, Saturdays, and Mondays without business in order to accommodate Members of Congress who live within commuting distance of the nation's capital. While we have all the sympathy in the world for our fellow Members who find it desirable to commute, it seems likely that longer hours and days of work early in the session would result in shorter sessions of Congress. The length of congressional sessions is becoming ridiculous; year-end sessions result in physically and mentally tired Members who often enact legislation which in their better judgment they would not even consider.

While each Congress should be able to decide for itself the length of its sessions, it would seem a good policy to insist on adjournment each year before the first of September. Lacking this, better scheduling should be followed in order to allow the Members certain pre-arranged periods in which they can be out of Washington. For instance, it might be well to suspend a session in the middle of the summer in order to allow Members to refresh their minds and bodies with a family vacation. Later in the year, perhaps another recess of two weeks would be in order to allow Congressmen to return to their districts for unhurried consultation with their constituents.

8. Finally, I would call attention to the privilege of Members to "revise and extend" remarks in the *Congressional Record*. The privilege is useful, and in the light of the very heavy burden today's Congressman carries, perhaps even necessary. In the interest of historical accuracy, however, I would recommend (1) that all remarks not actually delivered on the Floor of the House be set forth in different print from recorded debate, and (2) that the privilege of revising one's remarks be confined to grammatical correction and never allowed to alter the meaning or to misrepresent the circumstances of debate in colloquy between Members.

REFERENCES

1. Galloway, George B., *History of the House of Representatives*, New York, Thomas Y. Crowell Co., 3rd printing, 1962.
2. *Ibid.*, p. 52.
3. *Ibid.*, p. 53.
4. Deschler, Lewis, Preface to *Jefferson's Manual and Rules of the House of Representatives*, 89th Congress, 1st Sess.
5. See chapter of this book by Durward G. Hall.
6. Riddick, Floyd M., *The United States Congress: Organization and Procedure*, Manassas, Va., National Capitol Publishers, 1949.
7. *Ibid.*, p. 117.
8. See House Rule XXIV.
9. See House Rule XI.
10. MacNeil, Neil, *Forge of Democracy*, New York, David McKay Co., 1963.
11. Hearings, Joint Committee on the Organization of Congress, 89th Congress, 1st Session, Part 3.

DURWARD G. HALL, M.C.
7th District, Missouri

ELECTRIC VOTING IN THE HOUSE

by Durward G. Hall, M.C.*

"A slow sort of country," said the Queen. "Now, *here*, you see, it takes all the running you can do to keep in the same place."

From *Alice's Adventures in Wonderland.*

On "Bloody Monday," September 13, 1965, the U.S. House of Representatives set a record by remaining in session for 12 hours and 31 minutes. Nine of those hours were consumed just answering roll calls, 22 of them, each lasting an average of 24.5 minutes.

This kind of "filibuster," by individuals or the minority, is occasionally necessary to prevent a willful majority from forcing through resolutions discharging committees, limiting debate, eliminating amendments, and waiving normal procedure with regard to points of order and germaness. It has done so in 397 cases.

Still, one may ask, what kind of country is it where the people's representatives are running all the time just to keep in the same place!

From January 4 through October 23, 1965, the House was in session for a total of 798 hours and 25 minutes. Its Members answered 201 roll calls and an additional 182 quorum calls. The average roll call takes 25 to 30 minutes; a quorum call, on the average, takes 20 to 23 minutes. Reckoning with the lowest figures in each category, Members of the House last year spent 83 to 84 hours answering roll calls and another 60 hours responding to quorum calls. The two combined accounted for roughly one-fifth of the total time the House was in session. (Of course, all the time is not wasted by the individual after he answers or votes, to wit, the famous floor and/or lobby conferences.)

* Dr. Hall was first elected to Congress in 1960 from the 7th Congressional District of Missouri. He is a Member of the House Armed Services Committee and the Joint Committee on the Organization of Congress. Before entering Congress Dr. Hall was a practicing surgeon.

On the other hand, one Congressman has estimated that in the 1963 session, which ran into Christmas Eve, Members of the House spent 70 working days that year just answering roll calls!

It certainly seems strange that in this technologically advanced age the Congress of the United States has *not* been able to find an expeditious way to count its votes or ascertain its presence for duty. Indeed, when the bells ring for attendance in the House, the subterranean passageways connecting the office buildings to the Capitol are filled with scurrying replicas of Alice's White Rabbit:

I'm late, I'm late, for a very important date . . .

Would the installation of an electric voting system save wear and tear on the people's representatives and contribute to greater efficiency in the conduct of the nation's legislative business?

As a doctor in the House, I abhor the unnecessary waste of human energy occasioned by frequent running to the Floor and by the fretful wait while 435 names are called in alphabetical order. As a member of the Joint Committee on the Organization of Congress, I have been fascinated with the proposals for an electric voting system. But the more one studies the whole picture as it exists *under present rules*, the more one questions whether a system of automatic vote recording would in fact result in saving time without impairing the intricate functioning of the House's legislative process.

Congress first took cognizance of electric voting in 1914 as a result of the interest of Speaker Champ Clark. Since then, more than 30 bills and resolutions proposing some form of electric voting have been introduced in the House. Significantly, *not one* has ever been reported to the Floor. Clearly, there must be some unique considerations not present in the many state legislatures which permit electric voting that militate against an automatic system of vote recording in the Congress.

To begin with, the Congressman's job entails a great deal more than the activity in the Chamber. To the tourist in the gallery, the sight of so few Members on the Floor during debate may seem very disappointing. But to assume that a Member's absence from the Floor is proof that he is not fulfilling his responsibility is to ignore the range of that responsibility. There are letters, an increasing number of them, to be answered. There are constituents, an increasing number of them, to be greeted. There are committee meetings, an increasing number of them, to attend. And always there is the constant study of legislation that is not currently on the Floor.

Secondly, much of the activity on the Floor relates to routine matters. As noted in the chapter by Mr. Rhodes, the House has devised various methods of expediting its business without the necessity for the full Membership to be in attendance during the entire session. With urgent problems in his district, individual cases to be handled for his constituents, and piles of correspondence, reports, and reading matter stacked on his desk, Pandora's Box would be more inviting to most Members than a change in the Rules to make compulsory every Member's attendance while the House is in session.

According to testimony delivered before the Joint Committee on the Organization of the Congress last year by Mr. Charles Schwan, Director of the Council of State Governments, 31 of our States now have some system of electric voting. "The major argument in favor of electric roll call systems, Mr. Schwan noted, "has been that they save time in the conduct of legislative business. States with such equipment have reported that 30 seconds is the average time for their roll calls. Alabama and Louisiana estimate a savings of 10 to 12 minutes per roll call; Michigan estimates savings of 50 hours per session. Electric roll call voting assures an accurate account and a permanent, immediately available record of all votes. It is considered an aid in maintaining decorum, as all members must be in their places to vote, and the activity that often occurred during vocal roll calls has been largely eliminated."

It should be noted that unlike the state legislatures, there are no assigned seats in the U.S. House of Representatives. Furthermore, with the farthest reaches of the new Rayburn House Office Building located two full city blocks from the Chamber, there must be a lapse of time for the Member to get from his office to the Floor just to push his button. In itself, this delay would be self-defeating in a system designed essentially to save time.

Without getting into a highly technical discourse on the subject, the general sequence of events in an electric voting system is as follows: the Clerk illuminates the bill number on a Main Indicator Board. After debate, the Speaker states the question and pushes a button which unlocks the Member's voting switches. The Members vote simultaneously, and they can change their votes if they so desire. After asking if all Members have voted, or if any desire to change, the Clerk is then directed to take the record. The results are available within 10 seconds, both as to each Member's vote and as to the cumulative total.

The patent on the first electric voting device was granted to Thomas A. Edison in 1869. Very simply, it involved a switch at each desk which, when moved to the YES or NO position, would energize the Member's name in either the YES or NO column on a lighted board. The only major difference in today's electric voting devices in use in the states involves the legality of a third choice, PRESENT, in addition to the YEA and NAY switches. Apparently, no state constitutions authorize the Clerk to record PRESENT, although members may ask the Presiding Officer to have the *Journal* show them as Present but Not Voting or Paired.

The cost of installing electric voting systems has averaged about $80,000 in state legislatures which have recently had them installed. The larger size of the House of Representatives has prompted estimates ranging from $100,-000 to $200,000, and in all likelihood the installer would also contract for maintenance and upkeep.

The fact that the House has traditional methods of testing the strength of proponents and opponents through unrecorded votes involving physical movement by the Members argues against the adoption of an electric system.

One of these methods is called the *Division*. Here the Speaker asks for the "Ayes" to stand, and the Members literally stand up to be counted. Then the "Nays" stand, and the Speaker announces the results. The vote is not officially recorded.

If the Division proves inconclusive, the *Teller* vote may be resorted to, again a testing skirmish to avoid defeat on a roll call vote, at the same time affording Members the opportunity to learn which of their colleagues are for and which against a bill or amendment. In this process, "tellers" are appointed for each side, and the Members walk up the center aisle of the House to be counted, those in favor of the measure passing between the two "Aye" tellers, those opposed between the two "Nay" tellers. The Speaker is appraised of the informal vote, and the positions of the Members are clear without the necessity of the roll being called. (Incidentally, this procedural device is often shrewdly used to break up committee meetings, to force response to Whip calls, or to promote floor attendance.)

Perhaps the most persuasive argument for installation of an electric system involves the *Voice Vote*. This is the technique used by a majority to whoop through measures that might be very controversial and on which Members *do not wish* to be recorded. The bill is passed or rejected by sheer lung power, with the Speaker holding authority to decide whether the "Ayes" or "Nays" have it.

These are the methods employed while the House is in the Committee of the Whole House on the State of the Union. Under present rules, no roll call votes may be recorded during the amending process; rather, amendments are determined on the basis of the Oral, Division, or Teller votes described above. Only when the Committee of the Whole has been dissolved and the House has reconvened as the full House are roll call votes in order. As most of the major legislation is perfected while the House is in the Committee of the Whole, the efficiency accruing from an electric voting system would apply only part of the time.

In spite of these arguments against electric voting, it would seem that a compromise might be found by a body which recognizes that government itself is the art of successful compromise. With better scheduling of the congressional workload, perhaps by reserving certain days of the week for committee work, with other days given over wholly to Floor work, the procedural questions involved could be straightened out and the Members assigned seats for the purpose of casting their votes electrically, *after* proper and predetermined notice is given in each instance.

Under present rules of procedure, it is an open question just how much time, if any, an electric voting system would save. However, electric voting *could* save time if Congress would come up with a better schedule of business.

Sooner or later, the pressures of modern society will probably demand that the change be made, and the matter deserves careful consideration now.

REFERENCES

1. Figures on number of roll and quorum calls, time in session, from Daily Digest, *Congressional Record*, No. 15, 1965.
2. Hearings before the Joint Committee on the Organization of Congress, 89th Congress, Part 7, pp. 1067–1068.

ROBERT C. McEWEN, M.C.
31st District, New York

CONTESTED ELECTIONS TO THE HOUSE OF REPRESENTATIVES

by Robert C. McEwen, M.C.*

> "Each House Shall be the Judge of
> the Elections, Returns and Quali-
> fications of its own Members."
>
> (U.S. Constitution, Article I, Section 5)

Inherent in the structure of American government is a system commonly referred to as the "Separation of Powers." Actually, this basic principle is too often honored only in the breach. For while the Legislature legislates, it also judges and executes. The same can be said about the other two branches.

The Executive functioning in judicial and legislative areas is most obvious. Constitutionally–sanctioned veto power is an extension of the legislative function. Increased participation in the process of suggesting legislation is also a phenomenon of the twentieth-century Chief Executive. The modern Presidential "State of the Union" address, delivered to Congress in the evening before TV cameras, serves to highlight this role. In addition, administrative agencies in the Executive Department may appear to be in competition with the courts in producing findings and orders that are often quasi-judicial in nature.

The Judiciary, in the opinion of many, performs extra-judicial functions. An illustration of this is seen in the mandate to the State Legislatures to reapportion in a prescribed manner. It is also seen when the court sends out marshals to enforce its decrees.

---

* Mr. McEwen is the only freshman Member of the Task Force, having been elected to Congress in 1964 from the 31st Congressional District of New York. He is a Member of the House Public Works Committee and served in the State Senate of New York before entering Congress.

The Legislature also operates in the executive and judicial spheres. The administration of each house is itself a major executive task. In the area of judicial action, the House of Representatives sits as a Court of Impeachment, can issue contempt citations, and also acts to judge the qualifications of its elected members. This last area is one of the hidden tasks of the legislator, often out of public visibility and, consequently, frequently ignored. The framers of the Constitution empowered each House of Congress to be the sole judge in the seating of its own Members. This principle, intended to safeguard the self integrity of Congress, has frequently been invoked to challenge a claimant's right to a seat as a Member or Member-elect. In the House of Representatives, this has occurred more than 100 times since the turn of the century.

Issues of "contested seats" have been diverse. Some, easily determined, have been clear-cut issues; others have been complex, raising fine points of parliamentary and constitutional law. On occasion, emotion and partisanship have tended to muddy the waters.

From the very beginning of our Republic, Congress has been the sole arbiter of the seating of its Members. This has been constantly reaffirmed by the Judiciary. The distinguished jurist, Learned Hand, stated the case succinctly. Contested House elections are ". . . justiciable by the House, and by the House alone."[1] This power is a direct legacy of the British Parliament, wary of external interference in its proceedings.

Requirements for membership in the House of Representatives, as set forth in the Constitution, are that those elected be (1) at least twenty-five years of age, (2) seven years a citizen, and (3) an inhabitant of the state from which elected. Congress has also included other and varied criteria in its constitutional function to judge "the Elections, Returns and Qualifications of its own Members."

In point of time, Congress can act (1) not to seat a claimant on account of a dispute in the election itself, (2) not to seat a claimant on the basis of personal conduct or failure to meet constitutional requirements, or (3) to unseat or expel a Member from the House. In theory, expulsion of a Member, as opposed to the failure to seat a Member, comes under different categories of legislative action. The former requires a two-thirds vote of the House, the latter a majority. Yet, there have been a few meaningful precedents laid down in this area that would give the scholar of congressional government much basis to speculate, with assurance, as to the manner in which Congress would deal with one or another of these situations. In point of fact, there is little that one could tell from its history that would provide any insight as to how Congress might act in the future. This judicial function of the Congress has been confused by the consideration of expediency that necessarily enters into legislative judgments. Congress has sought political equities more often than individual ones. And in the past more than one prospective House Member has been prevented from taking his seat because his point of view was at variance with that already prevailing in the House.

Similar failure to seat duly elected legislators, because their unorthodox beliefs were unacceptable to the majority of their colleagues-to-be, has also occurred at the state level. An example is the exclusion of Julian Bond from the Georgia Legislature because of his views on the draft and the war in Vietnam. Several decades ago, a parallel dilemma presented itself in New York, when its legislature refused to admit Socialist Members-elect. Thus, the people, voting in full awareness of the position of their legislator-to-be, may be denied the type of representation they apparently desire.

Challenges to a person's being seated in Congress nearly always are based upon three allegations; namely, failure to comply with a qualification as delineated in the Constitution itself; failure to have won the election on the basis of the election returns; and lack of qualification on the basis of individual conduct or point of view. On the whole, most challenges have been of the first two types. The emergence of third parties, running candidates outside the mantle of either of the two major parties, could conceivably change this. The House might then be faced with cases such as those which confronted the Georgia and New York Legislatures.

The seating challenge usually occurs when the Congress convenes. In such cases, the challenged Representative-elect is asked to step aside while the other Members are sworn in. Then, the House might immediately vote on the question of seating the Member-elect. More often, however, he is sworn in provisionally and the matter is referred to the Committee on House Administration. A challenge might be instituted by a private citizen's "memorial" or "protest," a Member's "motion," or a challenge instituted by the defeated candidate under an 1851 statute as amended. Despite this apparent clarity, however, the area remains clouded. Each case is dealt with on an *ad hoc* basis, and experts in the area are able to tell what has been done but are little able to predict for the future.

A case in point involves my distinguished colleague, Rep. James C. Cleveland (R., N.H.), who tried to pursue the issue of whether or not the campaign manager for a defeated incumbent could avail himself of one or another of the remedies on behalf of his claimant. At each step of the way, he was met with increasing difficulties that were only resolved when one staff member of the Office of the Clerk of the House was able to reach a decision as to how the rules of the House were to be administered.   His "solution" and advice were eagerly adopted by the majority and made the rule. I might add that the rule was completely at odds with what Mr. Cleveland and the Legislative Reference Service of the Library of Congress had been led to believe was the state of the "law" on the issue. Many members of the minority party concluded, with some fair reason, that political decisions were primary in the conclusion of the issue. The claimant, acting on behalf of a defeated Republican, was prevented from bringing his case before the House. I should note here that the same solution might have been forthcoming had the parties been in opposite positions.

Contested Seating Cases in the House

The eighty-nine Congresses in the history of the Republic have been the scene of numerous contests involving the admission of individuals to membership in the House of Representatives. In exercising the power granted by Article I, Section 5, the House has asserted the power to inquire into the activities of the Member-elect prior to the election as well as the disputed election itself. Causes for these contested seat cases have ranged from charges of "stuffing" the ballot box to a Member-elect's polygamy, from fraud and bribery to allegations of disloyalty to the country, from being under the required minimum age to failure to qualify as a citizen.

The more prominent cases in this area generally have fallen into three categories:

(1) LACK OF CONSTITUTIONAL QUALIFICATIONS

The case of failure to live up to a constitutional mandate of qualifications has been dealt with in cavalier fashion by the House. Rarely does a member come seeking admission who is not 25 years old, or seven years a citizen, or a resident of the state from which elected. When he does, however, he is generally admitted despite the "disability."

Two cases of Congressmen who were admitted to membership while not possessing constitutional qualifications can be found prior to 1800. Representative-elect William Smith of South Carolina was admitted to membership during the 1st Congress although he had been abroad during the American Revolution. Though he had subsequently returned to his native South Carolina, he clearly had not resided in the country for seven years prior to his election. Yet, the House held him to be a qualified citizen.[3]

William C. Claiborne of Tennessee, said to have been born in 1775, took his seat in the House on November 23, 1797. No question appears to have been raised; although if his year of birth is correctly listed, he was only 22 years of age when elected.[4]

More recently, in the *Estep* v. *Ellenbogen* contest, former Member Estep, who was not a candidate, challenged the seating of Representative-elect Ellenbogen on the ground that he had not been a citizen for seven years at the date of election. Nor would he have been at the commencement of the term, March 9, 1933, when he would have been a citizen only 6 years and 8½ months.

Mr. Ellenbogen, of Pennsylvania, stood aside when the House convened and did not present himself until January 3, 1934, by which time he had been a citizen for 7½ years. He was promptly sworn in and took his seat. The committee which examined the contest held that he qualified at the time the oath was administered. The citizenship requirement was equated with the age requirement in that it could be met subsequent to election.[5]

(2) Contests Based on the Vote Itself

A close vote in the general election has often been the basis for a contest. Numerous challenges have been initiated because of the lack of a decisive election victory at the polls. As a general rule, it might be said that:

a) The official returns are *prima facie* evidence of the regularity and correctness of official action;

b) Election officials are presumed to have performed their duties loyally and honestly;

c) The burden of coming forward with evidence contrary to a) and/or b) rests with the contestant.

d) Fraud is never presumed, but must be proven.

e) The mere closeness of the result of an election raises no presumption of fraud, irregularities, or dishonesty.[6]

However, contests based on the closeness of the election results are costly and time-consuming. Such disputes are not only difficult to adjudicate but can also deprive constituents of true, effective representation. Such a contest took place in the 75th Congress. At issue was the seating of the Representative for the 1st District of New Hampshire.

On November 3, 1936, the Republican candidate, Arthur B. Jenks, was elected to the House by a plurality of 550 votes, according to the state's official returns. His opponent, Alphonse Roy, a Democrat, sought a recount by the New Hampshire Secretary of State as provided by state law, and the result was declared to be a tie. Both candidates then appealed to the state's Ballot-Law Commission, which considered 108 contested ballots in question. As a result, the Commission decided that Mr. Roy had a majority of 17 votes. Prior to the issuance of the required certification of election to the Democrat, Mr. Jenks disclosed that there were 34 missing ballots in a particular precinct. The Ballot-Law Commission then held hearings on the missing ballots. After hearing witnesses, it concluded from the testimony that all 34 votes had been cast for Jenks, and he was declared the final winner by ten votes. The Secretary of State then certified that Republican Jenks was the final winner by ten votes.[7]

On January 5, 1937, an unsuccessful attempt was made in the House to prevent Member-elect Jenks from being sworn in. Roy filed a petition with the House, contesting the election and seating of Jenks based on the 34 ballots and the recounts. The matter was referred for investigation to the appropriate House committee, which declared Roy to be the winner by 20 votes. A minority report from the committee disagreed with the majority report, which advocated seating Roy.

After considerable debate, on August 19, 1937, the House recommitted the case to committee and directed the taking of further testimony concerning the ballots in dispute, appropriating $5,000 therefor. On the following April 28, after concluding its hearings, the committee recommended that Alphonse Roy, not Arthur Jenks, should be sitting as Representative in the House from the 1st District of New Hampshire. After debate, the House voted on June 9, 1938, to seat Mr. Roy and he was sworn in.[8] It seems paradoxical that Republican Jenks served the first 17 months of a 24-month term and Democrat Roy the last seven. Perhaps in this case, it was true that "some defeated candidates go back to work and others say the fight has just begun."[9]

The 1960 Presidential election provided a razor-thin nationwide margin of victory in the popular vote for President and Vice-President. The 5th Congressional District of Indiana vote for U.S. Representative was equally thin. In that district, tallies filed by the county clerks with the Secretary of State of Indiana showed a plurality of three votes for Republican George O. Chambers. The Secretary of State, on the basis of returns corrected to November 15, 1960, certified that Chambers had a plurality of 12 votes over the Democratic candidate.

The Democrat, J. Edward Roush, thereupon instituted a contest. When Congress convened, Representative Davis of Tennessee objected to the oath being administered to Mr. Chambers. A resolution not to administer the oath to either contestant or contestee was passed and the matter of the election was referred to the Committee on House Administration. The issue involved a recount by that Committee since the laws of Indiana did not provide recounts for a legislative office. After adopting a set of criteria for determining which ballots were correctly marked in instances of questionable ballots, the Committee determined Mr. Roush to be the winner by 99 votes. On June 14, 1961, after a sharp debate which questioned the failure to seat Mr. Chambers on the basis of the state's official returns and the method of conducting the recount, the Democrat was seated in the Democratic-controlled House.[10]

(3) CONTESTS DUE TO AN INDIVIDUAL'S CONDUCT OR BELIEFS

This type of contest can have several sources of origin. The Member-elect may hold views contrary to the majority of his "colleagues-to-be." A third party may contest his seating on grounds other than a clear-cut question of "close vote." Allegations against his character or conduct may be the issue. His previous actions or beliefs may be deemed to be in opposition to the consensus of viewpoint held by other Members. The numerous contests of this nature offer a vast array of justifications, or lack thereof, for challenges having been instituted.

The era immediately following the Civil War witnessed House seating disputes concerning Members-elect and allegations that they had been disloyal to the Union. Although they possessed the constitutional qualifications for U.S. Representatives, the House refused to grant membership to John D. Young and John Young Brown, both of Kentucky, because of charges of disloyalty during the War.[11]

The 41st Congress denied a House seat to Frank Whittemore of South Carolina on June 21, 1870. When a resolution for his expulsion had been offered in the House the preceding February (because of his selling appointments to the Military Academy), he had resigned and then run for re-election. Upon receiving his new credentials, the House refused to allow him to be sworn in for the new term.[12]

On December 4, 1899, amidst the organization of the House for the 56th Congress, the validity of seating the Representative-elect from Utah was challenged. An Ohio Member objected to the swearing in of Brigham H. Roberts on the grounds that Roberts had been convicted of polygamy and was still a polygamist. Accordingly, the Member-elect from Utah was ineligible for House membership because of the statutory disqualifications of current Federal law. Mr. Roberts was not administered the oath of office and a special committee of nine appointed by the Speaker investigated the allegations made by the Ohio Representative. A subsequent vote resulted in the gentleman from Utah not being sworn in, the House voting 302 to 32 against seating him.[13]

An interesting and important contest for membership arose during the organization of the 66th Congress in May, 1919. Victor L. Berger, the Austrian-born Socialist editor of a Milwaukee newspaper, had been elected to the 62nd Congress in 1910 and served in the House from 1911 to 1913. He was elected again as a Socialist to serve in the 66th Congress, but this time his seating as a Representative was challenged. During World War I, Berger had been an executive committee member of the Socialist Party and his Wisconsin paper had printed articles over his signature that were critical of the war effort. A grand jury indicted him and a Federal Court in Chicago found him guilty of violating the 1917 Espionage Act.

On February 20, 1919, Berger was sentenced to 20 years imprisonment and an appeal was still pending on May 19, 1919, when he attempted to be sworn in as the Representative of Wisconsin's 6th District. The House refused to seat him, apparently agreeing with its investigating committee that ". . . if the House is satisfied that Representative-elect Berger did give aid or comfort to the enemies of the United States, he is ineligible to a seat in this House, and it is not only the right but the constitutional duty of the House to exclude him."[14]

The 89th Congress met for organization and oath-taking on January 4, 1965. Following the election of the Speaker by the Members-elect and their being sworn in, two separate challenges were made concerning six Members-elect. Mr. Ryan (D., N.Y.) objected to the entire five-man Mississippi delegation being seated and Mr. Cleveland (R., N.H.) contested the oath being administered to Representative-elect Richard L. Ottinger of New York. The six gentlemen whose seats were questioned stood aside as the rest of the House was sworn and seated. Thereafter, they, too, were seated following a brief debate and vote.[15] However, all six faced additional difficulties concerning the validity of their membership. The challenges to the seating of the six men were based on dissimilar circumstances, but they were similarly adjudicated.

Mr. Ottinger, a Democrat, had been challenged because of reported excessive campaign expenditures. The five Mississippi Members had been challenged because of allegations that nearly the entire Negro population of their state had been excluded from the electoral processes.

In the Ottinger contest, James R. Frankberry, the New York campaign manager for defeated incumbent Republican Congressman Robert R. Barry, contested the seating of the victorious Ottinger. The challenge was based upon the allegation that Representative Ottinger had spent more money in his 1964 congressional campaign than was lawfully permitted under both State and Federal statutes. Frankberry brought suit in the New York State Supreme Court against Ottinger and also wrote to the Committee on House Administration and the House Special Committee to Investigate Campaign Expenditures, requesting that they investigate the Ottinger campaign. In addition, he instituted a contest before the House under the 1851 statute, as amended, regarding contested congressional elections. On January 19, 1965, after a debate replete with constitutional and parliamentary issues, the House approved a resolution dismissing the Frankberry challenge to the Ottinger seating on the grounds that the former was not a contestant in the election and therefore not justified in using the statutes[16] to bring a contest before the House. The vote on the resolution dismissing the contest was 245 for, 102 against, 3 present, and 84 not voting.[17]

The Ottinger decision was to have a direct bearing on a subsequent 1965 challenge involving the Mississippi delegation in that the contest was instituted by others than a direct party to the election. On July 29, the Clerk transmitted to the Speaker a communication including testimony, exhibits, and notices of contest brought by the predominantly Negro Mississippi Freedom Democratic Party against the validity of the seating of the entire Mississippi delegation in the House of Representatives. The lack of Negro participation in Mississippi's electoral processes was cited as grounds for the challenge. The Speaker referred the matter to the Committee on House Administration, which reported back to the House on September 15. Its opinion and recommendation—the Members whose seats were now being contested should remain duly seated; they possessed valid certificates of election and the contest against them should be dismissed.[18] The House followed this advice.

The Future and Contested Seats ?—

Questions have been raised concerning the propriety of the House in refusing to seat a duly-elected person who has met the qualifications required by the Constitution—at least 25 years of age, seven years a citizen, and an inhabitant of the state from which elected. From this has developed the contention that the power to rule upon the validity of a Member's election should have been conferred on the Judiciary rather than upon the Congress. In support of this argument, one can note the power originally vested in the British House of Commons to be the judge of a Member's election to that body. In time, this prerogative was abandoned and such authority was conferred on the Judiciary, with more satisfactory results. However, throughout the history of our Republic, Congress has had its constitutional right as sole arbiter in the seating of Members constantly reinforced by the Judiciary. Whatever the merits of the claim that the House should not be able to refuse to seat someone duly elected and constitutionally qualified, the argument remains moot unless a constitutional amendment to the contrary is adopted. It is doubtful that such change would be enacted, depriving the House of a prerogative it has exercised since the First Congress met in 1789.

Present statutory guidelines covering procedures for contesting House elections are not only confusing and questionable but in obvious need of updating. The existing statutes relative to contested elections merit a thorough and unified revision, for the laws as they now stand are cumbersome and unclear to both contestant and contestee alike. Evidence of this can be seen in the Ottinger and Mississippi contests.

From the tangled web of contested election cases, several obvious improvements seem to be indicated. It would appear that a complete review, revision, and codification of both statutes and House rules governing contested congressional elections are long overdue. The precedents themselves are frequently contradictory. Determination of contests should be less partisan in decision. Both the Members and their consituents are entitled to updated, fair, and uniform standards for the determination of the manner in which individuals are seated, or not seated, in the House of Representatives.

On March 1, 1966, Representative H. R. Gross (R., Iowa) introduced a bill (H.R. 13163) designed to revise and update provisions of the law governing election contests. Hopefully, this bill may serve as a catalyst for other needed reforms in this area.

As things now stand, I see three possibilities. Either the Legislative Branch must enact the needed reforms itself or else it should invest the Judicial Branch with the authority to adjudicate contested elections. The third alternative is that the Judiciary, at some future time, might enter the once-avoided "political thicket" and, on its own initiative, decide such cases. While I am very much opposed to this latter possibility, I strongly advocate review and reform of existing contested election guidelines. It is a matter which cannot be ignored much longer.

House membership is not merely the concern of the Members. The citizen constituents have a right to question the seating of their Representatives. This is a privilege that grows more difficult with each new session of Congress. Our Nation has the right to hope that the House will put this segment of its own affairs in order. The composition of the Congress cannot be regarded as only of interest to its Members. The votes of a district, the basic tenet of effective representation, and the nation as a whole, are directly affected. Because of this, contested elections must not be regarded as political-legal jousts between a contestant and contestee in which the constituent is reduced to a passive observer and often a secondary consideration.

REFERENCES

1. *In re Voorhis* (D. C., N. Y., 1923), 291 F. 673.
2. *Congressional Record*, January 18, 1965, p. 795.
3. *Hinds' Precedents*, Vol. I, p. 390.
4. Second Session, 5th Congress, *Journal*, p. 84.
5. 73rd Congress, *House Report 1431*.
6. 73rd Congress, *House Report 893*.
7. 75th Congress, *House Report 1521*.
8. 75th Congress, *House Report 2255*.
    81 *Congressional Record*, pp. 8842–8846, 9356–9374, 9501.
    83 *Congressional Record*, pp. 5960–5961, 8642–8662.
9. Quip attributed to the American newspaperman and humorist Mark McKinney.
10. 87th Congress, *House Report 513*.
    107 *Congressional Record*, pp. 10377–10391, 10160, 10186.
11. *Hinds' Precedents*, Vol. I, pp. 444, 451.
12. *Hinds' Precedents*, Vol. I, p. 487.
13. 33 *Congressional Record*, 53.
    In the 46th Congress, Mr. Cannon of the Utah Territory was not admitted as he also was a polygamist.
    Hinds' Precedents, Vol. I, pp. 503, 527.
14. 66th Congress, *House Report 413*.
15. *Congressional Record*, January 4, 1965, p. 17 ff.
16. Revised Statutes 105 to 130, as amended, 2 U.S. Code 201–226.
17. *Congressional Record*, January 19, 1965, p. 934.
18. First Session, 89th Congress, *House Report 1008*.

LAURENCE J. BURTON, M.C.

1st District, Utah

THE COST OF GETTING THERE
AND LENGTH OF STAY

*by Laurence J. Burton, M.C.**

Term of Office

On January 13, 1966, a Gallup Poll taken before the President's State of the Union Message (containing a proposal for lengthening the term of Representatives to four years) found that 65 per cent of the Democrats in the country and 59 per cent of the Republicans favored a four-year term for Representatives in Congress. The population as a whole, without regard to political parties, stood 61 per cent in favor and 24 per cent opposed. Fifteen per cent expressed no opinion. (An earlier poll, taken in 1961, showed that only 51 per cent of the people surveyed were in favor of extending the term of Representatives to four years. Thirty-four per cent of those polled were against the proposal.)

As of March 1, 1966, twenty-two proposals had been introduced in both Houses of the current Congress to extend the term of office for Representatives. One proposal, H.J.R. 630, introduced by Rep. Herbert Tenzer (D., N.Y.), would provide for all House Members to run every three years in such a manner that they would run concurrently with the President every twelfth year. The remaining 21 bills provide for extension of tenure to four years. Six of these provide that the congressional elections shall take place concurrently with the Presidential election; the remaining 15 provide for staggered elections, with one half the membership running every two years. (Of the bills providing for staggered elections, the majority would initiate the

* Mr. Burton was an administrative assistant to former Congressman Henry Dixon of Utah before entering Congress in 1962. A former Assistant Professor of Political Science, Mr. Burton represents the state's 1st District and is a Member of the House Agriculture and Interior and Insular Affairs Committees.

proposal by casting lots to see which seats would be up for re-election during a concurrent Presidential campaign.)

Both Senate joint resolutions introduced provide for concurrent election with the President every four years. In addition, these two bills provide that an incumbent Representative shall not run for the Senate at mid-term without resigning his House seat before the election. (Twelve of the House Members sponsoring bills have included such a proviso, realizing the importance of such a clause in getting a bill through the Senate.) There is serious question, however, whether such an additional qualification for a U.S. Senator can be established without an amendment to the Constitution.

The division of the Members over whether or not to have the four-year term run concurrently with the President's term has sparked a great deal of debate on proposals for any extension of tenure for Representatives. Hearings on proposals extending the term were held by both the Joint Committee on the Organization of Congress and the House Judiciary Committee in 1965. Most of those who testified were interested, first, in whether any change at all was desirable, and second, if so, should the new terms run concurrently with the President's term.

In his State of the Union Message, President Johnson noted that most Representatives today spend a great deal of time and money getting ready for the next election. His second point was that the complexity of modern government makes it necessary for the individual Member of Congress to put in far more time on his committee work than was the case in earlier years. Finally, the President argued (as had Madison in the Constitutional Convention) that a longer term would attract better qualified candidates for office.

The counterargument to point one holds that if a four-year term would increase the importance of the office as the President suggests, it would seem likely that the increased desirability of the office would prompt all candidates, incumbents or otherwise, to spend *more* time and money in their bid to be elected or reelected.

All Members of Congress can testify to the truth of the President's statement that the workload of the Representative has vastly increased. However, there is again question as to whether a four-year term would be a corrective. In a survey conducted by Professor Roger H. Davidson of Dartmouth College, only three per cent of those Congressmen questioned felt that campaigning took up the majority of their time. Fourteen per cent ranked it as an important secondary activity. Seventy-seven per cent felt legislation and committee work was their most time-consuming activity. Twenty per cent felt casework and constituent relations took most of their time, and 96 per cent ranked casework and associated chores as their most important secondary activity.[1]

Obviously, a longer term would not cut down on the amount of casework and constituent mail a Representative must deal with. As the population in-increases, casework and constituent mail will also increase, regardless of tenure.

The same argument applies to campaign costs. Campaign costs in terms of cost per vote have increased very little over the years. As pointed out by George Agree, Executive Director of the National Committee for an Effective Congress:

> No special interest that budgets its political giving, at so much per year, will reduce its budget because the terms are longer. It will just give twice as much when the election comes around, and perhaps even more, because the stakes will be higher and the competition will grow. The people whose contributions will be discouraged are the little givers, who respond only at election time, in the heat of campaigns. They will give only half as much because half as often. The $10 givers will not bank their money in order to be able to give $20 four years later.[2]

Mr. Agree's latter point is particularly important when it is noted that both parties are attempting to shift their focus in fund-raising to the small contributor, as will be discussed later in this chapter.

With regard to the assertion of Presidents Johnson and Madison that the longer the term, the more qualified the candidate attracted to the office, the point could be made that any candidate must run the risk of *not* being re-elected whether every two years or every four. To date, no House seat has remained vacant for lack of candidates, and although some Representatives may not seem as qualified as desirable, there is little evidence to support a contention that the Senate has a higher proportion of "qualified" (an extremely subjective word) Members. And while there is question that a longer term would attract better qualified candidates, there certainly is no question that the votors under the four-year plan would have twice as long to wait to remove "unqualified" incumbents.

The strongest argument for a four-year term is that running concurrently with the President would make Representatives far more sensitive to the Presidential platform. As a consequence, party discipline would be improved. It is also argued that the four-year term would make Representatives far more aware of national, rather than local, interests.

To have Congress elected at the same time as the President would certainly increase the control of the executive over the legislature. Which, however, is more important: the chance that the President's party in Congress will lose some of its seats, or that the people will have the chance to exercise a sort of "referendum" on what has happened during the first two years of the President's term? Any reading of the Federalist Papers or the debates at the Philadelphia Convention will show that the House of Representatives was meant to be the branch of government most directly responsible to the people. As it stands at present, the average Representative (with the exception of those holding "safe" seats) must remain close to his constituents. The four-year term would surely reduce the incumbent's motivation to guard these ties with his District.

As for effective party control, there is no guarantee that because a disciplined party system works in the English political environment that it would necessarily work in the United States. Is making Congress "effective" the same thing as making it a speedy "rubber stamp" for the Executive? Congress is the place where broad policy decisions are reached through majority rule with consideration of the rights and interests of minorities. Congress was originally meant to be "slower" in its operations than the Executive Branch. When one considers that once a law is passed it is only very rarely repealed, the necessity for careful and unhurried debate on broad policy decisions is understandable.

It is certainly true that congressional operations need improvement, but the real question is whether improvement means making the present constitutionally ordained *modus operandi* more effective or radically changing the whole system. If the former is the more correct approach, then a concurrent four-year term is out.

The staggered plan presents various technical problems. Most sponsors of the staggered arrangement would decide which Representatives would be elected in which years by the drawing of lots. Would the drawing of lots prove to be a meaningful choice? Suppose fate has it that all urban districts, or all rural districts, or all "safe" districts, are elected at one time? Five states have only one Representative. This would mean that these states could only exercise their vote every four years, and if this vote fell at the same time as the Presidential election, there would be no chance at all of a mid-term referendum for these voters.

Another argument is that the public as a whole would have difficulty expressing its views each election since only half of the total number of Representatives would be up for re-election. (Those advocating the concurrent plan stress the same argument in terms of the President's not being able to get a working majority.)

Finally, the effects of reapportionment every ten years could frustrate the staggered system since it would have to be decided when the new districts would vote. If all terms were to end at the election following reapportionment, Members would serve two four-year and one two-year term.

The greatest concern, however, is that staggered elections for the House could easily make the body more divisive than it already is. Some districts would become purely "coat tail" districts, while others would become "referendum" districts. In addition, as Rep. Donald Rumsfeld (R., Ill.) pointed out in a statement before the House Judiciary Committee, those Members who were elected in a non-presidential year would be likelier to attain positions of seniority than Members who could be damaged from the coat tail districts.

Besides the four-year plans of both the concurrent and non-concurrent variety, two other proposals have been voiced for extending the tenure of Representatives. Rep. Tenzer's bill, H.J. R. 630, would provide for a three-year term. Under this plan all Representatives would stand for office concurrently with Presidential candidates every twelfth year. Tenzer's plan, as the plan for all Representatives to run for office in off-year elections every four years, would seem to have the disadvantage of going in the opposite direction: it would subtract from the minimal amount of coordination between the Executive and Legislative Branches which is genuinely needed to enact a legislative program. Moreover, critics of the three-year plan point out that there is not enough difference in adding only one year of tenure to make the change worthwhile.

One other suggestion (which, like the proposal for election of all Representatives every four years in off-year elections, has not yet been put before the Congress in bill form), comes again from Rep. Rumsfeld. He suggests that Members of the House run for alternating two-year and four-year terms. In this manner, they would remain closer to their constituents than in the four-year plan. In addition, the problem of seniority would be avoided. Rumsfeld believes that his proposal takes the best points from the other proposals while avoiding their disadvantages. The sponsor would implement his plan by providing that all congressional elections in a given state would be contested during those years that the senatorial candidates from the state are running. (Another method would be to divide the 435 seats into thirds and have one-third of the total number run every two years, alternating 2-year and 4-year terms.) Both methods would avoid the pitfalls of overresponsiveness or underresponsiveness to the Executive. Problems of redistricting under the Rumsfeld plan would be avoided in that all Congressmen in a particular state would be up for election in the same year. Also, the referendum value of a mid-term election would be preserved. The sponsor also believes that having the Representatives run for election at the same time as a statewide race for the Senate was taking place would provide for greater public interest and voter participation.

So far, the proposal which has received the most support has been the staggered four-year proposal introduced by Rep. Frank Chelf (D., Ky.) and others. However, Professor Robert L. Peabody of the Johns Hopkins University believes that both the concurrent and the staggered plans suffer from too many of the defects outlined above. The concurrent plan would give too much power to the Executive Branch, while the staggered plan would result in making one-half the House Presidentially-oriented, the other half unresponsive to the executive. He feels that the Rumsfeld proposal may be a good compromise:

> One possible way out of this dilemma has been suggested by Rep. Donald Rumsfeld, Republican of Illinois. . . . Over a twelve year period a Member would run four times, as compared with the present six elections: twice during presidential years, and twice in nonpresidential years. This would seem to mitigate a division of the House into two classes, one overly responsive and the other unresponsive.[3]

Nevertheless, Professor Peabody, a sharp student of the electoral process, realizes that both the Rumsfeld plan and the Tenzer plan run the risk of confusing the voter.

In the long haul, any plan that is adopted must take into account the historic nature of the House of Representatives as the branch of government closest to the people. All proposals for extending the term of Congressmen involve an extremely important value judgment on how our government is to operate.

Financing Political Parties

In the early days, most national and local elections in the U.S. were preceded by a caucus of concerned citizens who selected the candidate of their party to run in the election. Later, the political convention was introduced. As the American electoral system became more democratic, the primary election came into being and today it has all but replaced the local and state conventions in most areas. As more and more citizens have become involved in selecting their party's candidates, the costs of electioneering have risen correspondingly; in fact, under the primary system, a candidate for all practical purposes must run his campaign twice.

Air travel has added greatly to the expense of campaigning. Advertising costs—radio and television, newspaper and magazine, billboard and poster—have increased. More and more campaigns today are assisted by public relations and polling organizations, and the services of these experts do not come cheap. Additionally, paid professional manpower hired for the duration of the campaign is replacing the "volunteer army" of former days, and I think that is unfortunate.

Where Does the Money Come From?

There are three main sources of campaign funds. First, there are the candidates themselves. The 1960 election clearly demonstrated the advantages of personal wealth in running for the Presidency. Second, there are the so-called "Fat Cats," i.e., wealthy contributors to the political campaign. Until recent times these individuals have coughed up the lion's share of national campaign budgets. A third source of campaign funds is the "small contributor" of the community, the fellow who donates to the campaign because he likes the candidate(s) and/or party.

Three additional sources of campaign funds are gone but not forgotton: in the late 19th century, big business alone financed many campaigns at all levels of government. After a good deal of public outrage, legislation was was passed in 1907 forbidding corporate donations at the federal level. Labor unions also have been prevented by law from contributing to campaigns for federal office. (In 33 states similar laws prevent contributions from business at the state and local level; four states prevent contributions from labor at state and local level.)

Political fund-raising in the United States has employed most of the techniques known to man for making a dollar—campaign dinners, cocktail parties, theater benefits, movie premieres; all offer the loyal party supporter something for his money that direct mail solicitation does not have. One new wrinkle in political fund-raising is the "gala," an event which, because of its size and production costs, is usually held for the benefit of the national party organization. Washington is the favored location for such affairs, with New York second, followed by Chicago, Los Angeles, and San Francisco. Generally the party sponsoring the event draws on a large number of popular entertainers to provide their services either free or at the lowest price possible.

Another new approach to raising funds is the small select private party. This consists of inviting a small group of one's friends to meet in one's home with a particular incumbent or candidate. Cocktails and dinner may be served. In some cases the possibility of a donation is mentioned in the invitation, but generally no specific amount is set as the atmosphere is informal and the guests invited can usually be expected to come up with $100 or more for the candidate. (In some cases amounts of even $1000 to $5000 may be the average donation.) Washington and New York are again the favored locations for these gatherings.

Matthew McCloskey, Democratic financier, has been credited with developing the idea of the "Presidents' Club," an organization conceived during the Kennedy Administration. A very select group of Democrats who would contribute $1,000 or more to the party comprised the original club. Today the club has well over 4,000 members with "chapters" in many states. Republicans have likewise sought contributions of $1,000 from the wealthy for a war chest for congressional candidates.

Corporate Advertising

At their $2 million convention in Atlantic City in 1964 (three times the cost of their own 1960 convention and three times the cost of the 1964 Republican gathering in San Francisco), the Democratic Party employed with marked success another way to raise funds. In 1960 they had sold advertising to industry in their convention program at $5,000 per page. (This book advertising was the same price the Republicans charged in 1960 and at their 1964 convention.) In 1964 the Democrats hiked the price to $15,000 a page and the venture raised $1 million.

The success of the convention advertising led the Democrats to repeat the idea in the post-election period and in December of 1965 it was announced that the Democratic National Committee would publish a book entitled, *Toward An Age of Greatness*, extolling the achievements of the Johnson Administration. The book's creator was Richard Maguire, former Democratic National Treasurer. Maguire succeeded in selling advertisements at

$15,000 each to such likely customers as Lockheed Aircraft, Sperry Rand, Martin Marietta, General Motors, and Ford. Robert S. Boyd in *The Washington Post* summed up the situation as follows:

> International Telephone and Telegraph used its page to brag of its accomplishments at the Camp Kilmer Job Corps. Elsewhere in the book appears an article by Poverty War Chief Sargent Shriver, who holds the strings on ITT's contract. A number of businesses subject to federal regulation bought ads—like railroads, airlines, pipelines, and shipping lines eager for government subsidies. . . . Las Vegas' gaudy Sahara Hotel, and New York's upper-crusty Carlyle, favorite of the Kennedy clan, coughed up for the Administration.[4]

The public concern over the use of advertising revenue finally prompted the Democrats to announce that the funds from such advertising would be put into a special "educational fund" to support Voter Education Committees in each state. Washington newsman Walter Pincus notes that from the outset such committees appeared to be far from nonpartisan:

> In each state, VEC organizations are made up in part by a representative of each Democratic Congressman and the party's state committee. There is no mention of including Republicans.[5]

By early 1966 criticism of Democratic fund-raising techniques prompted the Democratic National Committee to announce that $600,000 worth of revenue from the "Age of Greatness" was being transferred to a bipartisan foundation which would match funds raised in a similar manner by the Republicans. This arrangement fell through, however, when the foundation refused to accept the money. The Democrats are still pondering the question of what to do with the $600,000. (In the meantime, Maguire enjoyed some very unfavorable publicity when it was revealed that Administration employees were being solicited for tickets to a $100-a-plate dinner.) Originally, the Democrats had planned to use the advertising revenue to help out Democratic candidates and incumbents who were to distribute the books at party film premieres in their districts.

Sen. John Williams (R., Del.) early in 1966 put a crimp in the publications field when his amendment to an appropriations bill was passed. It prohibits corporations from taking out advertisements in political publications and treating them as business expenses for tax purposes. The amendment is expected to have wide-sweeping effect in many states, where for years state political committees have published "guides" or "yearbooks" which were loaded with business ads and produced considerable revenue for state organizations.

Direct Mail Solicitation

In 1962, the Republican National Committee succeeded in obtaining three-quarters of a million dollars through direct mail solicitation. In 1963 the Committee enjoyed even greater success when it received over $1.1

million from "small contributors." In 1964, even before Senator Goldwater announced his candidacy, the National Draft Goldwater Committee had received $750,000 in contributions from "small contributors" contacted through mailings. From January of 1964 (when Goldwater announced his candidacy) until convention time the various Goldwater committees attracted $5 million in funds, primarily from "small contributors."

Several conclusions regarding political fund-raising can be drawn from the 1964 campaign. First, the direct mail approach, if properly organized and administered, does work. Second, big business, although normally faithful to the Republicans, is not beyond switching its contributions to the Democrats when it is felt investment in a Republican candidate would yield little return. This points up the fact that, third, big money is usually bet on a winning horse. (Occasionally both candidates receive equal sums. In these cases the contributors are "playing it safe.")

Proposed Legislation Affecting Campaign Financing

Shortly after the Kennedy election, the House Committee on Campaign Expenditures of the 86th Congress held hearings on possible revision of the Election Laws. Even before the great expenditures of 1960, various proposals had been introduced on both sides of Capitol Hill for a general "updating" of the laws regulating campaign expenditures. Under present regulations, a candidate for the Senate may spend only $25,000 in the final election. A House candidate is limited to $5,000. Finally, a limit of $3 million is set on the amount which a party's national political committee may spend in any calendar year.

These limits have been ineffective from the start. The fact is that candidates have historically lived within the letter of the law while the spirit of the law was forgotten. The limits set by the law apply only to what the candidate himself spends; not to the amounts spent by his friends or relatives in promoting his candidacy. Thus, the many independent committees formed to support each candidate are not included in the candidate's personal expenditures. (The proliferation of "independent" committees also aids loyal contributors who by law can give only $3,000 to a particular committee without paying a gift tax.)

Political committees are required to file statements four times a year with the Clerk of the House of Representatives. Legally, these committees are defined as organizations which accept money to influence the election of candidates in two or more states, or within a single state when such a committee is a branch or division of a national organization. Such committees must report the names and addresses of those individuals who gave more than $100, the grand total of all contributions, the names and addresses of those persons or organizations to whom disbursements of $10 or more were made, and the total amount of expenditures.

A recent example of committee multiplication which aroused considerable unrest in the House and indeed in the national press was the case of Rep. Richard Ottinger (D., N.Y.). What made the Ottinger case so interesting is that while no laws were broken, the Representative succeeded in raising $187,000, of which $160,000 came from the candidate's mother and sister alone. What was done was to set up over 30 different committees for the receipt of contributions. Since federal law limits contributions to $5,000 for each committee, and to $3,000 if a gift tax is to be avoided, both the mother and sister gave $3,000 each to 27 different committees.[6]

Since the reporting laws of both New York State and the United States and indeed the limits set by the Federal Corrupt Practices Act were all complied with, the disclosure of Ottinger's sources of funds provoked perhaps even greater public interest than if the candidate had actually violated the law. An editorial in the *New York Herald Tribune* of December 23, 1964, pointed out that it was not Ottinger or candidates like him that were primarily at fault.

> The trouble is, first, that these limits are so absurdly low as to be totally unrealistic; and, second, that the laws have loopholes large enough to drive a Brink's truck through. The upshot is that candidates don't even try to conform to the spirit of the law . . .

To make the laws regulating campaign expenditures more realistic has been a goal of both parties for some time. As early as 1908, Theodore Roosevelt suggested federal contributions to campaigns. First of all, however, there is the problem of what constitutes a reasonable limit on expenditures. Senator Paul Douglas, writing in the August, 1952, edition of *Atlantic Monthly*, suggested a ceiling of 10¢ per registered voter for the Presidential, senatorial, and congressional candidates. Today this figure would probably be too low.

In recent years there has been a revival of Roosevelt's proposal to provide some funds for federal campaigns out of the national treasury. In 1956 this suggestion was put before Congress by the late Senator Richard Neuberger of Oregon. Since the death of her husband, Senator Maurine Neuberger has sponsored this proposal on several occasions. The difficulty here, of course, is in deciding which parties would be eligible to receive such funds. Most proponents would give funds only to the two major parties, which would discourage competition by third parties. (However, if a membership quota were used, perhaps this method could be made more equitable.)

A more practical approach is found in proposals for giving tax incentives.

An equally frequent suggestion is the modernization of the campaign laws so that a more realistic limit would be placed on the amount of money a candidate for a particular office might legally raise without resorting to complicated networks of committees set up merely to circumvent the present law. In addition, it has been suggested that more adequate reporting be required of all candidates for office on the Florida model. Herbert Alexander writes that:

. . . an effective publicity system can be self-regulatory. The experience gained under Florida's 1951 who-gave-it-who-got-it-law, which appears to command the respect of practioners and public alike, is that candidates have watched each other like hawks, sending their workers regularly to copy lists of contributors and amounts for their opponents, and then carefully checking for violations and compliance. Moreover, Florida reporters are said to eagerly await the arrival of financial reports in order that they may send accounts of fair contents to their offices for publication.[7]

During the 1960 hearings before the House Committee on Campaign Expenditures, Robert W. Sarnoff, of the National Broadcasting Company, Inc., spoke out in favor of shortening the campaign period. At that time Sarnoff suggested that the present campaign period was established in a time when the railroad was yet to be developed. He noted that the first conventions were held in September and December of 1831, one year before the election. Until the 1860's they were held in May and finally, as transportation improved, moved up to July. Sarnoff's reasoning is as follows:

A shortened campaign would cut costs not only in the areas of paid political broadcasts but for electioneering of all kinds. It offers numerous other advantages. It would cut down the extraordinary physical strain and drain on the candidates themselves. It would enable Congress to extend a session in which there is usually a heavy backlog of unfinished business. . . . It would invite a closer concentration of public attention on the essential issues, free of repetition and overexposure risked by the candidate in a long, drawn-out campaign.[8]

At the same time, Sarnoff made it quite clear that he was not in favor of giving away free broadcasting time to the candidates, which has been done at network discretion, on an equal-time basis, for the two major candidates in the past.

President Kennedy's Committee on Campaign Costs rejected the idea of shortening the campaign period on the basis that little-known candidates need as much time as possible to appear before the public. The President's Commission took difference with Mr. Sarnoff, who emphasized that his network had done all possible to lower costs and provide a reasonable amount of free time for political programs. However, the Commission did advocate a measurement for a specified amount of free time to be provided by the broadcasting industry. It was their feeling that every campaign was different and further study would be given to such a proposal.

Additionally, the President's Commission suggested:

(1) Bipartisan contributions by corporations and labor unions to encourage political participation through voter education and registration activities. Such contributions should be tax deductible.

(2) A tax credit for individuals of up to $10 in credits per year in all years should be allowed. This limit would establish a broad base, where if larger credits were to be allowed they would only encourage the "Fat Cats." Such contributions could only be made to the national committee of each party and/or to one committee in each state designated by the national committee while, at the same time, the "meaningless ceilings on an individual contribution and on total expenditures by political committees be abolished."[9]

(3) That an effective system of public disclosure of political fund-raising and disbursement be implemented. Also, individuals contributing over $5,000 per year should be required to submit a similar report.

The Commission also recommended maintaining and strictly enforcing the law forbidding *partisan* political support by unions and corporations alike and that all other laws regulating campaign fund-raising and spending be rigidly enforced. Finally, it urged further research in this area in order to improve methods of fund-raising by the political parties, concluding that after a "trial period with the changes proposed, a second evaluation of campaign finance should be made."[10] Most important, the Commission suggested that, if the proposals set down failed to raise enough money for the parties, perhaps a "matching incentive system be attempted whereby the government would match (with specified limitations) a percentage of the money raised by the two parties."

Conclusion

Both the Democrats and the Republicans have demonstrated their ability to raise money (and to spend it) in recent years. In some cases candidates have ignored the law; in other cases the candidates and their parties have circumvented the law. The Federal Corrupt Practices Act is known today for its loopholes rather than for its positive contribution to the American electoral system. The law should be made more realistic. At the same time, existing laws governing reporting should be strictly enforced. Although both corporations and unions are now forbidden to contribute to political campaigns, there is no reason why they could not work together to "get out the vote" in fairly administered bipartisan programs. The examples of AMPAC (American Medical Association Political Action Committee), COPE (Committee on Political Education of the AFL/CIO), and BIPAC (Business-Industry Political Action Committee) have demonstrated the effectiveness of work in this area. Finally, the parties themselves should investigate new ways to raise money from the "small contributor" within the law.

At this time it does not seem advisable, in my opinion, to proivde for a direct federal subsidy to political campaigns. Elections are by nature a thing of the people, not of the government. If worse comes to worst, the parties themselves must find ways to economize without impairing their effectiveness. There is a tendency today to "go overboard" in campaigns. Electioneering has become a major business in itself and a modern business deserves modern management techniques, not only in conducting the campaigning itself, but also in the management of the party finances. A direct subsidy would also involve the control of the opposition's pocketbook by the party in power at that time. If government aid should be provided to the American political parties, it should be provided indirectly, in the form of some kind of tax incentive.

Most important, any such legislation should encourage financial support from citizens at all economic levels.

Finally, every American should feel an obligation to provide a check on abuses in fund-raising. Our parties are made up of and directed by individual citizens. Our government is composed of and run by individual citizens. If, as citizens, we become apathetic about campaign financing and fair election practices, no amount of legislation can improve either.

With the problems discussed in this chapter in mind, I believe there are two major categories in which change is needed. The first category of proposals deals with the prevention of abuses. The second is for the purpose of stimulating or assisting parties and candidates in adequately financing campaigns.

Insofar as the prevention of abuses during a campaign is concerned, I suggest that the following steps be taken:

1. Cost ceilings should be removed completely.
2. An effective limit on the size of an individual's contribution should be established.
3. There should be full disclosures of contributions and expenditures made to influence the outcome of national elections. (Right now national committees must report, but contributions to committees within a state for national campaign use need not be reported.)
4. The report should be filed with the Comptroller General of the United States and not with the Clerk of the House or Senate.
5. The Justice Department should enforce the laws on contributions and reporting.
6. An amendment to the Hatch Act should be made to authorize the Civil Service Commission to take action against any federal employee who solicits political contributions. (Under the present law high-ranking federal employees are not subject to the Civil Service Commission. Congressman Ancher Nelsen (R., Minn.) has recently introduced a bill to help plug this loophole.)

In order to better stimulate and assist parties and candidates in financing campaigns I suggest the following:

1. Amend the equal-time provision (Sec. 315, Federal Communications Act) to enable T.V. and radio to grant more free time to major party candidates without having to give the same treatment to minor parties.
2. Allow the official party committees in each state the privilege of sending free of charge one statewide mailing during the course of each biennial campaign. This could be done by providing to such committees the required quantities of a special envelope which could be mailed without postage during a 30-day period preceding the election.
3. Provide government aircraft without charge for the travel of the Presidential and Vice-Presidential candidates of the major parties for three or four months before a Presidential election.
4. Provide that political contributions up to $100 per individual would be tax deductible. This would help encourage small contributions.

References

1. Hearings, House Judiciary Subcommittee No. 5, "Congressional Tenure of Office," 89th Congress.
2. *Ibid.*

3. *Congressional Record*, March 30, 1966, pp. A1841–1844.
4. December 8, 1965.
5. *Washington Star*, September 27, 1965.
6. *Congressional Record*, 89th Congress, 1st Session.
7. *Money, Politics, and Public Reporting*, Princeton, N.J., 1969.
8. Hearings, House Committee on Campaign Expenditures, 86th Congress, 2nd Session, 1960.
9. *Financing Presidential Campaigns*, Washington, D. C., 1962.
10. *Ibid.*

BOB WILSON, M.C.
36th District, California

CONGRESSIONAL ETHICS

*by Bob Wilson, M.C.**

At the outset, it should be understood that Congress *does* now have a "Code of Ethics." On July 11, 1958, it passed such a code setting forth ten tenets to which "any person in Government service should" adhere.[1]

Although it is difficult to understand how the words "any person in Government service" could be misconstrued to leave out officials and employees of the legislative branch of government, Senator Lyndon B. Johnson, on the day the Code was passed, reminded Congress:

> The committee understands and intends that this resolution apply to every servant of the public whether he be the President, a Member of Congress, a lifelong career employee, or an employee engaged only on a temporary basis . . .[2]

Incredibly, the interpretation came to be that the Code applied only to officials and employees of the executive branch of government. In an attempt to re-establish the application of the Code to Members of Congress, and to make it the "sense of the Congress that it should be emphasized to the public . . . that (1) the operations of the Government generally, including the legislative branch, are characterized by devotion to duty in accordance with high moral and ethical principles; and (2) these principles have been set forth in detail in House Concurrent Resolution 175, 85th Congress (72 Stat. B12), providing a Code of Ethics for Government Service," I introduced, on July 18, 1963, a concurrent resolution reiterating the tenets of the bill originally introduced by Rep. Charles Bennett (D. Fla.). The text of the resolution was released to the press, and a few days later, in the absence of any discernible stir on the Floor of the House, I sent out a mimeographed letter to Members calling their attention to the resolution (and the existing

---

* Mr. Wilson was first elected to Congress in 1952 and represents the 36th Congressional District of California. He serves on the House Armed Services Committee and has held a number of leadership posts in the Republican Party, including the chairmanship of the National Republican Congressional Committee since 1962.

Code). My file contains two responses: one colleague offered his support of the measure; another thanked me for calling the matter to his attention.

The Code lacks teeth and may even be grossly naive. In view of the widespread misapprehension that Congress has no "Code of Ethics," however, I here reprint the text of the "Code of Ethics for Government Service."

Any person in government service should:

I. Put loyalty to the highest moral principles and to country above loyalty to persons, party, or Government department.

II. Uphold the Constitution, laws, and legal regulations of the United States and of all governments therein and never be a party to their evasion.

III. Give a full day's labor for a full day's pay; giving to the performance of his duties his earnest effort and best thought.

IV. Seek to find and employ more efficient and economical ways of getting tasks accomplished.

V. Never discriminate unfairly by the dispensing of special favors or privileges to anyone, whether for remuneration or not; and never accept, for himself or his family, favors or benefits under circumstances which might be construed by reasonable persons as influencing the performance of his governmental duties.

VI. Make no private promises of any kind binding upon the duties of office, since a Government employee has no private word which can be binding on public duty.

VII. Engage in no business with the Government, either directly or indirectly, which is inconsistent with the conscientious performance of his governmental duties.

VIII. Never use any information coming to him confidentially in the performance of governmental duties as a means for making private profit.

IX. Expose corruption wherever discovered.

X. Uphold these principles, ever conscious that public office is a public trust.

The problem in trying to deal with congressional ethics through disclosure of "personal holdings" or the establishment of a rigid code was summed up by former Congressman Oliver Bolton (R., Ohio) in a report to his constituents on May 20, 1963:

While I respect these efforts, they all have two common failings; first, they are unenforceable; and second, they foolishly attempt to legislate moral conduct and ethics.

During a debate on the floor of the House of Representatives in 1811 . . . John C. Calhoun pinpointed the problem when he said, "The very essence of a free government consists in considering offices as public trusts, bestowed for the good of the country, and not for the benefit of an individual or a party."

If, through various legislative means, we were to close off every avenue of temptation, would we not destroy the entire concept of "public trust" in the process? Can a teacher imbue a true code of honor in her pupils if she suspiciously hovers over each of them during an examination in an effort to catch the occasional cheater?[3]

At the same time, a fair and reasonable outline of conduct for the members of any group can hardly be considered an evil. Most groups in society find it advisable at one time or another to adopt some written standard of conduct, from the Hippocratic oath of the medical profession to the oath required of Boy Scouts. (Incidentally, Mr. Bolton's analogy to the teacher may contain some inadvertent humor: "The teaching profession," says the Danforth Foundation's Merrimon Cuninggim, "is the only profession that has no definition for malpractice."[4])

I believe Congress should have some variety of code of ethics for its Members. If the existing one is not acceptable to most Members and/or the public, study should be given to the drafting of a new and better one.

Unfortunately, the best of codes will not provide a guarantee against occasional misbehavior by Members. Recalling an impassioned speech on the House floor by William Jennings Bryan citing the Roman Senate, "whose power was eroded and corrupted by the Roman Emperor, and they sank into oblivion with presents, gifts, luxurious chariots, villas, and nepotism," Professor Erwin Krasnow points out:

> Although the prophecy of doom may be part of congressional histrionics, no one disputes the harmful potential of conflicts between the official duties of a Member of Congress and his personal economic advantage. Basically, the problem is not whether to have a system of legal restraints on conflict of interest, but how to design a system which achieves the maximum protection for both the Members of Congress and the public, and a minimum of undesirable collateral results.[5]

Those who advocate stringent enforcement provisions governing misconduct by officials of the Legislative Branch *equal* to those applied against officials of the Executive Branch would do well to keep in mind that Members of Congress, unlike the latter officials, are subject to discipline of the voters every two years. In any case of misbehavior by a Congressman, the citizens whose interests he represents have an opportunity to "throw the rascal out" at the next election. The question of "who watches the watchers" is easily answered: the people. This is the very foundation of our democratic system of government, and the opportunity to pass judgment on one's Representative in the national legislature is not the least of several compelling reasons for retaining the constitutional provision of a two-year term for Members of the U.S. House of Representatives.

The *standards* of conduct for government officials should apply equally to those of the executive and legislative branches. However, the provisions for enforcing adherence to those standards may, and I believe should, be different. Indeed, enforcement provisions governing the conduct of Members of the House may be less stringent even than those applied to Members of the Senate, as the latter are subject to recall by the people only every six years.

Moreover, we should note that Members of Congress are subject to prosecution for violation of certain existing laws: "Members of Congress are subject to the prohibitions against bribery (sections 204 and 205, Title 18 of the U.S. Code), against 'procurement' of Government contracts (sec. 216), and against acceptance of compensation for services in connection with proceedings before Federal agencies (sec. 281)."[6]

The existing Code of Ethics, the opportunity for recall by the people every two years, and the statutory provisions cited above notwithstanding, the people are entitled to some better safeguards against abuse of the public trust by *all* officials of the government. As Senator Kenneth Keating said on the Floor of the Senate a couple of years ago:

> It has never been more important than it is today—when we are engaged in a life and death struggle with tyranny—to maintain confidence in our government and to strengthen the moral fiber of our nation. Even though the abuses are infrequent, the danger from low ethical standards in any branch of government has never been more serious.[7]

In the last twenty years, more than one hundred measures have been introduced in both Houses of Congress (42 of them in the 88th Congress) aimed at providing answers of one sort or another to the "ethics problem" in Congress. More than 20 Members of the House and a number of Senators addressed themselves to the need for tighter standards of conduct for officials of the legislative branch in testimony before the Joint Committee on the Organization of Congress in 1965. Probably as an outgrowth of questions raised in the press recently concerning fund-raising activities of one of its members, the Senate in 1965 established a Select Committee on Ethics.

Similarly, it is time for the House to appoint a committee (or commission) to review existing codes and statutes with a view to establishing clear guidelines and enacting provisions for enforcement of laws governing the conduct of its members. In light of the fact that the Senate already has established such a committee, and in consideration both of the differences between the two bodies and the constitutional provision that "each house shall be the sole judge of the . . . qualifications of its own members . . . (and) may . . . punish its members for disorderly behavior," a joint committee would seem less desirable at this time than separate studies conducted by both houses.

As it is extremely difficult, if not impossible, to "legislate morality," I suggest it would be desirable also for the committee or commission to include in its membership a number of private citizens. This would both militate against charges of "rigging" or "whitewash" and bring expert, dispassionate judgment to bear on an admittedly complex subject.

As an illustration of just how frustrating it is to deal in this area, I recall the following excerpt from testimony by former Congressman John Lindsay before the Joint Organization Committee last year:

> I must say that one of my assignments as a member of that Ford Foundation–sponsored committee (to review conflict-of-interest laws for the executive branch) was to write the British Government and get all the rules and regulations covering their Members of Parliament on this subject. I dutifully wrote a letter to the right people and expected a truckload of material to come back. Instead of that, I received a one-paragraph letter back saying, "Dear Mr. Lindsay, we expect our Members in Parliament to act like gentlemen."[8]

In fact, the British Parliament takes a very strict view of the relations of its members ito outsde interests. Professor K. C. Wheare, former Member of Parliament, writes:

> The power of the two houses of the legislature in the United Kingdom to punish for contempt of themselves is a strong power and is by no means a dead letter. . . . It acts as a restriction upon the press and the public in their freedom to criticize the conduct of members of the houses.[9]

Most legislatures accept certain limits governing the conduct of their members, although they differ widely in their specific approaches to the problem.

In my own view, six considerations are of major importance in dealing with the matter of ethical standards for Members of the U.S. Congress. First, each house should have a *standing* committee on ethics, both to insure that the public interest will be safeguarded and to serve as a protective device for Members of Congress against unwarranted charges leveled at them. (A joint committee would be acceptable, but for reasons cited earlier in these pages, separate committees would seem preferable at present.)

Second, any committee or commission so established (by both houses separately or together) should include private citizens sitting as active members of the unit, this to contribute expertise and unbiased judgment and also to counter charges of "rigging" or "whitewash."

Third, the guidelines contained in the existing Code of Ethics are vague, to say the least. It would be to the benefit of the Members as well as to the public to have more clearly defined guidelines.

Fourth, a law is hardly sufficient without adequate enforcement provisions for penalty in the event of failure to comply. Therefore, we should add teeth to the code by making sure that violators will be subject to discipline and that such discipline can in fact be imposed.

Fifth, I believe the legislation should be aimed at disclosure rather than restriction. A Member of Congress is also a citizen, and hopefully an active participant in the affairs of his community. He should not be barred from sitting on the Interior Committee because he represents a western district, or from sitting on the Agriculture Committee because he is a farmer, or from serving on the Judiciary Committee because he is a lawyer. Let the public decide for whom a Member speaks by making his *major* financial activities a matter of public record. Privacy is a precious thing, but a Member of Congress no less than an official of the executive branch is a public servant, and as such the public has a right to know what his major financial investments and obligations are.

In May, 1966, President Johnson sent a message to Congress proposing that Members of Congress disclose annually income received for personal services and gifts of $100 or more in cash or kind. Unfortunately, the President's proposal is deficient. As explained by Senator Clifford Case (R., N.J.), long distinguished for his efforts to strengthen congressional ethics:

I am delighted by the President's recognition that disclosure is the most effective way to protect the integrity of elective office. I am deeply disappointed that the recognition is only skin deep.

In the area of campaign financing the President, pointing out in his message the weakness and narrowness of existing law, called for "full disclosure." The whole thrust of his message, so far as campaign contributions and expenditures go, was a vigorous endorsement of the fullest possible reporting. "Artificial limits breed, artificial disclosures," he said. I agree, and I have long supported legislation strengthening our Corrupt Practices Act to this end.

Regrettably, the specific recommendation of the President with regard to Members of Congress, apart from campaign financing, falls far short of complete disclosure. Here he proposes to require disclosure only of income received for "personal services" and gifts of substantial value. It would not require reporting of transactions in real property, or any other kind of property for that matter. It would not require a statement of assets or liabilities such as loans.

Omission of such vital information would drastically limit the effectiveness of any disclosure requirement. For my part, I believe we would be adding "more loophole than law," as the President characterized current legislation governing campaign contributions and expenditures.[10]

As the Senator summed up the matter:

To those who say half a loaf is better than no bread, I answer: Perhaps, but not if acceptance of half a loaf sets back, perhaps indefinitely, our chance of getting the whole loaf in the form of really effective disclosure legislation.[11]

I associate myself with the Senator's views and argue for a strong bill the first time around.

Finally, ethics in the broader sense encompasses a great deal more than disclosure of Members' financial dealings. If Congress is really sincere about improving its public image, it must look to the correction of several other practices, such as the increasing tendency to hold committee hearings in executive session (see chapter by Mr. Griffin), the continuing prohibition against telecast and broadcast coverage of proceedings on the Floor of the House and of public hearings of committees (see chapter by Mr. Ellsworth), and the willful distortion of salary figures of congressional office employees under the "basic rate" method of determining and reporting clerk hire (see chapter by Mr. Broyhill). "The whole is equal to the sum of its parts," and that equation speaks also to the public image of our national House of Representatives.

REFERENCES

1. 86th Congress, 1st Session, House Document No. 103.
2. *Congressional Record*, July 11, 1958, p. 13557.
3. "Nevertheless," Mr. Bolton continued, "the people are entitled to expect from their elected representatives in the Federal Government and the employees of the legislative branch a standard above that of the market place, for these public servants are entrusted with the welfare of the nation, often the world. As a lawyer, I believe disbarment procedures by Bar Associations offer a possible solution . . ."

4. *Time* Magazine, May 6, 1966.

5. "Congressional Conflicts of Interest: Who Watches the Watchers?" *Congressional Record*, Sept. 29, 1964, Erwin G. Krasnow and Rep. Richard E. Lankford, pp. 22327–22330.

6. U.S. House of Representatives, Subcommittee No. 5 of the Committee on the Judiciary, Staff Report, 85th Congress, 2nd Session (1958).

7. *Congressional Record*, July 2, 1964, p. 15315.

8. Hearings, Joint Committee on the Organization of Congress, Part 3, p. 446, 1965.

9. Wheare, K. C., *Legislatures*, Oxford University Press, 1963.

10. Partial Test of Remarks by Senator Clifford P. Case, Annual Mid-Year Conference of New Jersey Conference of Mayors, Princeton, New Jersey, June 1, 1966.

11. *Ibid.*

PART 4
Information, Technology, and Citizens' Rights

ROBERT F. ELLSWORTH, M.C.
3rd District, Kansas

THE CASE FOR TELEVISION AND RADIO COVERAGE

*by Robert F. Ellsworth, M.C.**

The doors of the United States Congress are, in an alarmingly real sense, closed to the American public.

This is so despite the fact that Members of Congress are the direct representatives of the people and that the people have an inherent right to witness their national legislators at work.

The U.S. constitutional guarantee of freedom of the press means more than freedom to express dissenting views; it also means freedom to have immediate access to debate and discussion in the supreme legislative body of the land, the Congress.

Full access to the actions of Congress realistically implies full access by the nation's mass news media—newspapers, periodicals, television, and radio.

But a policy of discrimination exists in the Congress today. Even though television and radio have created a revolution in communications techniques in recent years, television and radio do not have the same full access to congressional activity enjoyed by the print media, newspapers and periodicals. Indeed, for television and radio, the doors of Congress are closed.

Nine of my colleagues and I introduced resolutions in the House of Representatives on January 12, 1966, (see Appendices V and VI) to (1) allow televising and broadcasting of proceedings on the Floor of the House, and (2) permit television and radio coverage of public hearings of House committees.

To the extent that the adoption of these resolutions would establish a vehicle for furthering public understanding and appreciation of the workings

---

* Mr. Ellsworth is a member of the Post Office and Civil Service and Veterans' Affairs Committees of the House and of the Joint Economic Committee. He was first elected to Congress in 1960 from the 3rd District of Kansas.

of the legislative branch of our government, they constitute an important first step in the effort to shape a twentieth-century Congress.

Repeatedly, television and radio personnel have sought permission to broadcast "live," or to record by film, sessions of the Congress. And Congress has been persistent in its refusal to permit such broadcasting. In making its own rules and establishing its own precedents, Congress has explicitly prohibited radio and television coverage of the House and Senate chambers. Consequently, the Congress itself must shoulder much of the blame for its current nondescript image in the eyes of the American people.

The arguments in favor of telecasting and broadcasting in Congress are sound. The major arguments might be listed as follows:

1. That the people have a right to see and hear what is happening in their national legislature;
2. That *all* news media should be permitted equal access to activities of the Congress, *with* the tools of their trade;
3. That there is an urgent need for Congress to be on a more equal footing with the executive branch in terms of communicating its involvement in national policies, programs, and issues.

The decision to shield the activities of Congress from the public eye is totally unjustified and a break in faith with the American people. The policy of secrecy leads to the natural question, "What does Congress have to hide?" And perhaps even more damning, the prohibition of electronic coverage of Congress implies to many that the national legislature has become so far overshadowed by the other branches of the federal government that "live" coverage would be of little importance.

As an editorial in *The New York Times* summed it up:

The immediacy of television makes it an ideal instrument for giving the citizen a sense of participation in governmental affairs. There is, of course, the risk that legislators will succumb to the temptation to "ham it up" for the unseen audience. And there are the mechanical difficulties of keeping cameras, wires and other equipment from making a shambles of chambers designed before the electronic era. But none of these obstacles should outweigh the gains to the democratic process that could flow from wider use of TV to link citizen and lawmaker.[1]

There is increasing evidence today that a significant proportion of the population has only the most meager knowledge of the functions and responsibilities of Congress. A recent Gallup Poll indicated that 57 per cent of the American people do not know the name of the person who represents them in Congress, 41 per cent do not know to which political party their Representative belongs, and 81 per cent do not know how their Representative voted on any major issue!

Clearly, the public is uninformed when it comes to the Congress. As the Gallup figures show, public ignorance is widespread. And the prohibition of television and radio coverage contributes to the public's ignorance of Congress.

It is my opinion that the electronic media people have been exceedingly restrained and patient under a system which grants their competitors—newspapers and periodicals—unfair advantages in reporting. The Congress provides quite adequate facilities for coverage by the print media; a large portion of both the House and Senate galleries is restricted to use by pencil-and-paper reporters.

But the Congress does not permit television and radio reporters equal access. Oh, yes, television and radio reporters are allowed admittance to the press galleries, *but* they are not permitted to bring along the tools of their trade, the camera and the microphone. Interestingly, the President of the United States recently invested many thousands of dollars in equipping the White House with the latest facilities for the electronic media.

Members of Congress have been heard to complain about the diminishing influence of the legislative branch as compared to the executive. Yet, the Congress is unwilling to adapt its rules to changing times. The President is well aware of the importance of television and radio in accurately reporting his positions; in fact, spokesmen for the President have publicly acknowledged that he prefers to use television and radio over newspapers and periodicals in the belief that there is less chance for misinterpretation and greater opportunity for person-to-person communication. The President has a point, and the Congress ought to recognize it.

In the absence of written rules governing television and radio coverage in Congress, the decision concerning broadcasting, at least in the House, rests with the discretion of the Speaker.

No Speaker has ever allowed live broadcasting of a House session. Other standards, however, have been applied to committee hearings. In the 1951–52 session, Speaker Rayburn ruled that committees had no power to authorize telecasting or broadcasting of their public hearings on the grounds that the Rules of the House, which are expressly made the rules of its committees, are silent on this subject. In the 1953–54 session under Speaker Martin, the opposite position was taken and committees permitted live coverage. In the Senate, the committee chairmen possess the power to decide whether or not live coverage will be allowed.

The Congress cannot continue to stand still in a world which is moving faster and faster. And the Congress cannot continue to deny television and radio coverage of its activities by simply citing the hollow fear that it may trip over an electric cord or be "distracted" by a bright light. Modern televising techniques require no special lights or equipment or other disturbing factors which might result in interference with the normal debate.

The lessons taught in the executive branch ought to be heeded. Through its wise utilization of the mass media—*all* mass media—the executive has succeeded in pushing Congress into the background. It is a rare American who can say that he has not seen the President in action over television. Rarer still is the American who can say he *has* seen his Congress in action.

As *The New York Times* correspondent Tom Wicker put it:

The essential fact of the Executive-Congressional balance today is not that the Executive is too big, but that Congress has let itself become too small. The Presidency has evolved in changing times and necessities as a remarkable instrument of governing power; but Congress has not similarly grown and adapted itself to new conditions.[2]

Mr. Wicker may have made this observation with the knowledge that as of May, 1964, the U.S. Bureau of the Census reported that 93 per cent of the homes in this country had one or more television sets. Indeed, more homes in this country are equipped with television sets than with telephones![3]

Congress has a responsibility to preserve its prestige and influence under our system of separation of powers. It has a responsibility to grant equality in its treatment of the mass communicators. It has a responsibility to keep the people informed, for an informed electorate is the very cornerstone of American democracy.

Truly, Congress has a responsibility to open its doors to the American people.

REFERENCES

1. *The New York Times*, April 21, 1966.
2. *The New York Times*, August 24, 1965.
3. Wattenberg, Ben J., and Richard M. Scammon, *This U.S.A.*, Garden City, N.Y., Doubleday & Co., 1965.

CHARLES McC. MATHIAS, JR., M.C.
6th District, Maryland

MANAGING THE DISTRICT OF COLUMBIA

by Charles McC. Mathias, Jr., M.C.*

This year the people of the District of Columbia will pay about $260 million in local taxes and fees. In 1964 the District's tax receipts totaled $216 million, exceeding the tax revenues of sixteen states and all but two American cities.[1] Yet these Washington taxpayers, unlike the residents of the fifty states and all other cities and towns, do not elect any of the public officials who collect and spend their public purse. The citizens of the Nation's capital today enjoy far less self-government than did the American colonists who, two centuries ago, rebelled against "taxation without representation."

The captive condition of the District's citizens can be traced to the desire of the Founding Fathers to protect their new nation's capital, not against the people, but against the states. In the 1780's two factors, state rivalry and congressional security, decreed the establishment of a federal capital under the exclusive jurisdiction of Congress. First, while states and cities competed for the seat of government, all recognized that undue influence could be exerted by any state which legally embraced the capital. Because interstate suspicions were intense, the goal of competition became the privilege of ceding territory for the capital to Congress. Second, the need for direct federal law-enforcement authority in the capital was dramatized in June, 1783, when the State of Pennsylvania failed to provide adequate protection for the Congress, then assembled in Independence Hall, against a threatening crowd of soldiers who had gathered to demand overdue pay. Thus in 1787, under Article I, section 8, of the new Constitution, Congress was granted

> exclusive legislation, in all cases whatsoever, over such district (not to exceed ten miles square) as may, by cession of particular States and the acceptance of Congress, become the seat of the Government of the United States.

* Mr. Mathias was first elected to Congress in 1960 from the 6th Congressional District of Maryland. He is a Member of the House Judiciary Committee and of the Committee on the District of Columbia.

It is clear that, in removing the District of Columbia from the control of any state, the framers of the Constitution did not intend that the citizens of the District should be deprived of the political rights enjoyed by citizens of the states. James Madison observed in the *Federalist* that "the State will no doubt provide in the compact for the rights" of citizens of the ceded lands, and further noted that "a municipal legislature for local purposes, derived from their own suffrages, will of course be allowed them."[2] In fact, when the District was established on the banks of the Potomac River, Maryland and Virginia did expressly protect the rights of residents of the ceded cities of Georgetown and Alexandria, while Congress granted the new city of Washington an elected council in 1802, and an elected mayor in 1820.

Self-government in the young Nation's capital was plagued, however, by recurrent racial tensions and financial difficulties arising from overly optimistic commercial ventures and public works. The Congress was repeatedly obliged to service District debts. After the Civil War, when former slaves crowded into Washington, local political problems were multiplied. After several years of turmoil, Congress in 1871 suspended self-government in favor of a modified form of territorial rule, under which the District retained an elected legislative house and a non-voting delegate to Congress. In 1874, a Congressional committee recommended that legislative authority over the District be returned to Congress, and that administrative power be vested temporarily in a board of three Presidentially appointed commissioners, including an Army engineer responsible for public works. This system, enacted in 1874, was incorporated into the Organic Act of 1878, which established the District as a municipal corporation. Intended as a temporary expedient to restore the fiscal and political stability of the capital, the commission form of government has remained in effect for the last eighty-eight years.

As both the federal establishment and the city of Washington have grown, the government of the District has become less compact, though not more democratic. Public policies are now influenced by a collection of advisory commissions, councils, committees and boards, whose members try to reconcile the national interests unique to Washington and the local interests which residents of Washington share with people in all other major cities. The Zoning Commission, for example, is composed of the three District Commissioners, the Architect of the Capitol, and the Director of the National Park Service. The important Policy Advisory Committee, which deals with highway policy, is composed of the Chairman of the National Capital Planning Commission, the Director of the National Park Service, the Engineer Commissioner of the District, the Administrator of the National Capital Transportation Agency, a representative of the Federal Department of Housing and Urban Development, the Chairman of the Fine Arts Commission, and the Administrator of the Federal Bureau of Public Roads. Recently, expanded interest in regional planning has generated new clusters of planning and coordinating agencies. In this vast complex, the only element not clearly represented is the people.

Today, although political rights have been secured in law and generally in fact for almost all other adult Americans, the 800,000 citizens of the District of Columbia are still subjects of Congress and its creations, and are governed ultimately by men and women elected by voters somewhere else. Congressional control far exceeds the federal financial contribution to District government, for while the annual federal contribution has declined to less than 12% of the municipal budget, congressional control is potentially almost absolute. The greatest power is exercised, formally and informally, by the fifteen Senators and thirty-one Representatives from thirty-three states[3] who comprise the Senate and House District of Columbia Committees and the District of Columbia Subcommittees of the House and Senate Appropriations Committees.

The jurisdiction of the two standing Committees on the District of Columbia embraces nearly all municipal questions except appropriations. The House District Committee, for example, is expressly assigned all legislative proposals dealing with health, sanitary, and quarantine questions; holidays; protection of fish and game; regulation of the sale of intoxicating liquors; the adulteration of food and drugs; taxes and tax sales; insurance; public safety; harbor regulations; wills and divorces; juvenile courts; the incorporation and organization of societies; and amendments to the criminal and corporation codes.[4] Traditionally, implementation of the local police power has been delegated to the Commissioners, but the District Committees have retained jurisdiction over most other legislation, including proposals to alter the form of District government.

The power exercised by the Appropriations Subcommittees is also great, for they appropriate every dollar of the municipal budget and wield authority to approve or disapprove specific programs, such as welfare programs, and specific capital expenditures, such as school construction. In general, active members of these strong subcommittees can exert even more influence over District policy than members of other Appropriations Subcommittees can hold over the federal agencies whose budgets they approve.

Despite their central roles in national capital affairs, the two District Committees occupy low stations in the hierarchy of Congress. Both rank as minor committees, and assignments to them are not generally widely sought. In his study of the Senate in the 1950's, Donald R. Mathews found, for example, that the Senate District Committee ranked very low in Members' mean seniority, and very high in number of Members transferring to other committees.[5] Although the House District Committee presently includes several Members of long seniority, the Committee's attraction for freshmen Congressmen is also slight. Moreover, other committee work distracts even those Members who do choose to serve as city councilmen for the District, for each of the Members of the Senate District Committee has two other committee assignments, and each Member of the House Committee has one, with two Members of the House Committee sitting as chairmen of other committees.

With few exceptions, the quality and quantity of congressional attention to District problems reflect their relative importance in the context of the international, national, and constituent affairs entrusted to the Congress. The Appropriations Subcommittees do meet intensively each spring to refine the District budget. Because of the pressure and prestige of other business, however, the District Committees meet infrequently, and attendance is traditionally low. Not all Committee Members, and few Congressmen not on the Committees, become deeply involved in Washington matters. In the 89th Congress through March 2, 1966, for example, 76% of all measures referred to the House District Committee had been introduced by Committee Members, with 46% sponsored by just four Members.[6] Among these proposals were bills to establish home rule, to increase the local minimum wage, to establish institutions of higher education, to amend the Alcoholic Beverage Control Act, to incorporate various nonprofit organizations or exempt them from taxation, to regulate the practice of several professions, to increase salaries of teachers and policemen, and to promulgate special regulations for the 1966 American Legion National Convention in Washington.

Committee consideration of such measures, however sporadic, is extensive compared to the study they receive on the House and Senate floors. In the Senate, District bills are brought up for floor debate along with other minor items; in the House, District legislation can be called up on "District Days," the second and fourth Mondays of each month.[7] Attendance on such days is unusually slim, and measures are dispatched without elaborate debate. At times, the average attention given to individual bills approaches half a minute. Quorum calls on District Days are infrequent, and roll calls very rare. In the entire 88th Congress, in which 42 District measures became public laws, only six roll-call votes in the House (3.4% of the total) and five in the Senate (0.9%) were on District bills. The average Member of either House becomes involved in District arguments only on those scattered occasions when principles of public policy, such as civil liberties or public welfare, are being tested, or when his own local interest in Washington is aroused.

The present system of government of the Nation's capital is an essentially arbitrary one. Because congressional management of the District is neither comprehensive nor continual, decision-making on many locally important questions, such as the structure of public education and the location of freeways, is dispersed among the many appointed administrators and advisory boards. When Congress does act, or when individual Members of Congress exert influence, their preferences can override all other considerations. Since the President's involvement in District affairs is largely confined to the dispatching of occasional messages to Congress, and since District questions are seldom elevated to the status of national partisan issues, the primary determinant of congressional action or inaction is individual Members' senses of obligation. In the decentralized structure of Congress, the most influential obligations are those of four men, the Chairmen of the two District Committees and the Appropriations Subcommittees. At the moment, it is small exaggeration to assert that the greatest potential power over District government is held by the voters of the states of Nevada and West Virginia, and of particular congressional districts in South Carolina and Kentucky.

It would be optimistic to declare that communication between the Congress and the citizens of Washington has merely broken down, for there is little evidence that real communication has existed, in any sustained fashion, since 1874. The quality of District Committee Members has changed since the 1890's, when some Congressmen employed inside information, gained through Committee membership, as the basis for commercial speculation.[8] But it is difficult for the most conscientious Congressman, while representing more than 400,000 of his own constituents, to find time among his myriad duties for systematic concentration on District affairs. Congressional hearings, when held, are attended primarily by District and federal officials, and by representatives of those citizens' interest groups who understand the system's intricacies. Although more and more neighborhood groups are seeking to be heard, the District Committees still make little effort to solicit the opinions of the vast majority of Washington residents who pay the taxes, live in the public housing, send their children to the public schools, and endure the problems of inadequate education, recreation, housing, and transportation in the capital.

Nor is the District government, unfortunately, oriented primarily toward the citizens. Responsible to Congress, the Commissioners must spend tremendous portions of their time on congressional hearings and negotiations. Citizens who wish to be heard must far too often make their protests dramatically visible and audible, through demonstrations, public meetings, and complaints to the mass media. The overwhelming majority do not even try to convey their views on local policy issues and have serious trouble registering elementary grievances about trash collection, street repairs, housing code violations, and school deficiencies. The switchboard at the District Building is usually busy, and few District residents bother to write or call Members of the House and Senate District Committees for help.

Countless specific proposals for reform of District government have been offered in the three generations since the suspension of home rule. The plans which have persisted fall into three categories: the reinstatement of elected municipal self-government; the establishment of citizens' representation before the Commissioners; and the restoration of citizens' representation on Capitol Hill.

Although the right to vote is fundamental to American democracy, the citizens of Washington lacked any franchise at all from 1874 to 1964, when they obtained the privilege of voting in Presidential elections through the

Twenty-third Amendment to the Constitution, ratified in 1961. The continued absence of any elected District of Columbia Representative to Congress is a dual deprivation, denying Washington residents both any voice in national legislative policy and any advocate in the chambers of municipal rule. The two aspects, national and local representation, should not be confused. Providing voting representation for the District in both House and Senate, a step which would require constitutional amendment, would give Washington voters the republican rights enjoyed by all other Americans. Establishing the office of non-voting District Delegate to the House, a shorter step, would be an interim reform giving the District as much representation as has been traditionally granted to citizens of American territories. A non-voting delegate, however, would have only modest influence over municipal government. He would be simply another single voice and, in the present scheme of congressional operations, would not be the most important spokesman on District affairs.

Giving the people of Washington a representative at the District Building would be a similarly limited, but significant, reform. The great success of "Action Line," a local complaint service recently initiated by *The Washington Evening Star*, has emphasized the tremendous need for some central agency to which citizens can present their grievances. Many observers, including local station WTOP,[9] have urged the creation of a "public protector," or "ombudsman," a public officer empowered to investigate and resolve citizens' complaints. In the continued absence of any local officials directly responsible to the people, such an advocate could serve as a needed link between individuals and the District bureaucracy. His impact on major policy issues, however, would be minimal.

The only ultimate solution is for Congress to fulfill its constitutional responsibility to the Nation and the Nation's capital. The time has come for Congress either to manage the District of Columbia more effectively and equitably, or to delegate real authority to those who can.

Improvements can, of course, be made within the present pattern of District government. Congressional committee staffs could be expanded and employed to survey broad areas of policy, such as public education and housing, where the need for new approaches is especially immediate. Local public opinion could be far more actively sought, through the mass media and hearings held off Capitol Hill in various sections of the city. The many advisory boards could be made more representative of the entire District, and other channels of contact with the people could be developed. But in the most important legislative body in the world, in this demanding decade, there is little practical hope that Members of the appropriate committees could devote to District problems the full-time attention which they require. There is even less likelihood that many more Members of Congress could become amply informed about District government and the committees' work. Above all, no internal reforms or adjustments of attitudes would change the essentially arbitrary nature of direct congressional government of Washington. Even the most sympathetic administration would be grounded simply on good will, which is not a consistently reliable foundation.

By far the wisest course would be for Congress to implement James Madison's pledge once more, by delegating extensive authority over municipal affairs to a locally elected mayor and city council. This is the only reform which would provide the people of Washington a government fully and directly responsible to them and responsive to their needs for municipal public services.

Home rule has been advocated, of course, both by believers in democracy and by supporters of congressional reform.[10] While the meaning of home rule for the District is relatively clear, however, its import for the Congress is rather ambiguous. By divesting itself of direct legislative authority over Washington, Congress would not be eliminating a large portion of the minor tasks which now divert legislators from larger affairs. Few Members of the House or Senate now devote much time or thought to District problems, while floor debate and roll calls are minimal. On the other hand, it would be both unconstitutional and unrealistic to anticipate that the Senate and House District Committees would dissolve upon the advent of home rule. Congress would retain its constitutional mandate to oversee the management of the District, and congressional committees could be expected to exercise that privilege from time to time. Under some home rule proposals, Congress would continue to make annual appropriations of District funds, an assignment which could become the focus of general debate over the course of District government. Under all home rule plans, Congress would have the power to veto acts of the elected city council, and it is predictable that veto efforts would be made in the areas which now occasionally command general congressional attention. In short, home rule would reduce the congressional workload by about the amounts of time and effort now employed by a few Members of Congress in deciding whether to increase drivers' license fees or to legalize the sale of ice-cream bars.

Home rule, of course, would be a bold experiment, bolder because Congress has for so long denied the people of the District any experience in self-government. While the Senate has repeatedly shown its willingness to authorize the experiment, the House to date has been reluctant to abandon the established paths of congressional control. Last year, for example, a mayor-and-council home rule plan was approved overwhelmingly by the Senate, but was brought to the House floor only through the lever of a discharge petition. Faced with its first chance in eighteen years to vote upon home rule, the House hesitated and enacted instead a charter plan so different from the Senate-passed bill that reconciliation of the two measures has proved impossible. Because of a combination of privilege, prejudice and inertia, it appears that the House, at least, will continue to resist the extension of democratic local government to the citizens of Washington.[11]

In an era in which the United States has extended democracy at home and asserted its merits throughout the world, the American national capital should not be maintained as an exception to American faith in the right to local self-government. The congressional responsibility to the people of Washington is not to govern them, but to oversee their management of their own municipal affairs. The congressional responsibility to the Nation is not to maintain the capital as a federal preserve, but rather to encourage the growth of a great capital city. These obligations are not met as long as the District of Columbia remains a colony, part splendor and part slum, whose residents and rulers seldom meet. There is no guarantee that home rule will bring full prosperity, renewed vitality and perfect government to Washington, but there is every proof that continued congressional government will not. It is past time for Congress to start the experiment.

REFERENCES

1. U.S. Bureau of the Census, *Compendium of State Government Finances in 1965* (Washington, 1965), Table 7, p. 19; *City Government Finances in 1963–4* (Washington, 1965), Table 6, p. 57.
2. Madison, James, *The Federalist Papers*, No. 43, New York, Modern Library, 1938, p. 280.
3. The two Committees and two Subcommittees include three representatives from each of four states—New York, New Hampshire, Wisconsin, and Maryland; and two from each of six states—California, Illinois, Mississippi, Minnesota, Texas, and Virginia, and one representative from each of twenty-two other states.
4. Rule XI, Clause 5, Rules of the House of Representatives.
5. Mathews, Donald R., *U.S. Senators and Their World*, Chapel Hill, University of North Carolina Press, 1960, pp. 149, 153.
6. Legislative Calendar of the Committee on the District of Columbia, House of Representatives, March 5, 1966.
7. Rule XXIV, Clause 8, Rules of the House of Representatives.
8. Green, Constance McLaughlin, *Washington, Capital City 1879–1950*, Princeton, Princeton University Press, 1963, pp. 24, 180.
9. Jurey, Jack, "D.C. Public Protector I–III," WTOP editorials, broadcast June 2 through 6, 1966.
10. Little, Arthur D., Inc., "Management Study of the U.S. Congress," NBC Television broadcast (November 24, 1965), p. 27; "The Congress and America's Future," report of the 26th American Assembly (Arden House, N.Y., 1964).
11. After the House action last fall, columnist Art Buchwald wrote: "The citizens of Washington had a close scare last week. They almost got the right to have self-government. . . . It was stated that Washingtonians, who are more or less charged with running the United States Government and many parts of the world, had neither the intelligence nor the ability to govern themselves. . . . There is now a group of people here who feel that since Congress does such a good job of running the district, it should take over running all cities with populations of 500,000 or more. You would have a House Boston Committee, run by a Congressman from South Carolina, a House Los Angeles Committee run by a Congressman from Florida and a House Chicago Committee run by a Congressman from East Texas . . ." Art Buchwald, "Capitol Punishment," *Washington Post* (Oct. 8, 1965), p. A7.

DONALD RUMSFELD, M.C.
13th District ,Illinois

THE OPERATION OF THE CONGRESSIONAL OFFICE

*by Donald Rumsfeld, M.C.**

A careful study of today's Congress will reveal significant gaps in factual information on how this institution really functions as an instrument of government. There are several reasons for this lack of hard information.

1. During this century parliamentary bodies throughout the world have suffered a diminishing role as contrasted with executive branches. Professor David Truman believes the situation in the United States reflects the general trend of a " 'parliamentary crisis' that has affected the West for at least five decades."

The charges of "rubber stamp" against the Congresses of Franklin Roosevelt's first Administration have been matched by criticism from within and without the National Assembly of the Fifth French Republic, from critics of West Germany's "chancellor democracy," and even from within the British Parliament; the delays and debilitating compromises of other American Congresses have had at least their equivalents in the Third and Fourth French Republics, in Italy, and in most of the governments of Northwestern Europe.[1]

2. To this general trend may be added the differences in the nature of the two institutions. Whereas the executive branch is vertical in structure, with the President at the top of the pyramid, the legislative branch is organized on a horizontal plane, with the peaks of power and influence widely diffused among House and Senate leaders of both parties, the chairmen and ranking members of the powerful standing committees, and prominent political personalities of less seniority. For most, it is easier to stare at a mountain than to study the shadows and slopes across a rolling terrain.

* Mr. Rumsfeld is a member of the House Committees on Government Operations and Science and Astronautics. He represents the 13th Congressional District of Illinois and before his election to Congress in 1962 served as administrative assistant to an Ohio Congressman and also on the staff of a Michigan Congressman.

3. A long-standing attitude of mutual suspicion between political scientists and Members of Congress has inhibited the scholar's actual contact with, and therefore fuller understanding of, the legislative process. In a penetrating statement to the George Washington University American Assembly at Airlie House in Warrenton, Virginia, on May 14, 1965, writer-commentator Neil MacNeil observed that the dispute extends even to making it "difficult for anyone to stand between them as referee or as friend of the court, for he faces assault on one side as an apologist for incompetence and on the other for moralistic sophistry."[2] MacNeil may have exaggerated the case somewhat. Still, the suspicion that has existed has proved self-defeating for both sides, and deficiencies in information remain in part as a result of this lack of direct communication.

4. Other writers have only sporadically illuminated the governmental process on Capitol Hill, and again we may credit the deficiencies in part to an attitude of mutual suspicion, this time between Members of Congress and the working press. It is the deviation and not the norm which makes news. To reverse a phrase, "good news is no news." There is little "news" interest in the ordinary, workaday routine or in the high ethical standards adhered to by most Members.

A case in point is a front-page story in *The Washington Post* on March 14, 1966, under the headline: "GIMMICKS RAISE CONGRESSIONAL PAY." The article called attention to alleged improper use of allowance for office space by a handful of Congressmen and Senators. I would defend the story on the ground that disclosure of this type of information is in the public interest. However, totally ignored in the article was the fact that *most* Members of Congress exercise great care in the use of their allowances. (Indeed, as we shall see shortly, many are downright parsimonious, some to the point that the question could be raised as to whether such self-imposed frugality works to the detriment of their constituents and the Congress.) The point is that it is the occasional and questionable actions of a small percentage of Congressmen that make news, not the day-in, day-out labor of the vast majority.[3]

5. Certainly, the extensive use of radio and television by the President and the executive branch, coupled with the prohibition against radio and television coverage in the House and the Senate, have tended to encourage broader understanding of the executive's activities. This broader public understanding has contributed to the steady shift of power from the legislative to the executive branch. That the skillful politicians in Congress have failed to see that the prohibition against radio and television coverage has been self-defeating and has hastened the power shift is dumbfounding. Hopefully, this will be changed in the coming months.

6. Finally, Members of Congress and the people they represent have evidenced a less than thundering interest in volunteering and demanding better information about the way Congress operates. Considering the very heavy workload Members of Congress carry, they may possibly be excused for some

failure to volunteer facts about their activities. But what answer may be offered for an electorate of whose numbers less than half can identify the individual who represents them in the national legislature?

The problem of public access to information held by the executive branch is properly and at long last being corrected through legislation. It is time to lift the lid also on congressional secrecy, to provide the American people with a full and true picture of what the Congress is doing. And Congress must take the initiative: by translating the salaries of its employees into figures that are understood; by declaring ethical guidelines for financial disclosure and personal conduct of Members; by publishing the *Congressional Record* in a more accurate and easily read form; by conducting its work in such a manner that knowledge of the legislative process would be at least possible by the public in general; and by opening its doors to news coverage by the electronic media. These steps, and others, would make the Congressman's job simpler and would facilitate citizen participation in "government by the people,"

The Congressman's Job

Neither in the Constitution nor in the thousands of laws enacted by Congress does there appear any specific listing of the duties of a Member of the U.S. Congress. By definition a Representative acts on behalf of his constituents in helping to decide the issues of the day. By extension, he also assists them in their various relationships with their federal government. Beyond that, the Congressman's job is largely what he makes of it, and there are undoubtedly as many approaches to it as there are Congressmen. Certainly, there is nothing approximating a consensus among Members as to the definition of a Congressman's job.

In a letter to John Jay, Thomas Jefferson, then serving as a Member of the Continental Congress, wrote: "I think it a duty in those entrusted with the administration of their affairs to conform themselves to the decided choice of their constituents."[4] The opposite view was taken by Davy Crockett, Member of the House from Tennessee, 1827–31, 1833–35. As related by my colleague Jim Wright, several of Crockett's constituents had petitioned him not to get involved in the Texas dispute. Crockett wrote back: "I am going to Texas; you can go to Hell."[5] Most Members function somewhere between the extremes of Jefferson and Crockett.

In my view, the role of today's Representative in Congress can be broken down in five broad areas of activity:

1. *On the Floor of the House of Representatives.* It is here that a Representative joins with the membership as a whole in performing the last rites of the legislative process, debating, amending, and finally voting on the hundreds of bills and resolutions that come to the floor from various legislative committees. In the early days of the country, floor activity constituted the

bulk of the Congressman's work. There were no standing legislative committees and no individual offices for handling constituent mail and related business. In fact, the early Member had comparatively few constituents, the
constituents did not write very often, and the telephone had not been invented.
Today's Member spends less than a fourth, and possibly closer to a fifth, of
his time on the floor.

2. *In committee.* Since 1958 the House has had twenty standing committees, plus a Select Committee on Small Business and a varying number of
ad hoc and joint committees. Most of the standing committees have a number
of subcommittees dealing with specific areas of legislation under the committee's jurisdiction.

It is in committee and subcommittee that the substantive work of Congress is done. Here is where the legislation is hammered out, its fine points
negotiated, and the final language drafted. Witnesses are heard, staff reports
digested, and arguments continued for days, weeks, and months. With the
increasing complexity of today's legislative problem areas, not to mention the
volume and diversity of problems, plus a growing need to exercise the responsibility for oversight of the Administration, most Congressmen find themselves
spending more and more time on committee and subcommittee work. The
average Member has at least two committee assignments and usually serves
on several subcommittees.

3. *Serving His Constituents.* Today's Member fulfills an increasingly important role in serving as the human link between his constituents and the vast,
confusing maze of Boards, Commissions, Agencies, and Departments known
as "the government." This area of activity can be subdivided roughly into
three categories: (*a*) the informational and educational function; (*b*) district
problems and casework; and (*c*) public relations.

(*a*) By newsletter, press release, radio and television broadcasts, meetings
with constituents in Washington and the district, and by replies to the many
legislative inquiries and suggestions received daily both by phone and mail,
the Congressman keeps those he represents informed of the policies, programs, proposals, and activities of their federal government. Some Members
handle this function better than others, but all make an effort to bring some
understanding out of the confusion which stems from the sheer size of the
multi-layered, multi-faceted government.

(*b*) Congressmen are called upon to respond to a myriad of requests, to
solve constituent problems, and, in general, to act as expeditors and catalysts
between the federal government and individual citizens, organizations, and
communities. The matters on which a Congressman may be consulted range
across a broad spectrum: veterans' benefits and social security payments,
changes in postal facilities and services, and protests against jet aircraft noise
during church services, requests for tour information for visitors to Washington or perhaps to the House of Commons in London, for flags flows over the
Capitol, and even for guard rails on high speed highways!. For added spice and

variety, Members are requested to assist in securing compensatory payments for sonic boom damage, arrange transportation to Antarctica, or advise a fifth-grade class how to grow rice in an aquarium. The range is beyond imagination; the amount of work required is staggering.

(c) In response to the rise of a mammoth federal bureaucracy, today's Congressman also spends a good deal of his time attempting to "humanize" the relationship between the individual citizen and his government. Public relations is inextricably bound up with the personal needs of the Member in seeking re-election, but it is also an indispensable part of his over-all job as middleman between the citizen and his government in Washington, D.C.

4. *Serving the Public and His Party.* Most Congressmen, even though locally elected, become relatively prominent nationally and politically and are therefore called upon to engage in a variety of assignments not directly related to pending legislation or problems of the district. Such duties include speeches in other states, seminars at universities, television appearances, and attendance at dinners and meetings of all kinds. The American two-party system is part and parcel of our governmental process. The party system places certain responsibilities on those who shoulder a role in the management of government.

5. Finally, every Senator and Congressman faces the problem of getting re-elected. There is no way to measure how much of the time spent campaigning is extraneous to the job of a legislator. Any dereliction of duty that results from excessive campaigning may well result in defeat anyway. The point is, the Member must spend varying amounts of time in campaign or political activity, and the need is common enough that this area must be included in any attempt to describe his over-all job.

How Has the Job Changed Since 1789?

From an infant agrarian nation of 3.9 million inhabitants in the late eighteenth century, the United States has grown into a modern nation approaching two hundred million citizens, nearly three-quarters of whom live in and around her great cities. From a small "nation of immigrants," we have risen in the brief span of a century and a half to a commanding position of leadership in the world.

Particularly since 1900, changes have occurred with lightning-like rapidity. Noted author John Gunther observed:

> There have been more changes in the past sixty-five years than in all other centuries put together. . . . In the old days, we could deal with political affairs sector by sector. We could confront crises one at a time. Now, everything is inextricably conjoined and interlocked, and the sheer mass of what we have to take in is overwhelming.[7]

In the First Congress, the sixty-five Members of the new House of Representatives came from constituencies averaging 33,000 persons. The executive branch of the new government consisted of President Washington, perhaps with a few staff aides, and his Secretaries of Foreign Affairs (State), War, and the Treasury. The First Congress completed its work having enacted a total of 118 public and private acts and resolutions.

Today's Congressman represents an average of more than 450,000 constituents, and at the present rate of population growth it is expected that the average may double in forty years! The executive branch has grown into a vast bureaucracy comprising ten cabinet level departments (one of the original departments, Treasury, alone employs more than 85,000 people) and scores of independent agencies and bureaus. Today more than two and a half million Americans (excluding those in the military services) work in their federal government, which amounts to one employee for every 72 citizens.

In the First Session of the 89th Congress, a staggering 13,789 measures were introduced in the House of Representatives.[8] Members sat through countless hours of committee hearings on subjects ranging from salmon protection to salary increases for government employees; from defense appropriations to the poverty program; from manned flights to the moon to archeological expeditions to the Canal Zone. They answered 182 quorum calls, 201 Yea and Nay calls, and participated in hundreds of teller, division, and voice votes. They received thousands of visitors to their offices, made numerous trips to the executive agencies "downtown," and answered thousands of inquiries from their constituents.

Government has become so much a part of the individual American's life that it is impossible for any citizen not to find himself directly involved at some point or other with one or more of the numerous departments or agencies or bureaus. When he finds himself lost in the bureaucratic maze, when his case is unusual, or the decision is delayed or unfavorable, he turns to his Representative in Washington (generally as a last resort). Amid the impersonality of government, the Member of Congress is the personal factor, the human link between government and the people.

This role reaches far beyond a narrow definition of the word "legislator." As the contacts between the people and the federal government grow, the areas of legislative need broaden. As the areas of need broaden, the Member must study, interpret, and make decisions on a greater volume of legislation. Although it is true that the major work of the Congress is done in committee, every Member must weigh the issues involved in *each* measure in order to vote to approve or disapprove it. And he cannot do this conscientiously without extensive preparation, understanding, and an adequate office and staff organization. The importance of the congressional office is placed in perspective when one recognizes that the problems for the Members of Congress which result from these changes in our society promise to be compounded, rather than lessened, in the coming decades.

What Help Does the Congressman Have in Doing His Job?

To perform his job adequately, the Member of Congress must have information, manpower, and machinery. He has a certain amount of all three, an excess of none. Although the following chapter discusses this matter in depth, I should point out here that the Congressman gathers information and assistance from three major sources.

First are the staff and facilities available to Members within the Congress itself. These include the Library of Congress and its Legislative Reference Service, the Office of the Legislative Counsel, which serves the entire membership of the House, the staffs of the standing, select, and joint committees of Congress (although as Mr. Cleveland points out, severe deficiencies exist in the staffing of many committees), and finally, from the allowances for the operation of the individual Member's office, which will be discussed in detail.

The second major source of assistance to the Congressman is the executive branch of the federal government. Liaison offices specially set up to handle congressional inquiries are located in each of the departments and in many of the agencies and bureaus of the executive branch. These offices furnish information to the Congressman in connection with matters of interest to his district or to individual constituents. The function of these offices is discussed further under the heading, "An Ombudsman for Congress?"

Various Congressmen receive other types of assistance from the executive branch, some of which appears to be of questionable propriety. Some types of aid, in fact, raise questions relating to the separation-of-powers doctrine and to the specific qualifications laid down in Section 1913 of Title 18 of the U.S. Code (see chapter by Mr. Nelsen). However, much of the information supplied to Congress and to Congressmen by the executive branch is undeniably valuable both as grist for the legislative mill and for the insights it may provide into national problems.

In addition to the staggering volume of unsolicited information he receives, a Member of Congress may also obtain needed data from the executive branch upon request. This is not to say his requests are always complied with —the Administration *can* so successfully enshroud itself in cold silence, from the standpoint both of Congress and the public, that one may feel he is fighting the Second Ice Age. This "freedom of information" problem is a major and continuing concern in a free society. At this point, however, it is sufficient to say that the executive branch is a primary source of information and a secondary source of assistance to those in the legislative branch. Executive cooperation is generally satisfactory, and the results are usually mutually beneficial.

A third major source of assistance for the Congressman may be labeled "non-governmental." This category includes information in the press, both general background material and specific items which may lead to investigations or other inquiries; information and manpower occasionally supplied by the Member's political party; material and assistance proffered by various lobbyists and lobbying organizations; study papers, research help, and perhaps some speech-writing assistance, illuminating data from private institutions, foundations, and the like engaged in public policy research; and the help which comes sporadically and unpredictably, but often importantly, from individual citizens within and without his congressional district.

The amount of information available is enormous; the range of possible assistance extraordinarily wide. Unfortunately, with the exception of the services provided by the Congress itself, the sources available are largely on a catch-as-catch-can basis, and the task of coordinating the sources of information is alone a task of major proportions.

How is the Congressional Office Run?

There is no such thing as the "typical" congressional district. There is no such thing as the "typical" congressional office. And there is certainly no such thing as the "typical" day in the life of a Congressman (unless we can define a typical day as a busy, varied, somewhat disorganized series of events —or crises—depending on one's point of view).

In my own case, for example, the 13th Congressional District of Illinois is ranked by the Census Bureau as first in the nation in average family income, and is tied for first place in average number of years of education completed and in least unemployment. The residents of the 13th District of Illinois are well-read, well-traveled, and apparently above average in their awareness of and interest in national and international problems.

Having served as an Administrative Assistant prior to my election to Congress in 1962, I am probably not "typical" in the way I run my office. No doubt this experience has resulted in differences in the way I allocate the work between my staff and myself and in the techniques of handling both legislative and constituent responsibilities.

In the absence of statistical data to work with in understanding the operation of the congressional office, there follows a listing of the standard allowances for the operation of the Representative's office.

1. *Staff.* In June, 1966, the statutes on congressional staffs were broadened to allow each Member of the House of Representatives (and the Resident Commissioner of Puerto Rico) to hire a number of clerks, not to exceed eleven, with a basic allowance for their combined salaries of $32,000 per annum. (See chapter by Mr. Broyhill for explanation of "basic rate" method of determining clerk hire.) Those Members whose constituencies exceed 500,000 people may hire twelve clerks, with an over-all basic allowance of $34,500.

The Member determines the duties of each clerk and decides what salary each shall receive, provided no clerk receives more than $7,500 base ($20,-

578.39 gross). An analysis of 1965 clerk hire figures showed that less than half of the 435 Members used their full allotment for office staff. Careful study of such criteria as age of Member, length of service, or region of country failed to reveal any clear pattern in the use of clerk hire funds. Apparently, much depends on the personality and background of the Member, although, of course, the size and character of his constituency have a definite bearing on the amount of the allowance used—the bigger and more active his constituency, the more staff he needs, and hires, to handle the work. Most Congressmen maintain one or more offices in their districts, with the assignment of one or more of these staff employees to the district offices.

2. *Travel*. Each Member may be reimbursed for five round trips per year between Washington, D.C. and his district. (No funds are available for travel within the congressional district.) His assistant or another member of the staff may be reimbursed for two round trips. It is not uncommon for a Member from Illinois, for example, to find it necessary to make 25 to 35 round trips each year.

3. *Telephone and Telegraph*. This allowance is based on a "unit" system, with each word of a telegram comprising one unit, each minute of long-distance telephone conversation equal to four units. The total number of units allowed per Congressman is 100,000, whether the Member's district is large or small, near or distant. (No funds are available for the telephone expenses incurred by the Member's district office.)

4. *Stationery*. The stationery allowance for each Member is $2,400 yearly. This is a blanket sum and may be drawn upon for whatever supplies the Member needs which are available through the House Stationery Room. In large, active districts, this $2,400 allocation must be supplemented by private funds each year.

5. *Electrical Equipment*. Each office is allowed $2,500 for the purchase and use of whatever equipment it requires, in addition to five typewriters, one of which may be an automatic typing machine. In the event of defeat or retirement of a Member, his successor receives all of his office equipment plus whatever credit, if any, is left in the original account. This fund goes with the office, and the Member merely determines how it will be allocated. (The new Congressman, however, does not receive another $2,500.) There are no statistics on the total number of electrical pieces in use, although an employee of the Electrical Equipment Office estimates the number as "over 5,000 and rapidly growing." Old equipment is turned over to the General Services Administration for resale or disposal. In calendar year 1965, $30,560.58 was added to the U.S. Treasury from the sale of old office equipment.

6. *Postage*. The postage allowance for each Member is $500 per year, plus the franking privilege for first class "official business" mail. The postage allowance is not cumulative and must be used during that calendar year.

7. *Folding Room*. This service handles bulk mailing for all Members— folding, stuffing, and mailing—but, quite properly, does not handle political

or campaign materials. The estimated rate or pieces of mail in 1965 was 375,000 per day for the House during the period Congress was in session.

A "Typical" Day for a Member of Congress

In 1965, the American Political Science Association, working with the Joint Committee on the Organization of Congress and the Republican Task Force on Congressional Reform, surveyed the 435 House Members by questionnaire in an attempt to gain factual data on the operation of the congressional office.

While the results were far from complete, a tabulation of the first hundred questionnaires returned showed that the "average" Congressman, during a "typical" work-week while Congress was in session (1965), spent:

> 14.9 hours on the Floor of the House (24.9%)
> 10.9 hours on committee work (18.2%)
> 9.7 hours studying legislation (16.2%)
> 17.1 hours on constituent affairs (28.5%)
> 7.3 hours on public statements and party functions (12.1%)

On a daily basis, using a 5-day week (although many Congressmen open their offices on Saturday, and some on Sunday), this amounts to:

> 3.0 hours on the floor
> 2.2 hours on committee work
> 1.9 hours studying legislation
> 3.4 hours on constituent affairs
> 1.5 hours on public statements and party functions

This is a total of twelve hours a day, or 59.9 hours per week that the "average" Congressman devotes to his job. This figure is reasonably accurate. However, as I have said, there is no such thing as a "typical" workweek!

One deficiency of the above breakdown is the absence of a category relating to the Member's personal campaign activities. This is no fault of the survey because it was recognized at the outset that (1) it would be difficult to separate "official" congressional activities from those engaged in for purposes of re-election, and (2) even if such a line were drawn, one would hardly expect to receive completely reliable answers to such a question.

The problem in conducting such a survey lies in the fact that very few congressional offices keep accurate records on incoming and outgoing mail, number of visitors, or in short, reliable data on their routine operation. And even the most conscientiously-kept appointment book would not constitute an accurate time log of the Member's daily activities, as it would fail to show, for example, how often he leaves the floor to talk with constituents while the House is in session, or how many hours he spends, long past sundown, digging through the piles of reading matter stacked on his desk or taken home in his briefcase.

It is the almost total inability to compile accurate statistics on the operation of the congressional office that makes the task of coming up with intelligent recommendations to improve the situation so difficult. Nearly everyone complains about the workload on Capitol Hill, and there exists a strong feeling that something must be done. But what? The pattern from office to office fluctuates wildly. Office A has an Administrative Assistant, a Legislative Assistant, a Caseworker, an Appointment Secretary, two stenographers, a receptionist, and a file clerk. The work is compartmentalized, and each staffer knows his specific duties. Two additional staff people run the district office.

But in Office B next door, eight staff people are crammed into one room, two of them "sharing" a desk; whatever comes in gets done by whomever grabs it. There is no set division of work; no staffer has specifically assigned duties.

And down the hall is Office C, where three pleasant ladies work with a minimum of fuss and flurry and seem to get everything done that needs doing.

What sort of pattern can one draw from that! The dilemma is: any recommendations for improving the *general* situation must apply to *all* offices.

Some Recommendations

Nevertheless, there are certain administrative changes which, in the face of expanded activity in the congressional office, are certainly desirable. Some, in my opinion, are urgently necessary.

1. *Professional Assistance.* The Congress should retain competent office management and manpower consultant assistance to review, on request, congressional and committee office activities, procedures, methods, equipment, and administrative policies, and to devote particular attention to:

(*a*) Providing instruction for new Members of the House on office policies, procedures, and precedents;

(*b*) Offering time- and money-saving suggestions as they become apparent;

(*c*) Communicating to all Members ideas, techniques, and procedures which can be useful in the performance of their duties;

(*d*) Offering specific counseling, at the request of Members, on manpower and methods;

(*e*) Developing current, readily usable lists of sources of information, and

(*f*) Developing central office services for Members in appropriate areas such as autotyping, addressing, volume mailing, duplicating, and the like.

2. *Personnel.* The staff of a Congressman is a small and unusually hardworking, closely integrated group. Because of the unique demands on the Member's time, his staff must not only be extremely well qualified, but must also, collectively, provide the proper balance of the varied capabilities required by the Member, his district, his committee assignments and interests. Competent congressional staff members are a necessity. There is no central

office under the jurisdiction of the Congress where applications for employment can be accepted, screened, and referred and through which Members might work to secure needed personnel. Many would-be congressional staff members miss the opportunity to gain employment in the legislative branch of the federal government because of the lack of a central office, utilizing the talents of personnel experts who can match the needs of the Members to the qualifications of the applicants. A central personnel office should be established both to aid applicants and to help Members recruit qualified office personnel.

3. *Postmaster Appointments*. The time-consuming congressional role in the selection of postmasters should be eliminated by removing it from the political arena and placing it solely on a merit system basis. In the 89th Congress, I introduced H.R. 13586 to provide for appointment by the Postmaster General of postmasters "at post offices of the first, second, and third classes, in the competitive civil service without term." It is generally agreed that U.S. postal service has deteriorated in recent years. Postal appointments should be based on experience and merit, and the congressional office has no necessary role in the selection process. Either we continue to consider the U.S. Postal System as a political plaything and watch service continue to deteriorate, or we must recognize that rapid, reliable postal service is a necessity—not a luxury—in a modern commercial society and take it out of politics.

4. *Service Academy Appointments*. The service academies should handle appointments to these institutions. The processing of applications and the appointment procedures require an inordinate amount of staff work in the congressional office. Should it be determined that it is desirable to continue to assure geographical spread, the academies could easily work out a formula for the first 75 per cent of the class, fixing a percentage from each state on a population basis. The selections of the remaining 25 per cent could be flexible and based solely on merit.

5. *Immigration and Private Claims*. Such matters should be handled on an orderly, established basis, directly by the Immigration and Claims Subcommittee of the Committee on the Judiciary, and staff capability should be provided for that purpose.

6. *The Congressional Record*. The pages in the daily *Congressional Record* should be perforated for easy removal. It is my understanding that this can be done at no additional expense, following the cost of modifications to existing equipment. I suggest a cleaner, more readable format, perhaps clarifying the proceedings by bold-face type setting forth the different subject areas and with the actual thrust of the votes more clearly defined. The work of the Congress is complex enough without making it more confusing to readers of the *Record* by retaining out-of-date printing techniques and formats.

7. *Introduction of Bills*. Co-sponsoring of legislation is not permitted in the House of Representatives. Should a Member wish to sponsor legislation

that has been previously introduced, he must introduce an identical measure. The confusion which results from having to compare bills which often prove to be identical could be reduced by permitting co-sponsoring of bills. Added advantages would be substantial economies in printing costs and a more understandable Digest of Bills. Members responding to this question in the American Political Science Association Survey were overwhelmingly in favor of joint sponsorship of bills in the House. Of the first hundred replies, only nine were negative on this point.

8. *Office Supplies, Stationery Account.* As indicated, each Member is allotted $2,400 per year for stationery, office supplies, extra file cabinets, and the office supplies necessary to the operation of a congressional office. Some of the items which at present may be purchased through the Stationery Account are not directly relatable to the business activities of an office, even one as unique as a congressional office. I recommend that the allowance be increased to $3,000 per year. In addition, I suggest that the use of this fund be strictly limited to items necessary for the conduct of congressional business. Further, Members should not be permitted to withdraw funds from the account, and on the death of a Member, any balance in the fund should remain in the U.S. Treasury rather than be added to the deceased's estate. In short, this allocation should be handled as are staff funds, namely as Treasury funds, until expended.

9. *Electrical Equipment.* The present system results in unnecessary restrictions on the efficient conduct of a congressional office. With the growing population of the nation and the increasing demands on congressional staffs, every advantage should be taken of the strides made by the business machine industry. Each Member should be allowed the following *basic* equipment, exclusive of a purchase fund: one automatic typing machine, one electrostatic or photo copier, one mimeograph machine, and six electric typewriters (if his district is over 500,000 population, an additional typewriter would be in order). Each Member should have a basic purchase fund of $2,000, which may be used for other approved items, such as additional typewriters, dictating equipment, electric letter openers, sealers, folders, and the like.

The U.S. Senate utilizes a logical formula to balance the man *v.* machine problem. The plan permits a Senator to use staff funds for either clerk hire or office equipment if the latter proves more efficient. This has proved to be a workable and businesslike approach to efficient office management, and I endorse this procedure for the House of Representatives.

10. *Travel Allowance.* Recognizing that the Congress in recent years has stayed in session nine or ten months each year, it is apparent that the present five round-trip reimbursement standard is unrealistic. A more equitable approach would be reimbursement for one round trip between Washington, D.C. and a Member's congressional district per month for each month or part of a month that Congress is in session. (The present provision for staff travel appears adequate.)

An Ombudsman for Congress?

The word "ombudsman"[9] refers to an officer of parliament who looks into complaints of citizens who allege that they have been deprived of some right or benefit due them under the law or that they have suffered some kind of mistreatment by government. The office originated in Sweden over a century and a half ago and has been adopted in various forms by Finland (1919), Denmark and Norway (1955), New Zealand (1962), and most recently Great Britain. West Germany has an ombudsman for military affairs. Indeed, in the United States the Inspector General of the U.S. Army is a kind of ombudsman.

Other nations have been studying the concept for some years now, and in the U.S. bills to create an ombudsman at the state level are currently under consideration in several state legislatures. In addition, a bill is pending in Congress to establish an Administrative Counsel of the Congress, modeled somewhat after the Scandinavian ombudsman.

The concept is an attractive one and merits careful study by the Congress. Although the Interim Report of the American Political Science Association's Survey of the Congressional Office shows an average of only 17.1 hours per week spent on constituent affairs by the Congressman while Congress was in session in 1965, estimates of staff time devoted to handling various types of casework run from fifty to ninety per cent![10]

As the population of the United States continues to increase and as the Federal Government touches more and more the daily lives of all citizens, the people's representatives in Washington may find the casework load growing to almost unmangeable proportions. If a legislator is to have time to function as a legislator, both he and his staff will find it increasingly difficult to spend a major portion of their time responding to the growing volume of individual constituent cases. Also, it should be noted that a series of individual complaints against or difficulties with government agencies or departments often reveals a pattern pointing up the need for remedial legislation, or serves to correct an administrative mispractice within the agency concerned which might otherwise have gone unchecked.

At present the American citizen has only one obvious place to go for an investigation of any just complaint he may have against the administrative or executive arm of the federal government: to his Representative in Congress. "Write your Congressman" is as familiar as the old Army retort "See the Chaplain." But how efficiently and effectively can each case be handled, how much will it contribute to the congressional function of overseeing the administration of the laws, and to revising laws and procedures where appropriate, and how much time does it require of the individual Member of Congress, time taken from his legislative responsibilities?

What might be called the classical defense of the present method of handling casework is summed up by George Galloway in *The Legislative Process:*

Although many Congressmen privately deplore their "bellboy" activities, others frankly regard themselves merely as "the people's hired men" and seem reconciled to serving primarily as glorified lobbyists or Washington representatives for their home communities. They defend errand running as the road to reelection and as a means of humanizing relations between the people and a huge impersonal bureaucratic machine. The people must have some clearing house for their problems in the nation's capital, it is argued, and no other governmental agency could perform this function as cheaply or with the patience, understanding, and personal interest of congressional offices. Such services afford one of the few remaining direct contacts between the citizen and his elected representative. Constituent complaints also serve to keep Congressmen alert to the operation of the laws and administrative programs. In short, it is neither possible nor desirable, in the opinion of many members, to eliminate this nonlegislative business.[11]

While I would defend congressional handling of casework as a sometimes useful method of oversight or review and as a necessary part of the Congressman's role in providing a "human link" between citizens and their government, the following points argue for a better arrangement.

First, under the present system, the citizen is subjected to varying degrees of speed and effectiveness in the handling of his case, depending on the attitude, ability, and the time available to his Representative. The interest and skill of his Congressman and the quality of the Congressman's staff may have as much or more to do with the disposition of his case as the case's merits. I am *not* suggesting that any Member of Congress is guilty of favoritism or dereliction of duty in the handling of his constituents' problems; I *am* suggesting that the people's representatives are not equal in ability, expertise or knowledge, or in the time they have available for such matters, and therefore citizens possibly may receive unequal treatment in their legitimate grievances against the government.

Second, the argument that the constituent cases are "grist for the legislative mill" holds only if the Congressman has the knowledge and the perceptiveness to discover that a given case is part of a pattern which indicates that the law is deficient and follows through on it. No information exists as to the number of cases in which a law has been found to be deficient nor of the number of times the law has been successfully amended as a result of such cases being followed up. As a method of congressional oversight, individual handling of constituent cases is at best spotty and "a something thing."

Third, the present system is wide open to criticism on ethical grounds. The so-called congressional liaison offices, to which most cases are referred, have as their *primary* duty the responsibility of "selling" the Administration's programs on Capitol Hill (see chapter by Mr. Nelsen). Only secondarily are they engaged in assisting Congressmen with constituent problems. Some pertinent questions can and should be raised with respect to the same executive-directed lobbying offices having responsibility simultaneously for processing citizen complaints forwarded by Congressmen and for promoting the agency's programs and proposals on Capitol Hill. I am *not* suggesting that congressional liaison personnel curry favor by responding to some congressional requests or inquiries more quickly than to others; I *am* suggesting that the hard facts of the situation raise a serious question which remains unanswered.

Fourth, as to the "road to re-election" argument, I submit that it will be a sorry day for our system of representative government when and if Members of Congress find themselves campaigning on a claim that they can better protect their constituents against inequities by inept government officials than can their opponents. To claim to be equipped to advise the citizen of his rights under the law poses a legitimate question and the incumbent probably stands on advantageous ground. But certainly every citizen as a matter of right should receive efficient treatment in the handling of any just case and should not be totally dependent on which individual appears to possess the edge in being able to prosecute that case.

Fifth, the casework load imposes a disproportionately heavy burden on the time of both Congressman and staff. Although the Congressman has an implicitly official responsibility to deal with the individual problems of his constituents, this does not effectively argue against his being able to utilize the services of an "Administrative Counsel." Living institutions must adapt to changing times or stand as empty shadows of a dead past. "No procedural device is capable of guaranteeing good government," writes Professor Walter Gellhorn, one of the country's foremost authorities on administrative law and procedure, ". . . [but] this fact of organized life should conduce toward more rather than less experimentation with methods calculated to produce timely and well-informed administrative judgments."[12]

The present method of handling casework is sometimes inefficient, ineffective as a method of review or oversight, possibly unfair to the citizen, open to criticism on ethical grounds, and it imposes burdens out of proportion to the Congressman's duties as a legislator in the twentieth century.

Regrettably, we have come full circle to the complaint stated at the beginning of this chapter concerning gaps in research and information on the operations of Congress. In no area is the deficiency greater than in the operation of the individual congressional office. Ironically, this is where much of the work of the Congress gets done.

We do know that casework consumes a large share of the Congressman's time and even more of the time of his staff, but to date we have neither any statistical data on this subject nor even a commonly accepted definition of the term "casework." Before a better arrangement can be worked out, these gaps must be closed:

A tabulation of the number of actual cases, as opposed to other types of constituent mail, should be made. These cases should be broken down by type, agency involved, and whether the case involves a simple matter of administrative mispractice or points toward remedial legislation. Some measurement should be made of the time required by the Member and his staff in the handling of constituent cases and of their degree of success in following up on them.

Finally, I believe a thorough review of the operation of the congressional liaison offices is in order. During fiscal 1963, more than 800 employees of the executive branch were engaged in congressional information activities at a cost of well over $7 million. Data in the House Government Operations Committee files reveal that at least 24 different terms are used to designate information withheld from the public. There is no clear way to separate the "promotional" from the purely "informational" activities carried out by most federal offices, and there is some cause for suspicion that agency personnel are completely responsive or entirely accurate in supplying facts, figures, and information in this area.

Sooner or later, the U.S. Congress is going to have to deal with the doctrine of "executive privilege". In Sweden, for example, all government documents except those which clearly involve important matters of national security are open to the public. The "Public Records Law," which will take effect in 1967, is a major step in this direction, but it is only a first step.

The ombudsman approach has much to commend it, and I believe some modified version could work well in the U.S. Congress. However, the research gaps cited above must be filled and the differences between the governmental institutions of those countries which employ the concept and our own system must be carefully considered. It should also be noted that the genius of the ombudsman system is that the ombudsman personally oversees the investigation of all cases. In a relatively small country such as Sweden, this kind of personal supervision is possible. In a large nation such as the United States, it is obvious that one individual could not handle this function. Estimates of the staff he would need range from ten to more than 100 expert investigators. If the need for an ombudsman arises from the existence of a huge bureaucratic establishment within government, it could be argued that the solution hardly lies in the creation of yet another apparatus which might itself become bogged down in bureaucratic inefficiency.

Congressman Henry Reuss's (D., Wisc.) pioneering work to establish an Administrative Counsel of the Congress has done much to focus attention on alternative methods of handling casework. Hopefully, as more Members interest themselves in this problem area in the months ahead, a nonpartisan effort will get under way to close some of the research gaps cited above. Only then can an acceptable plan to improve the efficiency and effectiveness of the individual congressional office be developed.

Conclusion

That "Congress Needs Help," as a recent NBC special report was entitled, is, if anything, an understatement. Burdened by an increasing workload resulting from the population growth, the greater activity of the Federal Government, and the increasing complexity of the problems facing the Nation and the world, Congress has done little to meet the problems of these changing times. As a result of the failure to relieve itself of unnecessary work, adopt modern office techniques, and utilize up-to-date office equipment, the Congress and the individual Members find themselves working longer hours and yet failing, by a growing margin, to fulfill their constitutionally assigned responsibilities. The Nation could ill afford to see the motto of the Congress become, "The hurrieder I am, the behinder I get."

Without question, Congress could stumble along for a while more before withering and dying or falling into total disrepute. But if it is to fulfill its constitutional responsibilities, if it is to provide the check and balance so needed in our system of government, if it is to be, in fact, the voice of the people in a system of "government of the people," then it must act now to institute meaningful reforms.

If the Members of Congress fail the Congress, then they fail the people. If this happens, these simple lines from the poem, "My Congressman," by J. P. McEvoy, could well tell the sad tale of the fall of the Legislative Branch of our government:

> I know I have a Congressman
> in Washington, D.C.,
> For now and then he comes around
> To get a vote from me;
> He proudly shakes me by the hand
> And asks about my needs,
> And when he goes to Washington
> He sends me garden seeds.
>
> Whenever there's a bill for which
> I'd like to have him vote,
> I trust in him and tell him so
> By telegram or note;
> And he gets every one, I know,
> And every one he reads,
> For always when the Spring has come,
> He sends me garden seeds.

I think this will not be the fate of Congress, or of our system of government, or of this nation. As has been said, although our free system of government may not be perfect, it is the best form of government man has yet devised. Both its imperfections and its genius and unequaled success are direct results of the fact that it relies on the people. History has shown that at some point when the pendulum has swung too far, good people will become concerned and go to work to recenter it. Because our system of government provides, and in fact guarantees, that a mechanism for correction will always be available to the people, the people will prevail.

The American people are busy, but they are increasingly affected by government action. I believe the pendulum is swinging too far. Because I have great confidence in the fundamental good sense of the American people, it is my conviction that we are on the eve of meaningful congressional reform.

References

1. Truman, David B., ed., *The Congress and America's Future*, Englewood Cliffs, N.J., Prentice-Hall, Inc., 1965.
2. *Congressional Record*, August 5, 1965, pp. 18773–18776.
3. This would seem to be a good place to comment on the complex problem of "congressional ethics," the guidelines which determine the legality or nonlegality, the correctness or error in a Member's activity. For all the criticism, for all the discussion, there is no *binding* code of ethics. There is no specific set of rules or concrete source to which a Member may turn to determine whether or not the action he contemplates is proper and befitting the dignity of the office he holds. It would seem long past time for the formulation of a reasonably detailed statement setting forth basic guidelines on which a Member could rely and by which he may, if the need should arise, be judged.
4. *Jefferson Cyclopedia*, John P. Foley, ed., New York & London, Funk & Wagnalls Co., 1900.
5. Wright, Jim, *You and Your Congressman*, Coward-McCann, Inc., New York, 1965.
6. Perhaps the classic description of the Congressman's job is that contained in Edward C. Boykin's *The Wit and Wisdom of Congress*, New York, Funk & Wagnalls Co., 1961. "A Congressman has become an expanded messenger boy and employment agency; getter-outer of the Navy, Army, Marines; ward-heeler, wound healer, troubleshooter, law explainer, bill finder, issue translator, resolution interpreter, controversy oil pourer, glad-hand extender, business promoter, civil ills skirmisher, veterans' affairs adjuster, ex-serviceman's champion, watchdog for the underdog, sympathizer with the upperdog, namer of babies, recoverer of lost baggage, soberer of delegates, adjuster for traffic violators . . . binder up of broken hearts . . . good Samaritan, contributor to good causes . . . but it is getting harder every day to find time to properly study legislation."
7. "Inside the Twentieth Century," *Look* magazine, Jan. 12, 1965.
8. Unlike the Senate, the House does not permit joint sponsorship of bills. This accounts for part of the burden. See recommendation number 7 of this chapter.
9. From the Swedish word *ombud*, a person who represents or acts as spokesman for another individual. In a sense, the U.S. House of Representatives is composed of 435 individual *ombudsmen*.
10. Clapp, Charles L., *The Congressman: His Work As He Sees It*, Washington, D.C., The Brookings Institution, 1963.
11. Galloway, George B., *The Legislative Process in Congress*, New York, Thomas Y. Crowell Co., 6th Printing, April 1964.
12. "Administrative Procedure Reform: Hardy Perennial," *American Bar Association Journal*, March 1962. Dr. Gellhorn currently holds the Betts Chair of Law at Columbia University.

FRED SCHWENGEL

President

U.S. Capitol Historical Society

INFORMATION HANDLING: "FOR A VAST FUTURE ALSO"

by Fred Schwengel*

If all history were recorded, we would probably find that emperors and empires failed for want of some specific piece of information. In our own technological era, satirists picture governments going down to defeat, or at least paralyzed, not by too little information, but by too much.[1]

On November 24, 1965, the National Broadcasting Company presented an hour-length documentary entitled "Congress Needs Help." The opening scene showed stacks of reading matter collected from one Congressman's office that reached higher than stalks of Iowa corn at harvest time. As David Brinkley commented, a Member of Congress couldn't plow through all that if he did nothing else but read for a year.

Every congressional office today is deluged with information—material supplied by lobbyists, government publications of all kinds—with no small amount of the tonnage deriving from Congress' own sources. In some instances a Member gets neither as much nor the specific kind of information he requires, but his problem generally is that he receives *too much* information and has no efficient means of selecting what he needs from the turgid mass of documents, books, and reports spilling out of every nook and cranny of his office.

"Knowledge is power," a Congressman may remind himself. But what kind of knowledge? For what kind of power? The Constitution provides that legislative power shall be vested in Congress. Executive power, says Article 2, shall be vested in a President.

* Mr. Schwengel taught history before entering Congress in 1954. In the 88th Congress, in addition to serving on the House Public Works Committee, he served as Chairman of a Special Committee on Increased Minority Staffing. Mr. Schwengel has been President of the U.S. Capitol Historical Society since its formation and is currently a candidate for re-election to Congress from the 1st Congressional District of Iowa.

It would seem, then, that Congress should be primarily concerned with drafting the laws and the President with administering them. Yet it is estimated that as much as 80 per cent of the major legislation enacted today is not only initiated by but drafted within the executive branch.

While the Congress of the sixties is neither as weak as many of its Members claim nor as powerful as Presidents may complain, it is certainly a vastly different institution than that envisioned by the gentlemen who met in Philadelphia a century and a half ago to frame a government for the new nation. Perhaps as Professor Richard Neustadt suggests, "The separations between President and Congressmen are partly constitutional, partly political, partly attitudinal, and in no small degree a matter of semantics."[2] In any event, our system of separated powers is no longer the neat arrangement described in the civics books.

It is not my purpose here to debate the role of today's Congress. We face a growing population with urgent problems to solve, and whether the initiative for legislative action in all cases properly comes from the executive or not, the proposals must be sifted and weighed by the Congress.

* * * * *

Research and development have no longer been left to advance at random, to the curiosity of the scientist eager to learn more of nature, or to the unpredictable flash of inventive genius. Research-and-development has become the industry of innovation, the instrument of progress not as science for the scientists but science in the service of man. Composed of four hundred thousand scientists and engineers, working at hundreds of universities and nearly ten thousand industrial and government laboratories, research-and-development is undertaken in every one of our fifty states. R & D is sponsored by every major federal agency.

To understand this force of change, we must recognize the rapid growth of the activity itself. From less than one billion dollars annually in 1941, research-and-development has grown to $22 billion some twenty-five years later in 1966. Of this $22 billion, two-thirds, that is, over $15 billion, is derived from the Federal Government. At the same time, three-fourths of the nation's research-and-development is performed in industry or universities. A very important fact to recognize, therefore, is that research-and-development is a publicly funded but privately operated industry of innovation. It is thus characterized by a close and mutually reinforcing partnership between private industry, universities, and government. From this triad of institutions, each has contributed its strengths. Today, American science and technology—through entrepreneurship, scholarly inquiry, and alert public administration—set a pace and standard for excellence that the rest of the world seeks to follow.

Progress Also Has Thorns

Notwithstanding the enormous progress of the last two decades, the past is indeed prologue. Eighty-five per cent of all the scientists and engineers who ever lived throughout history are alive today. The writings from their research fill 35,000 technical journals with a literature growing at a rate of over one million articles a year. They offer promise of even more exciting discoveries that could be aided and abetted by proper congressional evaluation. Answers are being sought to basic questions about the composition of the atom, the origin of our solar system, the genetic code that controls heredity and the processes of life itself. The laser, the computer, new metallic or ceramic alloys will put man on the moon and probe the ocean depths.

As he applies this knowledge, however, man may inadvertently damage his own environment, soil his own nest. Automobile exhaust pollutes our air, cities and factories discharge sewage in all too convenient waterways, and solid waste is being generated faster than it can be disposed of. The silting of streams and rivers goes on almost unabated as watersheds are neglected. Urban crowding is producing social problems while it destroys aesthetics.

Science possesses no intrinsic morality. Practical applications may produce just as many harmful effects as benefits. The fruits of our progress are often accompanied by thorns. Of vital significance, therefore, is the recognition that with research and development so largely supported by government, what happens in this world in relation to or as a result of science depends far more on decisions of this nation's political leaders than it does on scientists and engineers. As science and technology have become new instruments for government policy, they have also become responsibilities. Improvement of human welfare is dependent upon the wise selection of public purposes to which science is directed, upon the allocation of public resources for their achievement, and upon the organization of government and prudent management of these funds.

Congress has responsibility to set public purpose, to allocate resources, to test the validity of proposals from the President against the wishes and mood of the people. In carrying out its legislative, oversight, and representative functions, Congress must have not only full and free access to information within the executive branch but the analytical capability to separate the "signals from the noise." Moreover, if Congress is to retain any degree of autonomy, it must equip itself with the necessary machinery and avail itself of adequate manpower for *independent* intelligence gathering, sorting, and analysis.

Improving the Committee System

Congress has always performed the substantive work of legislation through committees. Traditionally, committees have been the primary sources of information necessary to the Congressman. Now, committees have additionally taken on increasing responsibility for oversight of the Administration. As legislation has grown more complex, the need of technical specialists to assist the committees has become greater. As government programs continue to proliferate, the need of Congress for an over-all analytical capability to weigh existing programs against new solutions to national ills and both against national means, becomes more acute than ever.

Confined within the jurisdictions laid down in House Rule 11, the standing committees of the House concern themselves with only fractions of the total activity of government. No single unit of Congress is looking across the board at the sum of the nation's goals and resources. Funding is done piecemeal, with one committee granting authority, another actually appropriating the money, and yet a third left to find the means for assuring that money will be available for the program—with the whole process repeated on the other side of Capitol Hill. The simple fact is that as of now, Congress is patently unable to cope with the total expenditure by the government in relation to clearly defined priorities.

For example, federal assistance to education is carried out by more than 40 different agencies and departments of the executive branch, with the responsibility of overseeing the different programs scattered among most of the standing committees of both House and Senate. Indeed, we may question whether even the President can say precisely how much of the government's dollar is spent for education.

A second example is found in connection with the government's war on poverty: a score of executive agencies are involved with this problem in one way or another, each requesting sums of money for its programs. (One of my Democratic colleagues says the trouble with many of these new programs are that they are "grand shin plasters that fail to deal adequately with even the immediate problem.")

The role of a congressional committee in our system is to research complex problems and report back to Congress. If no effective distinction between majority and minority positions is made in committee, meaningful floor debate and a careful amending process are impossible. As a result of the investigative skill and exhaustive research efforts of our staff director, the Committee on Increased Minority Staffing of the 88th Congress was able to document a situation in which minority Members of Congress were receiving such limited assistance from expert personnel assigned to the standing committees that the wonder is that any differentiation at all was made on most of the issues before the national legislature that year. The situation clearly spoke to the very health of our governmental process.

In order that *all* participants in the legislative process may have adequate information and equal assistance at the committee stage, Congress should take urgent action to: (1) correct the imbalance of partisan staff available to minority Members of committees; (2) provide a measure of job security for minority employees through a guarantee that the hire and fire power of these people rests with the ranking and minority Members of each committee, and (3) clarify and upgrade the positions of all committee employees through the establishment of job descriptions.

The Legislative Reference Service

The second major source of information for the Congressman is the Legislative Reference Service (LRS) of the Library of Congress. Established in 1914 by administrative action within the Library, the Service has been in continuous existence for more than 50 years. The Legislative Reorganization Act of 1946 put it on a statutory basis, raised it to full-fledged departmental rank within the Library, expanded its staff, and spelled out its duties in broad language.

In essence, the Service was commanded to supply accurate and objective information, research, analysis, and evaluation of legislative matters of interest to the committees and Members of Congress. Implicit in the expansion of the Service and its functions was the belief that Congress must attain parity with the executive branch in access to information and expertise. The Service was to help Congress avoid over-reliance on the executive branch and other public or private sources, including lobbies, for the facts and research assistance it requires. Members of Congress receive from the Legislative Reference Service that rarest of all Washington products: the disinterested point of view, the undistorted fact, the impartial and nonpartisan analysis and evaluation of controversial public policy issues. Obviously, these are essential to intelligent and informed decision-making.

The language of the Service's statute speaks of "legislative proposals," "data . . . bearing upon legislation," "summaries and digests of public hearings . . . and of bills and resolutions of a public general nature . . ." If LRS dealt with nothing more than this, its value would still be inestimable and the weight of its burden staggering. With the encouragement of Congress, however, the Service has interpreted this language quite broadly and thereby approached its obligations more realistically. Congressmen, the Service recognizes, are not legislators alone—they are also educators, leaders of public opinion, and interceders between their often puzzled and desperate constituents and the awesome impersonality of a colossal Federal Government. In these areas, too, LRS attempts to serve the Members of Congress.

Because of its direct relationship with the Legislature, the problems encountered by the Service reflect the increasing and increasingly complex tasks faced by Congress. As summed up by the Service's former director, Dr. Hugh Elsbree, LRS "has too much of too many kinds of things to do, given its present resources."[3]

In 1946, the year of the passage of Reorganization Act, the Service handled 16,444 inquiries with a staff of 95. Nineteen years later, with little more than double that staff, it answered 113,628 requests, a workload increase of almost 700 per cent!

Clearly, the Legislative Reference Service cannot perform its functions effectively without sufficient manpower. Quality of research necessarily deteriorates under the pressure of an ever-mounting workload. Furthermore, as our nation's population increases, the extent of congressional activities will continue to grow, imposing still greater burdens on the Service. A substantial addition to its staff is imperative.

One aspect of the Service's workload problem that has received considerable attention recently is that involving constituent requests. The assistance given in connection with these requests is of great value to Members of Congress, not only because it helps them help their constituents, but also because such inquiries frequently prompt research of real value to the Member in connection with pending legislation, the exercise of legislative oversight, or matters of long-range interest. In terms of numbers, more than half the inquiries received by the Service originate with constituents. This is not to say that LRS spends half its time on such business; actually, constituent requests take up only about 19 per cent of the Service's total research time. They do, however, cut into the time available to the staff for dealing with legislatively related research. With additional staff resources, LRS should reorganize itself in a manner that will shift this burden away from subject specialists who should be devoting themselves to research.

Dr. Elsbree described the current workload situation in this way:

> The basic problem of the Service today is not that we do not do a great deal of legislatively related work—we do incalculably more than in 1946, thanks to the tremendous impact of the LaFollette-Monroney Act of that date and to the vigorous and imaginative leadership of Dr. Ernest S. Griffith who headed the Service for so many years. But first, the scope and the complexity of legislative activity, including legislative oversight of governmental operations, have increased enormously; and secondly, the individual Member's relations with his constituency have changed vastly, producing (a) a greater need of the Member to take a stand, and to brief himself on, more and more issues, and (b) a greater need of the Member for types of information and assistance connected with activities of his office but not so closely related to actual legislation—like answering constituent inquiries, keeping his constituents informed about issues they are interested in and his efforts on their behalf, preparing talks for public appearances, and so on. These are the trends that have created such a terrific problem for us.[4]

Obviously, the Service must have additional personnel to meet its present and growing responsibilities. But beyond this, LRS must expand the scope of its service in order to meet the varying needs of Congress. As the legislature becomes involved in more and more subjects, the Service must have a recruiting and hiring system flexible enough to permit it to employ at relatively short notice experts in those subjects. It should also have the capability of supplementing its core staff with outside consultants, advisers, and research organizations to deal with projects beyond its normal areas of specialization.

Furthermore, the Service must be encouraged to adopt new techniques in assisting Members and committees of Congress. These might include, for example, establishing a roster of *ad hoc* consultants who could be made available to Congressmen for short periods. Briefings and seminars for Members and their staffs on a variety of special subjects might also be useful.

Automated information retrieval is a *must* for the Service. Congress has been inexcusably slow in exploring the possibilities of electronic information systems to aid it in the legislative process. The functions of the Legislative Reference Service present a tantalizing number of opportunities for utilizing such devices.

The physical facilities now available to the Service are hardly conducive to creating the kind of atmosphere in which thoughtful research can best be carried out. Cramped quarters and second-hand equipment not only hamper the present staff but also hinder LRS in recruiting and retaining the top-level professional talent it must have. Congress should provide suitable facilities if it expects to attract the calibre of research personnel it wants and needs.

Finally, Congress should give some thought to unifying its research organizations. The Office of the Coordinator of Information, established solely for the use of the House of Representatives in 1947, largely duplicates the quick-answer function of the Legislative Reference Service. Congress should transfer the operations of this office to the Service.

Automated Information Handling

Since the development of the electronic computer shortly after the end of World War II, major emphasis in research and development has been placed upon evolving techniques and man-machine procedures, as well as developing equipment, that could aid a wide range of information consumers. Today, the dual impact of the "information explosion" and automatic data processing (ADP) is felt in all areas of American society—business, education, government, industry, and the professions. Through the concept of time-sharing and utilization of "on line" equipment, each is increasingly able to borrow from and contribute to the store of information of the others.

By way of caution, one is advised to bear constantly in mind that *the cardinal component of all information systems is the human element*, or, in the irrepressible style of my good friend Tom Curtis, "idiot input produces idiot output." The concept which should govern the utilization of ADP devices is based on the fact that they can sort, merge, compute, assemble, compile, translate, extract, store, and retrieve data, *but only at the explicit direction of the human controller*. Computers do not "think." They are also fantastically costly.

The subtleties of the information needs of the legislator in particular make requirements delineation for Congress a *sine qua non*. As Charles Dechert points out:

The problem of congressional access to information might be better defined as a problem of information management. What specific elements of information are needed to make what judgments? Where are these elements located? How are they to be retrieved? And how should they be presented in order to be meaningful?[5]

Four criteria determine the wise use of an automatic information system: completeness, accuracy, timeliness, and relevance of the information. Both technical and non-technical considerations must be taken into account when undertaking system analysis and design, and these factors, inextricably linked, should be recognized by all persons involved in the system. In order to utilize ADP systems in an optimum way, men must work *with* machines, using them selectively and on a priority basis.

ADP in Use in the Executive Branch

Although there have been identifiable needs throughout the federal community for increased utilization of automatic data processing equipment, the executive branch stands alone as the pioneer in acquiring both personnel and equipment. From only 90 computers in 1956, 2,188 electronic computers were projected for fiscal year 1965.[6] Thirty-five agencies own or lease ADP equipment (FY 1965),[7] and the investment of the federal government continues to rise—in fiscal year 1965, $1,132,000,000 was spent on ADP equipment and services.[8]

Since the need for machine support was identifiable readily in the Bureau of the Census application areas, one of the earliest ADP capabilities was created to help process statistical information on population, housing, construction, foreign trade, agriculture, business, government, industry, and transportation. Several types of computers have been used, and data has been stored in the form of punched cards, magnetic tapes, tabulations, and census and survey records.[9] Also, national and regional statistical samples are kept both on punched cards and computer tape.[10]

Because technological requirements related to national defense often required substantial ADP support, priority was established within the Department of Defense to conduct research (both basic and applied) and development in ADP equipment, techniques, and procedures. In some instances, special emphasis was placed upon designing complete systems; exemplary of this was the work in the command-and-control area of the Strategic Air Command and the North American Air Defense Command. Large, joint government-contractor teams comprised of military planners, programmers, systems analysts, and engineers worked long and hard in an intensive effort to provide the type of rapid response capability necessary to ensure military preparedness.

The services performed with ADP support by the Defense Documentation Center (DDC) are particularly noteworthy. This group, formerly called the Armed Services Technical Information Agency (ASTIA), is the organization which "seeks to keep ready at hand all of the research results obtained by or for the military departments and other DOD components."[11]

Through government sponsorship of Project LITE (Legal Information Thru Electronics), it has been possible to place the entire United States Code on magnetic tape.[12] The Bureau of Labor Statistics (Department of Labor) collects, analyzes, and publishes national, regional, and local data on retail and wholesale prices, wages and salaries, consumer expenditures, employment and unemployment, and other key data of acute interest to Congress.[13] In yet another significant area, the Internal Revenue Service continues to add to its ADP capability for the purpose of processing income tax returns. By 1967, in fact, the entire processing job of IRS will be computerized.[14]

Other application areas exist, such as in the Social Security Administration, where large-scale information handling systems using ADP have been established and developed. Clearly, with respect to government use of automatic data processing:

> . . . it is the executive branch, not Congress, that has taken advantage of the new information techniques; and in so doing, it has gained the advantage over Congress throughout the entire policy-making process.[15]

ADP and Congress

In projecting ADP support for Congress, one is faced with the usual discouraging array of considerations. The purchase, installation, and operation of equipment, both in terms of "hardware" and "software,"[16] is enormously expensive. In order to exact maximum efficiency at minimum cost, system design must be based on user need, both in terms of kinds of information and recurrence of use.

Who will be the users? To speak of "Congress" as a user is to speak of its committees, its Members, and its employees. What kinds of needs are felt by these different components? How much of the information needed by all three is of such a nature that it must be constantly updated and made available on a daily, even hourly, basis? Where should the systems operation be located? Who will govern its use and have responsibility for overseeing its personnel and upkeep? In light of the intertwined relationships between Executive and Congress today, do possibilities exist for "on line" sharing of information by the two branches?

The improvement of any information handling system should be performed in a modular (step by step) fashion, commencing with a thorough analysis of the existing system. This approach necessarily takes into consideration the essential criteria for evaluating system operation cost, performance, reliability, and maintainability.

Moreover, the attitudes of the information users must be conditioned to accept innovative methods while guarding against the tendency to throw out the baby with the bath water. Computers are a relatively new phenomenon, and as anything NEW tends toward an immediate polarization of reactions, both blind fear and blind acceptance characterize many discussions of ADP support for Congress.

Lost in the lexicon of such buzz words as "buffer storage," "random access," and "Williams tube," some people seem convinced that the complex information handling problems of the Congress can be solved by putting anything and everything on magnetic tape. Disks, drums, and tape together, the cheapest and most practical method of storing static (fixed in space and available at any time) information at present is between the covers of a *book*, of which the Library of Congress has millions.

As an illustration of the other extreme, one Congressman remarked recently that the last thing he wanted to hear was any talk of computers for Congress. "In my opinion, it will be a sorry day for the country when Congressmen have been replaced by computers." Although he probably could be replaced by a mimeograph machine, it is important to recognize that fear is no more conducive to practical decision-making with respect to automated information handling than infatuation with the new machines.

Suggested Applications

Many state legislatures are far ahead of Congress in the application of computer technology to the legislative process, and while Congress is unique in many respects, certain of its activities are common to all deliberative lawmaking bodies. As Sam R. Haley, Legislative Counsel for the State of Oregon, noted in testimony before the Joint Organization Committee:

> . . . it is also important that we realize that the business of assisting lawmakers has certain common denominators. The production of legislative drafts for introduction, their printing and reprinting from the time of introduction through enactment and compilation and, finally, the supplying of information regarding their status, disposition and content at these various stages is a common legislative operation.[17]

With the introduction of more than 13,000 measures in the House alone last year, it is difficult to comprehend how Congress could fail to take advantage of computer technology for the storage and retrieval of this most fundamental information while it allowed the executive branch to spend more than one billion dollars for automatic data processing in the departments and agencies!

Another application of ADP that seems to me overripe for study is in the matter of committee meetings, hearings, and reports. The workload of every Congressman is such that he scarcely has time to attend all the hearings and keep up with the reports of the committees on which he serves, let alone the activities of the other 17 or 18 committees of the House, not to mention those of Senate committees. As a result, he must rely in large part on the advice of his colleagues in casting his vote for or against a majority of the bills that come to the Floor. In some cases, legislation may be passed before printed hearings are available to all Members. With the aid of computers, the testimony of witnesses appearing on major legislation could be abstracted and printed out daily, reports stored for fast call-up in reference to past activity by the committee in this area, and records maintained of committee Members' votes. Additionally, conflicts in the scheduling of meetings could be diminished if not eliminated.

Certainly housekeeping functions, such as payroll accounting and the maintenance of employee records, should be automated without further delay. The laws governing the reporting of campaign expenditures and the activities of lobbyists should be tightened up and ADP applied to the collection and storage of this information.

A particularly fascinating application of computer technology to the Congressman's informational needs is the consideration of some SDI (Selective Dissemination of Information) system to support the Legislative Reference Service in keeping Members abreast of all new literature relevant to their individual fields of inquiry. One no longer describes information coming into the Library of Congress in terms of numbers of documents, books, and articles; material is wheeled in *daily* by the *truckload*. This information must be sorted, scanned, and catalogued eventually. Modern man-machine handling could speed the process, resulting in fast print-out of bibliographical material for use by the Congressman in keeping up with current writing in areas of his choice, whether the subject matter is directly related to his committee assignment or not. Reference retrieval is a relatively simple task for a computer, especially in response to pre-arranged search categories. What vast new horizons this could open up!

I have barely touched upon specific applications of automatic data processing to the legislative process. Yet, it is clear that Congress is far behind the times—behind the executive branch, the state legislatures, educational institutions, business, industry, and the professions—in the handling of information. Knowledge *is* power. The uses to which that knowledge is put determine the fate of our own nation and increasingly influence the destiny of others. Information is the key to wise decision-making. If the people would retain a voice in their government, if Congress would regain its stature as a co-equal partner with the executive branch, Congressmen must look to the improvement of their methods of gathering, sorting, and analyzing data. The need is fundamental. The case is urgent.

Congressional-Academic Liaison

Many ties exist between Congress and the academic community now, of course, but they are for the most part informal and short-lived. Congress could both improve the quality and variety of its information and contribute to a better understanding of the legislative process on the part of teachers and students, and ultimately the people, by strengthening the over-all relationship.

As an immediate step in the direction of improving professorial contact with Congress, I recommend that a special section of the House gallery be set aside for visiting scholars. While I stoutly defend the right of every citizen to watch his Congress in action, the simple fact of the matter is that gallery space is limited and heavy tourist traffic results in the scholar's being uprooted often after only fifteen minutes' observation. This is hardly enough time to witness the proceedings on the floor of the House that may be crucial to his understanding of a bill's passage or defeat. Special passes could be issued to scholars and a small section of the gallery reserved for them, much as a section of the House gallery is reserved for members of the press.

Second, I heartily endorse a proposal made by George Agree, Executive Director of the National Committee for an Effective Congress, before the Joint Organization Committee last year. Mr. Agree proposed:

> . . . any time a group of Members (of Congress) wish to undertake a particular study, the Congress itself should provide them with the facilities to do so . . . The present condition of Members who want to pursue some subject that may not be on the legislative agenda, or to make an independent study of a subject that is on, is one of almost complete frustration. The few "task forces" or "study groups" that are organized for such purposes too frequently founder for lack of staff and facilities.[18]

Mr. Agree's procedure would require that a minimum number of Members, say 15, perhaps with the qualification that no group be comprised of more than 75 or 80 per cent of the Members of one party, constitute such a group. After the purpose and scope of the group's inquiry had been approved by the Speaker and Minority Leader, the Members would be given office space, facilities, and funds for the employment of the necessary research and secretarial personnel to carry out their study. Additionally, funds might be authorized for such travel as Members of the group wished to undertake or to reimburse experts invited to Washington for consultation by the group. The unit would have no legislative or political authority; however, its work would become the property of the standing committees of most nearly related jurisdiction.

Mr. Agree's proposal is a step in the direction of a better informed Congress and improved communication and relations between scholars and Congressmen. The cost in consideration of the benefits to both would be negligible.

The fellowship program of the American Political Science Association is perhaps the most successful venture of this kind to date, and it augurs for the success of such a program as Mr. Agree has proposed. By itself, however, the APSA program should be expanded and better publicized. A similar fellowship program under the auspices of The Brookings Institution has proved immeasurably beneficial to both Congress and the participating scholars.

A collateral effort might be attempted by Congress based somewhat on the pattern established by the Nieman Foundation. Each year since 1938, thanks to a generous bequest of the late Agnes Wahl Nieman and an innovative decision by the university's president, James Bryant Conant, a dozen or so newspaper men spend a year on leave from their papers pursuing studies *of their own choice* at Harvard University. They may take any courses they want, or none at all if they can find a shorter route to the information they are after. No degrees are awarded; no credits are earned for the courses taken.

Obviously, a Congressman could not take a year of leave from his duties. However, he could take two weeks, or depending on the workload of the session, as much as two months, each year in November or December, to live on campus and pursue such studies as his time permitted and his interest dictated. As with the Nieman fellowships, the program would be limited to Congressmen who had served at least one full term and had been elected to a second; and as with Harvard University, the success of the program would be determined at least 50 per cent by the cooperation of the colleges and universities participating.

Subject to administrative procedures of each institution, the Congressman could audit any lectures, attend any lab sessions, and in general participate in any educational activities on campus. He would have free access to the resources of the university's library, and as the school's "Congressman in Residence," he would be expected to participate in weekend seminars and informal discussions with teachers and students.

Even though the press of his official duties would permit each Congressman only a brief residency and very limited study, the reciprocal benefits from such a program would seem to make it worth a trial run. In fact, the idea has been successfully tested. Former Congressman John Lindsay spent weekends "in residence" on the campuses of the University of Iowa and Washington University in St. Louis. John thoroughly enjoyed the experience and gained from it, and in both cases, the response of faculty, students, and—thanks to splendid reporting by the press—public, was uniformly enthusiastic.

In my capacities at various times as a history teacher, president of the U.S. Capitol Historical Society, and legislator at both state and national levels, I have visited hundreds of university and college campuses. During our residency in Washington, Mrs. Schwengel and I have hosted more than a score of college professors and over one hundred college students in our home. The contact in every case has been exhilarating for us, and we have been gratified by the letters from our guests expressing their appreciation of the opportunity these visits provided them to get a first-hand view of their government in Washington. I am convinced that a "Congressman in Residence" program would be welcomed by most colleges and universities across the country and would prove beneficial to every Congressman who participated in it.

Conclusion

As she entered the 1960's, America could count more than one-third of her population under twenty years of age.

These young people inherit the proud ideals and unfulfilled dreams of a strong and growing nation. They face the excitement of making new discoveries, crossing new horizons. They face as well the challenge of finding solutions to new problems.

As we labor to strengthen the machinery of our national legislature in order to cope with the problems of the sixties, we would do well to remind ourselves, as Lincoln reminded Members of Congress a century ago, that

The struggle of today is not altogether for today—it is for a vast future also.[19]

REFERENCES

1. From an address by Dr. Edward Wenk, Jr., Chief, Science Policy Research Division, Legislative Reference Service, before the Interparliamentary Union Conference held in Geneva, Switzerland, Nov. 5, 1965: "Information Required by Parliaments in a World Increasingly Dependent Upon Science."
2. Neustadt, Richard E., "Politicians and Bureaucrats," in *The Congress and America's Future*, David B. Truman, ed., The American Assembly, Columbia University, Englewood Cliffs, N.J., Prentice-Hall, Inc., 1965.
3. Hearings, Joint Committee on the Organization of Congress, 89th Cong., p. 1110.
4. *Ibid.*, p. 1114.
5. Dechert, Charles R., *Availability of Information for Congressional Operations*, Washington, D.C., American Enterprise Institute for Public Policy Research, 1966.
6. Executive Office of the President, Bureau of the Budget, *Inventory of Automatic Data Processing Equipment in the Federal Government*, Washington, D.C., June 1965, Chart 6, p. 11.
7. *Ibid.*, Chart 1, p. 6.
8. *Ibid.*, Chart 3, p. 8.
9. *Ibid.*, Table 2, p. 28.
10. National Referral Center for Science and Technology, *A Directory of Information Resources in the United States; Social Sciences*, Washington, D.C., Library of Congress, Oct. 1959.
11. Committee on Scientific Information of the Federal Council on Science and Technology, *Status Report on Scientific and Technical Information in the Federal Government*, Washington, D.C., Department of Commerce, June 18, 1963.
12. Office of Science Information Service, National Science Foundation, *Current Research and Development in Scientific Documentation*, Vol. 13, Washington, D.C., Nov. 1964.
13. *A Directory of Information Resources, etc., op. cit.*
14. Hirsch, Phil, "Computers and Tax Collection," *Datamation*, March, 1966.

15. Robinson, James A., *Decision-Making in Congress*, Washington, D.C., American Enterprise Institute, 1965.

16. "Software" refers to the techniques and aids (*e.g.*, programs, etc.) needed for the proper utilization of an ADP system. In terms of cost, the ratio of software to hardware is *at least* 50–50. Caveat emptor!

17. Hearings, Joint Committee on the Organization of Congress, 89th Cong., Part 13.

18. Hearings, JCOC, 89th Cong., Part 9.

19. Annual Message to Congress, December 3, 1861.

APPENDIX I

by James C. Cleveland, M.C.

As a sort of coda to this piece, I offer the following quotation from the Minority Views on S. 2084, the Highway Beautification Act of 1965.[1] The purpose is not to go over the merits or demerits of the bill but to present a vivid example of the total servitude in which the Congress can be (and was) put by a determined Executive, holding large congressional majorities in thrall.

The reader may readily picture for himself the tensions and frustrations of Committee members of both parties that lie behind these lines. The agony of having to sit by helplessly watching the rape of the legislative process is amply reflected in the Minority Views. In my own Supplemental Views on this bill, I stated: "Members should understand that the terms of this measure were dictated to our committee by a top presidential aide who came to Capitol Hill to sit in with Members. . . . It is painful to see the knowledge and expertise of the Public Works Committee brushed aside and ignored by the stubborn dictates of the Executive Branch."[2]

The adoption of the Ford proposal and increased minority staffing provisions would go far to blunt future opportunities for such shameful subjection of the Congress.

Minority Views on S. 2084

We support the concept of beautifying areas adjacent to highways, but we are opposed to the enactment of this bill in its present form, for three basic reasons:

1. It is not the product of careful, independent congressional deliberation. Instead, it is a poorly thought out proposal which was brutally forced upon the Committee on Public Works by spokesmen for the Administration who wielded the power and influence of the White House, to an extent which we have never

319

before seen, to make certain that the bill be reported, and reported *now*, regardless of the consequences.

2. The bill is replete with unworkable, unwise, and unfair provisions insisted upon by spokesmen for the Administration who did not know and probably did not care about the many ramifications and adverse impacts of such provisions.

3. The bill will unjustly penalize States which, in good faith, may attempt to control outdoor advertising and junkyards under the bill, but are unable to do so within the short time allowed, because of constitutional or other impediments; it will have a destructive impact upon small businesses, such as motels, hotels, restaurants, service stations, and the like, which depend upon patronage by the motoring public for survival, and it will deprive the motoring public of needed travel information.

White House Arm Twisting

On November 27, 1963, in his first address to a joint session of the Congress, President Lyndon B. Johnson made the following statement:

As one who has long served in both Houses of the Congress, I firmly believe in the independence and the integrity of the legislative branch. I promise you that I shall always respect this. It is deep in the marrow of my bones.

With equal firmness, I believe in the capacity and I believe in the ability of the Congress, despite the divisions of opinion which characterize our Nation, to act—to act wisely, to act vigorously, to act speedily when the need arises.

The manner in which spokesmen for the Administration, including officials from the White House itself, have brought pressure to bear upon the members of the Committee on Public Works raises considerable question as to whether the President has either changed his views or whether he was sincere at the time he made the statement set forth above. A brief chronology of the action taken with respect to the highway beautification proposal will serve to illustrate this.

By letter, dated May 26, 1965, the President transmitted his highway beautification proposals to the Congress. On the same day, bills were introduced to carry out the President's recommendations. Hearings were held on the four bills on July 20, 21, and 22. The hearings disclosed the existence of a number of problems and unanswered questions, and demonstrated rather conclusively that the bills would have to be substantially revised in order to provide for a workable program. At that time, it was the understanding of the Committee that, because of the great amount of revision which would be needed, the Committee and its staff would study the bills and not take final action with respect to them until early during the second session of the 89th Congress. This understanding came about, at least partially, because of the tremendous workload which has confronted the Committee on Public Works this session, including the Appalachian Regional Development Act of 1965; the Water Quality Act of 1965; the Pacific Northwest Disaster Relief Act of 1965; the Public Works and Economic Development Act of 1965; H.R. 6790, to provide for emergency relief for repair or reconstruction of highways; Senate Joint Resolution 81, to provide for apportionment of funds for the Inter-state Highway System and other purposes; and the Omnibus Rivers and Harbors and Flood Control Act of 1965; as well as other legislation.

Despite this prior understanding and the good and valid reasons support-ing it, a sudden decision was made to reopen the hearings on the Highway Beautification Bill. These hearings were held on Friday, September 3, and Tuesday, September 7. The hearings came immediately after the Subcommit-tees on Flood Control and on Rivers and Harbors had completed an exhaust-ing period of hearings on the Omnibus Rivers and Harbors and Flood Control Act and only one day after the full Committee on Public Works agreed to report the Omnibus Rivers and Harbors and Flood Control Bill. The hearings on highway beautification came at a time when the full efforts of the committee and its staff should have been devoted to preparation of the voluminous report on the omnibus bill. In addition to this, the hearings were split over the Labor Day weekend, when most of the members had plans and commitments of long standing.

The Subcommittee on Roads held executive sessions on September 13, 14, 15, and 16. On Wednesday, September 15, and Thursday, September 16, sessions were held both in the morning and at night. This was done in spite of the fact that the Senate was then considering the Highway Beautification Bill and the minority members of the Committee insisted that the matter was not so urgent that it could not wait until the Senate completed action and we had in our hands the bill to be passed by the Senate. On Friday, September 17, a meeting of the Committee was scheduled, but at the last minute was post-poned to await the Senate-passed bill. On Monday, September 20, and Tues-day, September 21, the full committee met in executive session to mark up the bill. A majority of the Committee agreed to report it out on Tuesday morning, just minutes before the members of the Committee were required to be on the floor of the House to take up the Conference Report on the Water Quality Act of 1965 and to debate the Omnibus Rivers and Harbors and Flood Con-trol Act of 1965. As if this were not enough, it was directed that the report be filed not later than midnight Wednesday, which allowed less than a day and a half for preparation of the report, including minority views, on this complex and controversial measure. During this day and a half, the members and staff were almost totally absorbed in the debate on the Omnibus Rivers and Harbors and Flood Control Bill, which was then going on.

Throughout this series of difficult and exhausting meetings, including the night sessions, representatives of the White House and of the Department of Commerce were gathered in the anteroom adjoining the committee hearing room. Of course they purported to be there for the purpose of giving technical aid and assistance to the committee. However, their answers to questions and their drafts of proposed amendments to the bill demonstrated to an embar-rassing degree their lack of knowledge and experience in the field of highway legislation.

Throughout this period, both the majority and minority staffs of the Committee worked nights and weekends in efforts to draft a bill which would accomplish the objectives of the President, as we understood them, without creating the problems and difficulties inherent in the administration bills before the committee. At one point, a committee print of a bill, prepared by the Chairman of the Subcommittee on Roads, was distributed to the members of the Subcommittee, and it contained provisions which could have been the farmework of a bill that might have been reported from the Subcommittee as a consensus bill. Overnight, however, without explanation, the bill was withdrawn and no further consideration was given to it. Instead, the subcommittee and the full committee reported a bill which has serious deficiencies, as will be discussed hereafter.

On January 4, 1965, in his address before a joint session of the House and Senate on the State of the Union, President Johnson stated: "Though total agreement between the Executive and the Congress is impossible, total respect is important."

The President has demonstrated his total lack of respect for the Congress by refusing to allow it to work its will upon highway beautification legislation.

Most of the members of the Committee on Public Works and its staff, on both sides of the aisle, have vast experience and knowledge of highway legislation and the federally aided highway program. Highway legislation has traditionally been handled by the Committee on Public Works in a bipartisan manner, and the Committee takes pride, and justifiably so, in the legislation that has been enacted as a result of its efforts.

The Committee on Public Works, with the help of its able staff, if left alone, could have, and we are sure would have, written an effective, acceptable, and workable bill.

The President and his advisers are not one whit more interested in highway beautification than the members of the Committee. The stampeded action on this bill has not been explained. At this point, we are sure of only two things: the bill is not a good one, and it is not the product of calm congressional reasoning and deliberation.

REFERENCES

1. House Report No. 1084, 89th Congress, 1st Session, pp. 45–47.
2. *Ibid.*, p. 56.

APPENDIX II

Robert McClory, M.C.

The most important attempted reform to date came in the creation of a Joint Committee on the Legislative Budget by the Legislative Reorganization Act of 1946. Like the Budget and Accounting Act of 1921, the 1946 Act came upon the heels of a destructive world war and was passed by a Congress concerned with the augmentation of power in the executive. A prime objective of the Act was to regain or restore Congress' power of the purse. Pursuant to this aim, the 1946 Act provided for the creation of a "legislative budget" and a Joint Committee on the Legislative Budget. It also provided for expenditure analyses to be made by the Comptroller General for the use of the appropriations committees and other financial committees to determine whether or not public funds had been economically and efficiently administered and for the expansion of the appropriations committees' staffs.

Sections 138 and 206 of the 1946 Act relating to the legislative budget and expenditure analyses were never successfully implemented by Congress. However, under Section 202(b) of the Act the appropriations committees' staffs were increased, although not to the extent intended or required.

Section 138 was one of the most comprehensive provisions ever enacted for improving the fiscal machinery of Congress. The Joint Committee on the Legislative Budget, composed of the Members of the four major fiscal committees of Congress (House and Senate Appropriations, House Ways and Means, and Senate Finance Committees), was to meet at the beginning of each session of Congress to formulate a "legislative budget" which would then be submitted to Congress. This budget would contain the "estimated overall federal receipts and expenditures" for the fiscal year, including a recommendation for the maximum amount to be appropriated for expenditures in such years. Subsection (b) provided that the committee report should be accompanied by a "concurrent resolution adopting such a budget and fixing the maximum amount to be appropriated for expenditures in such year."

Three attempts to carry out these provisions (in 1947, 1948 and 1949) failed. Many reasons are given for the failure of Congress to carry out Section 138. A recent report of the House Government Operations Committee on Financial Management in the Federal Government lists some of them:

1. The time allowed for preparation of the legislative budget was too short.
2. The joint committee was not adequately staffed to do the job expected of it, and the committee itself, with more than 100 members, was unwieldy.
3. Unpredictable expenditure demands render it impossible to keep total appropriations below the ceiling agreed upon early in the session.
4. The budget ceilings, though approved by Congress, are not binding.
5. The practice of separately passing from a dozen to a score of appropriation bills makes it difficult to enforce over-all ceilings.
6. A ceiling on total expenditures cannot be enforced as long as appropriations are based upon obligations whose liquidation in the form of expenditures is frequently spread over more than one year.[1]

Ironically, the provisions of Section 206 have never been carried out because of a lack of appropriations. While funds have been sought for this section, its implementation has been frustrated on numerous occasions by the House Appropriations Committee and once by the Senate, when offered as a floor amendment to the Independent Offices Appropriations Act of 1955. In any event, the provisions of Section 206 would only spell out an enhanced post-audit role for the GAO and would not allow it to play the active pre-audit role of examining budget requests sought by the drafters of the 1921 Act.

Why has Congress refused to develop the role of the GAO as intended in the 1921 Act? Saloma cites several reasons, which he summarizes as follows:

. . . the GAO has been restricted by congressional attitudes toward economy in government and the fear of establishing a legislative bureaucracy. Two essentially structural problems have barred full congressional utilization of the GAO: the central position of the House Appropriations Committee with unlimited staffing authority and the question of who will provide political direction and control of the budgetary actions of the GAO. These problems would seem to preclude the GAO as a serious reform alternative, although the Congress might reach the point of frustration with the House Appropriations Committee where it would act over its head.[2]

Section 202(b) of the 1946 Act represented an attempt at major reform of the appropriations process by significantly increasing the staff allowances of the House and Senate Appropriations Committees. The provision came about mostly as a reaction to the growth of the executive department staffs in the period since 1921: it was felt that the appropriations committees of Congress could more effectively counterbalance the role of the President in preparing the budget if they had an adequately large professional staff. As a result of this provision, the number of permanent staff members of the House and Senate Appropriations Committees has been increased from about eight for each committee to approximately 50 in the House and 30 in the Senate. While the appropriations committees have been given unlimited staffing authority, they have thus far been reluctant to use it.

As noted earlier, increased staffing of the appropriations committees is to some degree hindered by the seniority system, which allows senior members first call on staff assistants. There is also concern, especially among old-time committee members, that an increased permanent staff might develop into a staff bureaucracy independent of the committee. The late Clarence Cannon, former Chairman of the House Appropriations Committee and a member of the Committee for 30 years, summarized the latter point in these words:

> What happens when you put men permanently on the staff? They get lazy. They develop friendships with the departments. If you get misfits it is hard to fire them. They develop a camaraderie with the members of the committees and get their salaries raised. Everybody downtown knows them. When they enter the door the word is passed through the building, "Here comes that fellow from the committee." When there is no investigation they sit around cooling their heels and their time and their salary is wasted.[3]

Finally, there is the basic question of whether further increased staffing would actually enhance committee control of expenditures. It may not be advisable that appropriations committees be able to consider each and every budget detail to the exclusion of broader policy issues. Therefore, increased staffing may be significant only to the extent it will aid the committees in the quality, and not necessarily the quantity, of their work. It is generally conceded, however, that in either case, an increase in committee staff seems warranted.

Reforms outside the ambit of the 1946 Act have also been tried in an effort to improve the effectiveness of the appropriations committees in the congressional budget process. One of these has been the unsuccessful attempt to institute an omnibus appropriations bill for the consolidation of appropriations into a single measure. Such a procedure would have the advantage of allowing Congress to review comprehensively federal revenues and expenditures, effecting economies of time and money lost when the executive budget is considered on a program-by-program basis with funds being appropriated through a series of bills extending over a period of several months.

The omnibus appropriations bill procedure was first tried by the House on an experimental basis (*i.e.*, without changing the House Rules) in 1950. While it received wide public support by influential organizations such as the National Association of Manufacturers, the U.S. Chamber of Commerce, and other groups, and was sponsored by Senator Harry Byrd and Representative Clarence Cannon, it was nonetheless vigorously opposed by the rank-and-file Members of Congress, including most Members of the appropriations committees. Like the proposal for a legislative budget, it placed principal emphasis on appropriations rather than revenues and had as its objective the increased control of expenditures through a broader examination of government spending. However, unlike the legislative budget, the proposed omnibus appropriations bill placed no ceiling on expenditures and was to be drafted by the House Appropriations Committee rather than by the Joint Committee.

Advocates of the omnibus approach were quick to point out its merits—
a $2.3 billion reduction in the budget in 1950, fewer delays caused by amend-
ments, more informed consideration of the budget, and a record-setting early
report of appropriations. Its sponsors spoke glowingly of it. Senator Byrd
declared that

> . . . enactment of the single appropriation bill this year [1950] required less time,
> promoted fuller participation in debate, and resulted in savings rather than
> increases.[4]

In Rep. Cannon's opinion,

> . . . the single appropriation bill offers the most practical and efficient method
> of handling the annual budget and the national fiscal program.[5]

On the other hand, opponents of the omnibus bill pointed out numerous
defects. Harris gives the argument for the other side, as follows:

> It has also been charged that a consolidated bill would (1) not provide full
> information about proposed expenditures in relation to revenues, for it does not
> take into account supplemental and deficiency appropriations; (2) be too large
> and involved to be understood and debated intelligently by the members; (3) in-
> crease the likelihood of "pork barrel" items; (4) facilitate the use of percentage
> or "meat ax" reductions and other legislative riders; (5) impose excessive delays
> in starting department programs; and (6) unless it was accompanied by the item
> veto, deprive the President of his veto power.[6]

As Professor Harris notes, many of these objections could be overcome
by revision of committee procedure and organization to facilitate an omnibus
approach. Such revision entails making it possible for the appropriations committees to get a broader view of the budget and necessitates a more careful
examination of subcommittee recommendations by the full committee. It
would also require that the subcommittees give more attention to the program
and policy aspects of budget requests than to the details of departmental and
agency expenditures.

Like the legislative budget proposal, it was hoped by many that the omnibus appropriations bill would carry out the intent of the 1946 Act to increase
congressional control of the purse strings. However, unlike the legislative
budget, which was well received by the rank-and-file members of Congress,
the omnibus appropriations bill was given little support in Congress. A survey
has shown that more than 62 per cent of the House membership favored the
legislative budget proposal, while only 14 per cent supported the idea of the
omnibus appropriations bill.[7]

There have been several explanations made for Congress' lack of
enthusiasm for this proposal.[8] First, the omnibus approach, if it is to function
effectively, requires a radical revision in appropriations procedure and organization. Unlike the joint budget proposal, which would allow the Appropriations Committee to function as before only in joint capacity with the
other financial committees of Congress, the reporting of an omnibus appropri-

ations bill demands that the appropriations committees and Congress devote their entire energies to the consideration of a single measure rather than several individual bills. Besides necessitating revision of committee procedure and organization, this means that floor debate, usually spread out over several months, must be compressed into a matter of weeks. Appropriations bills that would normally pass without delay would be held up until debate was completed on the entire bill. This has led many to conclude that the omnibus approach injects unnecessary delays into the appropriations process, thus hindering the initiation of non-controversial programs. In the aggregate, however, the total time spent on appropriations was significantly reduced when the omnibus approach was tried in 1950.[9]

A second reason ascribed for the lack of popularity for the omnibus bill stems from the fact that rank-and-file Members of the House saw the omnibus appropriations bills as decreasing their power relative to that of the appropriations committees. It is true that the omnibus approach made for greater participation in floor debate, but such debate generally concerned the broad policy alternatives presented by the bill and not individual items. While this is a worthy effort in terms of the Congressman's role as a national legislator concerned with public policy, it appears to have limited his role as representative of the particular interest of his district or state, which demands that he have a more personal voice in projects and programs which may affect his area.

Finally, as noted in Professor Harris's examination of the omnibus bill, a single appropriations measure is much more susceptible to "meat ax" cuts and legislative riders. In considering one gigantic appropriations bill, the Congress is not presently equipped to make an item-by-item examination of the bill and is thus prone to make large reductions without regard to the consequences that such reductions may have on over-all administration policy. As the 1950 experience with the omnibus appropriations bill will attest, such reductions, particularly when made via the legislative rider or "tacked-on" amendment, may simply be a reduction without reference to any specific items in the bill. This was clearly seen when Senator Byrd offered an amendment to the 1950 omnibus bill calling for a $550 million appropriations cut in such agencies and programs as the President may designate.[10]

Another major proposal for budgetary reform is in the bill to create a Joint Committee on the Budget, first introduced by Senator McClellan in 1950. This measure, aimed at circumventing the objections raised to the 1946 Reorganization Act which provided for a Joint Committee on the Legislative Budget, would further amend Section 138 of the Act to establish a 14-member committee to provide a more effective means of enabling Congress to assume greater control of the budgetary and fiscal business of the federal government. It would be composed of 7 Members each from the House and Senate Appropriations (4 majority; 3 minority), chaired by a House Member in even-numbered years and a Senate Member in odd-numbered years, with a Vice-Chairman to be chosen from the opposite house. Staff assistance would be provided by a Director appointed from the majority party and an Assistant Director appointed from the opposition party. The Committee could also appoint such professional and clerical help as necessary to carry out its work.

The responsibilities of the Committee would require that it inform itself of all areas of the federal budget; provide the appropriations committees of Congress with detailed information regarding budget items and their justification through an examination of expenditure reports and an investigation of federal agency operations; review the President's State of the Union Address, Economic Report, and pertinent revenue information, and survey changing economic conditions, in order to hold expenditures to a minimum in relation to revenues; recommend needed changes to the legislative committees of Congress to eliminate waste and to bring authorizations in line with appropriations; and submit to Congress at the beginning of each session over-all cost estimates of all authorized programs and projects for the current and for succeeding fiscal years. Amendments to the original bill provide for inclusion in the Federal budget of fiscal analyses of long-term construction and development projects authorized by Congress; authorization for representatives of the Bureau of the Budget to sit in on executive sessions of the appropriations committees and their subcommittees, when invited to do so by the committee or subcommittee, and submission of budget requests on an annual accrued expenditure basis.

These provisions would enable the Congress to establish its own budget, a legislative budget. In addition, this measure would (1) give the Congress a means of continually evaluating the federal budget in a comprehensive and coordinated fashion; (2) permit additional staff aid for certain committees and for the GAO in order that it could make a pre-audit examination of the budget; and (3) eliminate some of the conflicts that arise as a result of the pluralistic influence of two appropriations committees and the division between the authorization and appropriation function.

Despite these advantages, several attempts to implement this reform (in 1952, 1953, 1955, 1957, and 1963) have failed in the House after having passed the Senate. Saloma explains the failure of the Joint Committee to materialize in the following excerpt:

> Drawing as it does on three of the approaches already considered by Congress—the use of a joint committee mechanism, the increase of appropriations staff, and the development of a role for the GAO in budget review—the McClellan bill has drawn together a range of opposition. This opposition stems from the House Appropriations Committee, jealous of its prerogatives in the Appropriations process; from the traditional reluctance to expand staff personnel, whether within the Appropriations Committee or as an external supplement, and from the various congressional reservations against assigning the GAO a budgetary pre-audit role.[11]

Many scholars feel that the establishment of an active pre-audit role for the GAO would result only in needless duplication of effort and could be justified only if Congress felt that it could no longer rely on the accuracy of the budget presentations of the BOB. This position would seem to ignore the legislative history of the Budget and Accounting Act, which intended for the GAO to play such a role. However, some Members of Congress hold the belief that an increased congressional budget staff might unduly influence the decisions of the appropriations committees. In addition, the staff might seek competition and undue controversy in their relations with the BOB and other executive departments in an effort to justify their existence.

For various reasons, attempts at major reform through the legislative budget, the omnibus appropriations bill, and the Joint Committee on the Budget have for the most part failed. These by no means exhaust the list of attempted reforms, which would also include the item veto, capital expenditure budgets, authority to impound funds, the use of revolving funds, and other proposals. However, the reforms discussed in some depth here do illustrate a few of the major problems and objections encountered in attempting to fashion a remedy (or remedies) to Congress' shortcomings in regard to expenditure control and fiscal policy.

REFERENCES

1. U.S. Congress, Senate, Government Operations Committee Staff, *Financial Management in the Federal Government*, 87th Cong., 1st Sess., 1961, p. 32.
2. Saloma, John S., III, *The Responsible Use of Power: A Ctirical Analysis of the Congressional Budget Process*, Washington, American Enterprise Institute, 1964, p. 44.
3. Harris, Joseph P., *Congressional Control of Administration*, Washington, The Brookings Institution, 1964, p. 74, citing passage quoted by Douglass Cater, "The Power of the Purse and the Congressman," *The Reporter*, Dec. 11, 1951, p. 26.
4. Galloway, George, B., *The Legislative Process in Congress*, New York, Thomas Y. Crowell, 1953, p. 123.
5. *Ibid.*
6. Harris, *op. cit.*, pp. 109–110.
7. Saloma, *op. cit.*, p. 59.
8. *Ibid.*, pp. 59–62.
9. U.S. Congress, *Financial Management*, etc., *op. cit.*, p. 50.
10. Saloma, *op. cit.*, p. 62.
11. *Ibid.*, p. 65.

APPENDIX III

89th Congress
1st Session

H. R. 9252

In the House of Representatives

JUNE 21, 1965

MR. MICHEL INTRODUCED THE FOLLOWING BILL;
WHICH WAS REFERRED TO THE COMMITTEE ON RULES

A Bill

To provide that the majority of the membership (including the chairman) of the Committee on Government Operations of the Senate and House of Representatives, respectively, shall be composed of members of a major political party other than the political party of which the President of the United States is a member.

Be it enacted by the Senate and House of Representatives of the United States of America in Congress assembled, That the respective amendments made by the following sections of this Act are enacted by the Congress—

(1) as an exercise of the rulemaking power of the Senate and House of Representatives, respectively, and shall be considered as one of the rules of that House of Congress to which specifically applicable; and

(2) with full recognition of the constitutional right of such House to change such rule at any time, in the same manner, and to the same extent, as in the case of any other rule of such House.

SEC. 2. Clause (j) of rule XXV of the Standing Rules of the Senate (relating to the Committee on Government Operations of the Senate) is amended by adding at the end thereof the following:

330

"(3) The majority of the membership (including the chairman) of such committee shall be composed of members of a major political party other than the political party of which the President of the United States is a member.".

SEC. 3. Clause 8, of rule XI of the Rules of the House of Representatives (relating to the Committee on Government Operations of the House of Representatives) is amended by adding at the end thereof the following:

"(e) The majority of the membership (including the chairman) of such committee shall be composed of members of a major political party other than the political party of which the President of the United States is a member.".

SEC. 4. The foregoing provisions of this Act shall become effective at the beginning of the next regular session of the Congress which follows the date of enactment of this Act.

APPENDIX IV

89th Congress
2nd Session

H. R. 12004

In the House of Representatives

JANUARY 12, 1966

MR. BROYHILL OF VIRGINIA INTRODUCED THE FOLLOWING BILL;
WHICH WAS REFERRED TO THE COMMITTEE ON HOUSE ADMINISTRATION

A Bill

To improve payroll administration with respect to payment of compensation from clerk hire of Members of the House of Representatives.

Be it enacted by the Senate and House of Representatives of the United States of America in Congress assembled,

CONVERSION OF HOUSE MEMBERS' CLERK HIRE AND EMPLOYEE COMPENSATION PAID THEREFROM TO SINGLE PER ANNUM RATES

SECTION 1. (a) Beginning with the effective date of this Act—

(1) subject to paragraph (2) of this subsection, the aggregate compensation paid from the clerk hire of each Member of the House of Representatives and the Resident Commissioner from Puerto Rico to each employee on the employment rolls of the House of Representatives on such date whose compensation paid from such clerk hire was fixed or adjusted prior to such date shall be a single per annum (gross) rate in an amount which is equal to the sum of the rate of the per annum basic compensation from such clerk hire of such employee in effect immediately prior to such date and the rate of his per annum additional compensation from such clerk hire in effect immediately prior to such date, adjusted to

the lowest multiple of $60 which will provide a single per annum (gross) rate of compensation from such clerk hire for such employee which is not less than the amount of aggregate compensation which such employee was receiving from such clerk hire immediately prior to such date; and

(2) the aggregate compensation paid from the clerk hire of each Member of the House of Representatives and the Resident Commissioner from Puerto Rico to each employee on the employment rolls of the House of Representatives on or after such date whose compensation paid from such clerk hire is fixed or adjusted on or after such date shall be at a single per annum (gross) rate constituting the aggregate compensation of such employee from such clerk hire, fixed at a multiple of $60.

(b) Section 11(a) of the Legislative Appropriation Act, 1956, as amended (2 U.S.C. 60g–1), is amended to read as follows:

"(a) Notwithstanding any other provision of law, the clerk hire of each Member of the House of Representatives and the Resident Commissioner from Puerto Rico shall be at a single per annum (gross) rate, as follows:

"(1) in the case of each Member and Resident Commissioner the population of whose constituency is less than five hundred thousand (as currently estimated by the Bureau of the Census), such single per annum (gross) rate shall be $73,320, and

"(2) in the case of each Member and Resident Commissioner the population of whose constituency is five hundred thousand or more (as currently estimated by the Bureau of the Census), such single per annum (gross) rate shall be $80,320.

No person shall be paid from such clerk hire at a single per annum (gross) rate in excess of $20,040. Not more than one person shall be paid at a single per annum (gross) rate of $20,040 from such clerk hire at any one time.".

Conforming Amendment to Provisions of the Dual Compensation Act Affecting Payment of Employee Compensation from House Members' Clerk Hire

Sec. 2. Section 301(c) of the Dual Compensation Act (5 U.S.C. 3105(c)) is amended—

(1) by striking out "Unless" and inserting in lieu thereof "(1) Except as provided by paragraph (2) of this subsection, unless"; and

(2) by adding at the end thereof the following new paragraph:

"(2) Unless otherwise authorized by law, no money appropriated by any Act shall be available for payment to any person of salary from more than one civilian office if the aggregate (gross) compensation from such offices exceeds the sum of $20,040 per annum and if one of such salaries is paid from the clerk hire of a Member of the House of Representatives or the Resident Commissioner from Puerto Rico.".

Saving Provision

Sec. 3. This Act shall not be construed to—

(1) reduce the amount of clerk hire which any Member or Resident Commissioner is receiving immediately prior to the effective date of this Act;

(2) limit or otherwise affect any authority for the making of any appointment to, or for fixing or adjusting the compensation for, any position for which the compensation is paid from the clerk hire of a Member or Resident Commissioner;

(3) affect the continuity of employment of, or reduce the compensation of, any employee paid from such clerk hire; or

(4) affect the authority provided by H. Res. 294, Eighty-eighth Congress, as continued by H. Res. 7, Eighty-ninth Congress, and enacted as permanent law by section 103 of the Legislative Branch Appropriation Act, 1966 (79 Stat. 281; Public Law 89–90), for the employment of an additional clerk by any Member or Resident Commissioner.

Policy Statement Concerning Future Compensation Increases for Employees Paid From House Members' Clerk Hire

Sec. 4. It is the sense of the House of Representatives that, unless otherwise subsequently provided by law, whenever future salary increases for employees in the legislative branch generally are provided by the Congress by appropriate legislation, the salary increases for those employees whose compensation is paid from the clerk hire of Members of the House of Representatives and the Resident Commissioner from Puerto Rico shall be provided for in such legislation by means of an appropriate provision for increasing the single per annum (gross) rate of clerk hire of each Member of the House of Representatives and the Resident Commissioner from Puerto Rico.

Effective Date

Sec. 5. This Act shall become effective at the beginning of the first pay period which begins more than ninety days after the date of enactment of this Act.

APPENDIX V

89th Congress
2nd Session

H. Res. 641

In the House of Representatives

JANUARY 12, 1966

MR. ELLSWORTH SUBMITTED THE FOLLOWING RESOLUTION;
WHICH WAS REFERRED TO THE COMMITTEE ON RULES

Resolution

Resolved, That the Rules of the House of Representatives are amended by adding at the end thereof the following:

RULE XLIII.

TELECASTING AND BROADCASTING OF PROCEEDINGS IN THE HALL OF THE HOUSE

1. Television and broadcast coverage of sessions of the House of Representatives shall be permitted, consistent with guidelines established by the House Committee on Rules, under the supervision of the Speaker and the minority leader of the House of Representatives.

2. No editorial broadcast commentary shall be made with the televising or broadcasting of sessions of the House of Representatives.

3. No telecast or broadcast, nor film or sound recording, of a session of the House of Representatives shall be used at any time by any person or political party for political or campaign purposes.

4. No broadcast or telecast, nor film or sound recording, of a session of the House of Representatives may be used for commercial purposes, but this

shall not be construed to prevent the broadcasting or telecasting of any such session in connection with a bona fide newscast, bona fide news documentary, or coverage of any such session as a bona fide news event.

5. Any person, company owning a radio or television station, or any radio or television network violating this rule may be liable for punishment for contempt of the House.

APPENDIX VI

89th Congress
2nd Session

H. Res. 651

In the House of Representatives

JANUARY 12, 1966

MR. ELLSWORTH SUBMITTED THE FOLLOWING RESOLUTION;
WHICH WAS REFERRED TO THE COMMITTEE ON RULES

Resolution

Resolved, That the Rules of the House of Representatives are amended by adding at the end thereof the following:

RULE XLIV.
TELECASTING AND BROADCASTING OF PROCEEDINGS
BEFORE COMMITTEES OF THE HOUSE.

1. Television and broadcast coverage of legislative and investigative committee sessions (including any subcommittee thereof) of the House of Representatives shall be permitted, consistent with guidelines established by the House Committee on Rules, under the supervision of the chairman and the ranking minority member of the committee.

2. No editorial broadcast commentary shall be made with the televising or broadcasting of committee (or subcommittee) sessions of the House of Representatives.

3. No telecast or broadcast, nor film or sound recording, of a committee (or subcommittee) session of the House of Representatives shall be used at any time by any person or political party for political or campaign purposes.

4. No broadcast or telecast, nor film or sound recording, of a committee (or subcommittee) session of the House of Representatives may be used for commercial purposes, but this shall not be construed to prevent the broadcasting or telecasting of any such session in connection with a bona fide newscast, bona fide news documentary, or coverage of any session as a bona fide news event.

5. If any subpenaed witness shall decline to have broadcast or telecast any portion or all of his testimony, or shall decline to have film or sound recording of his testimony, the chairman of the committee shall order that no broadcast or telecast nor film or sound recording be made of such witness.

6. Any person, company owning a radio or television station, or any radio or television network violating this rule may be liable for punishment for contempt of the House.